Indian Education in Times of Global Change

Indian Education in Times of Global Change

J.S. Rajput

SHIPRA

Rs. 1450

ISBN: 978-81-7541-851-6

First Published in India in 2016

Indian Education in Times of Global Change

Published by:

SHIPRA PUBLICATIONS
LG 18-19, Pankaj Central Market,
I.P. Ext., Patparganj, Delhi 110092, India
Ph.: 011- 2223 5152, 2223 6152
Email: info@shiprapublication.com
www.shiprapublication.com

Preface

Human evolution and civilization are a consequence of unbroken chain of transfer of accumulated knowledge and wisdom to the generations ahead. Structures and procedures have evolved over centuries so as to systematize this process that hinges upon two main 'humane' aspirations: the generations ahead may lead a better, peaceful, harmonious and integrated life; and further, it must add to the knowledge, wisdom and skills acquired so far and, thus, progress ahead in human evolution and growth. Man is the only species amongst the living beings who remains ever unsatisfied with the present and realizes his potential to 'create a better tomorrow'! History reveals how varied systems and approaches, developed over centuries in different parts of the world under varying conditions are now subsumed under education. This 'Education' is the indispensible asset in the eternal human quest to create conditions that enable every individual to lead a just, dignified and humane life, irrespective of innumerable diversities that illuminate the essential unity of mankind. Consequently, global unanimity has already been achieved that primacy must be allocated to extend education universally to one and all. That is the first possession everyone deserves to own and acquire for the very survival as a human being in the 21st century. In a fast changing scenario, in the age of globalization and connectivity facilitated by the unprecedented advances in the information and communication technology, education systems, per force, have to be alert, dynamic and ready to accept the new and reject the obsolete, without any delay! It is the level of outreach of education and its quality that directly impact the socio-economic growth and advancement that are essential for a better life, lifestyle and human dignity.

In continuity with its great traditions of knowledge quest, Indian freedom fighters realized over a century ago the urgency of extending education to all. 'Hind Swaraj', authored by Mohandas Karamchand Gandhi in 1909, very clearly unfolds this urge. The Constitution mandated it: 'free and compulsory education within ten years to all children till they attain fourteen years of age'. The subsequent developments require no repetition as these are very well known to everyone. It is impossible to locate any one who would not like his children, both boys and girls, to receive good quality education in a good school. Is our present education system professionally equipped to respond to various facets of academic elements and motivated sufficiently to harmonize these to transform a 'board certificate and university degree' oriented system into 'man-making education'? It needs serious analysis whether the education policies enunciated after independence suffered from perceptional inadequacies; or there was lack of political will; or the implementation strategies suffered due to lack of coordination and lethargy of work culture. Policy changes are necessary but these would bear fruits when duly provided for with adequate resources, professional leadership, academic support and an inbuilt dynamism and motivation in the system. The canvas before educational planners is huge, vast and varied. Consequently, policy formulation at one end and preparing reading material at the other for a particular region are highly professionalized tasks that can be carried out only by motivated experts.

One of the most pertinent issues that requires an in-depth analysis is: how far the present system of education is responsive to the emerging national needs, and aspirations of the young? There is a widespread belief that it has created a seemingly irreversible gap between haves and have-nots! This scrutiny becomes far more relevant once one studies the evolution of the Indian system of knowledge quest, its creation, utilization, and transfer to next generations. It is an interesting and fascinating journey that revolves around the Gurukula system. It is elevating to realize the international credibility that the universities of Taxila, Nalanda and Vikramshila and others enjoyed in their times. Reverting to contemporary context, one finds the traces of this tradition in the educational ideas of Swami Vivekananda, Swami Dayananda Saraswati, Mahatma Gandhi, Sri Aurobindo, Rabindranath Tagore and several others. They knew India, its diversity, its strengths and also its weaknesses. They all were aware of the need to develop a system of education that would be rooted in culture and committed to progress. Any nation that decides to embark upon its own ideology of progress and development, first of all, needs to develop its own indigenous system of education that assimilates the global requirements. When this is attempted, issues of curriculum development and renewal appear very prominently before the academics. The professionals to perform this sensitive job come from teacher-training institutions; which are effectively the power plants for quality not only in the education sector alone, but eventually in every sector of human action, activity and endeavour. The process of curriculum preparation and teaching as also that of developing the teaching learning materials has a very prominent task that is specific to India: every child must internalize genuine appreciation for otherness; respect for religions other than his own; respect for the language, traditions and cultural practices of his peers. Generations ahead deserve an environment that abounds with 'social cohesion and religious amity'. Human and democratic values as also the Fundamental Duties enshrined in Article 51-A must be imbibed and internalized by one and all. Without these two, India would always confront serious impediments in its march towards progress and development. And education is the only ray of hope.

In the times of glitter and glamour of materialistic pursuits overshadowing the eternal spiritual quest, practically everyone suffers in one way or the other because of value erosion. Should every citizen of tomorrow not be familiar with the vision of Mahatma Gandhi that nature has sufficient to meet the need of everyone, but not the greed of anyone? It is education alone that could sow the seeds of value inculcation, nurture and development in the sensitive years of life. Once the teacher realizes that he continues to remain a role model; in spite of alternatives emerging from sports and media; the process of value erosion can not only be checked, but also reversed effectively. Globalization is a reality and so is the mobility of young persons to destinations abroad. As institutional networking with international agencies is necessary in education as India has a prestigious global presence, which has created opportunities abroad for more young persons. National requirements and international opportunities could very well be met through a dynamic, futuristic and value-based system of education. Essentially, it all could be summarized as the 'pursuit for institutional leadership and academic excellence'!

Several of these aspects are dealt with in the chapters of this book. I acquired and assimilated the contents from literature, personal interactions with the learned, long discussions with students and questions posed to me by young persons in schools and institutions of higher education. I also derived immense learning experiences from several of the assignments in universities, Government of India, international agencies and national level organizations. Special thanks are due to Astha Bharati and IC Centre for Governance and the NHRC. They provided space in print for the dissemination of my views on various educational issues. I claim no originality for the ideas contained in the book which is being presented with the sole intention of generating discussions on specific concerns before education.

Gratefulness just cannot be expressed in words to Professor Sarla Rajput who reads every word that I write and publish.

March 21, 2016 **J.S. Rajput**

Contents

1

Education Policy Formulation

The Decade Ahead

> *"The real difficulty is that people have no idea of what education truly is. We assess the value of education in the same manner as we assess the value of land or of shares in the stock exchange market. We want to provide only such education as would enable the student to earn more. We hardly give any thought to the improvement of the character of the educated. The girls, we say, do not have to earn; so why should they be educated? As long as such ideas persist there is no hope of our ever knowing the true value of education."*
>
> *—Mahatma Gandhi*

India inherited a transplanted system of education at the time of her independence, and continued with it because of several omnipresent elements in the education discourse in the post independence period. While Radhakrishnan and Mudaliar Commissions were the initial efforts to have a look in to specific stages of education, the first National Commission on Education (1964-66); popularly known as the Kothari Commission, resulted in the formulation of the National Policy on Education (NPE) in 1968. The next major change came in the shape of the National Policy on Education (1986) which, after enduring a short period of instable governments at the centre, was revised in 1992. Presently, the NPE 86/92 is the guiding policy document for those involved in the education in India. The system of education need to remain dynamic in view of the all-round changes taking place in the socio-cultural and economic aspects as also the political upheavals and impacts of developments in science, technology and their impact on the curricula, evaluation systems, and management aspects. The need for a policy review and reformulation remains paramount. The next phase of policy formulation, already delayed considerably, has to incisively analyze the experiences gained since Independence.

Priorities in the national education endeavour have to be reset to ensure that the promises made and the assurances given in the Constitution of India are implemented in letter and spirit. In the times of drastic erosion of values, ever-increasing insecurity, increasing bigotry and violence, tyranny of the rich, injustice, aberrations in functional democracy, education that imparts knowledge, inculcates values and provides opportunities for skill acquisition could be the 'only ray of hope' for the suffering humanity. What stands out with disturbing prominence is the startling phenomenon of education getting divided into two distinct partitions: for the haves and for the have-nots! For ensuring inclusive growth and development, it just cannot be allowed to divert from its basic premises and objectives. A sustained combat needs to be launched against all forces that continue to deprive children of their natural rights of equality of opportunity of access and success in education.

Context

The great Indian tradition of knowledge generation, dissemination and utilisation for human welfare, an outcome of the search for truth and the ultimate reality, is of eternal relevance. Continuity of learning to 'serve others' and strive for the welfare of 'All' shall remain the foundation stones of education policy of India that would celebrate the diversity of India and emphasize the inherent unity of the nation and its people in diversity.

The pre-British system of education in India neglected none in acquiring education on the basis of caste, creed or any other discrimination or diversity. India was more literate than Britain before the Englishmen destroyed the Indian system of education and transplanted their own.

True to the duty assigned to them, the alien educational planners merit praise for the objective-based strategies they designed to suit their masters. These really worked very effectively to serve their interests. It was meant for a few and it worked for the benefit of the colonial powers. As intended, it proved disastrous for India and Indians. It aimed at delinking Indians from India, its culture, history and tradition. The objective was achieved with great success. It meant destruction of the Indian system of education, loss of traditional expertise in arts, crafts and work skills in other sectors and the ruin of decentralised production activities. Widespread poverty was the natural consequence, resulting in unprecedented miseries being inflicted on the masses, who were left totally disillusioned and demoralized.

Indian independence struggle is a unique example of its leaders being conscious of the role that education was to play in free India. Swami Vivekananda elaborated it so beautifully—in Independent India, it shall be "Education. Education and Education". Not only this they realized the importance of girls education. Luminaries like Raja Rammohan Roy, Ishwar Chandra Vidyasagar, Mahadev Ranade, Mahatma Phule, Acharya Karve, and others put their ideals into practice. Mahatma Gandhi made that famous speech in Chatham Lines London in 1931, daring any one to achieve Universal Elementary education in India in the 'next hundred years' by following the 'existing' model of education. His plans were ready—a school in each village of India for both: every boy and every girl in free India. Education, Gandhi Ji always reiterated, was the only ray of hope for India's resurgence.

Gandhi did not only preach on education or designed plans for the future. He put these in practice. He invited his colleagues to refine these, experiment with ideas suitable to the Indian context and put the results before the nation.

The conceptualization of 'Basic Education' and '*Nai Talim*' had the essential ingredient of working with the hand and acquiring learning and knowledge in the context of 'continuity and progress'. It could also be articulated as one education policy that "is rooted to the socio-cultural heritage of our country and committed to progress and development". Traditional skills were not to be discarded but there was to be no aversion to the acquisition of new ones. Gandhi's model had development in focus and it revolved around the "Village". He undertook a comprehensive view of education; as an integrated development of the head, hand and heart i.e., simultaneously contributing to intellectual, emotional and spiritual development. He wanted them to be as self-dependent as possible. In 1946, he pleaded with Jawaharlal Nehru to make the village as the nodal point of India's development after India attained Independence. Nehru rejected it. The rest is history.

Even after over six-and-half decades, Independent India could not re-create and put in place an Indian education system to replace the legacy left over by the alien rulers at the time of their departure. Sporadic changes made now and then have proved totally ineffective to find solutions that people expect to emerge from education. It has created more problems. Instead of bridging the gap, these have perpetuated inequality creating two sharply different segments: Public Schools for the resourceful and influential and consistently-ignored government schools for the children of over seventy per cent of the population. There are exceptions of certain genuine initiatives undertaken in the right spirit by organizations and individuals. These suffer from government apathy and bureaucratic restrictions that inhibit innovations and experimentation.

India is under global watch, not only for its much-hyped economic growth rate (which is now swiftly falling downwards to alarming levels) but also for the golden age of demographic advantage. Its youth power is now being seen as its strength, unlike the 'burden' it was treated earlier, particularly by the developed countries. Education policy must aim to create conditions for rightful and planned utilization of the young manpower.

The higher education system in India has not kept pace with the emerging demands that are specific to India even in the times of globalization. Sixty-six years after is a time gap sufficient enough to review the state-of-art position in matters 'how India looks after its young generations'.

After over two decades of the last Policy Formulation, Indian education system has yet to serve effectively the vast majority of children. The constitution had mandated free and compulsory education for every child till they attain fourteen years of age. The same remains the position of the higher education in which the participation of the young persons is just around 17-18 per cent only.

The report of the National Education Commission "Education for National Development" made a thorough analysis of the existing system—the reforms needed to extend the outreach of the system to all on the basis of 'equality of opportunity irrespective of any conceivable diversity' and to prepare manpower necessary for the growth and development of India into a developed nation. Its several major recommendations, including those on "Common School System" and vocationalization of education, unfortunately remained ignored and neglected even after these were incorporated in the National Policy on Education-1968 and reiterated subsequently on various other occasions. It paved the way for the girls to study science and mathematics, which was earlier considered a taboo for them!

The process of curriculum formulation continues to be sequential; preparing every learner for the next higher grade or the stage of education. It has its relevance but the stark reality that not all of them would go to the next higher stage after the universal elementary stage of up to fourteen years of age just cannot be ignored. Those who move out of the learning process, require a self-contained curriculum that would help them later in life.

The National Policy on Education-1986, modified in 1992, made several significant recommendations and brought in schemes and programmes. Schemes like Operation Blackboard (OB) and Strengthening and Restructuring Teacher Education could have transformed the entire scene in school education. Most of these suffered considerably at the implementation stage and the outcomes remained far below the expectations. The level of commitment and work culture were just not upgraded to requisite levels.

India amended its Constitution in 2002 to make education a fundamental right. The RTE Act first passed by the Parliament in 2002 was amended in 2009 and implemented w.e.f. April 01, 2010. The target was to be achieved within three years. As per official records over 92 lakh children are still out of schools. If one estimates the numbers of these added to the dropouts after one or two years, it could easily be around 30 million. The challenge before the nation is still enormous in magnitude.

The use and assimilation of ICT in teaching learning process is accepted in principle but the vast majority of children still remain deprived of it, mainly because of the inadequate resource allocations and lack of putting well trained personnel at the right place. Politics has entered the arena through practices like distribution of free laptops to children instead of establishing computer laboratories in schools and colleges.

The Basics

In an emerging knowledge driven economy and a globalised materialistic world, the education system in India must be strongly rooted to the culture and committed to progress and development. It must prepare children to imbibe constitutional values, develop an empathetic acquaintance with the culture, history and heritage of India and develop a sense of pride and self-assurance in being Indian. The culture of acceptance of all possible diversities of faith, culture, religion, practice, traditions and others is unique to Indian civilization. It has been successfully practised for over two millennia. Every Indian must imbibe a sense of responsibility and a bounden duty to strengthen it further and take it ahead.

Learning to live together and strengthening social cohesion shall have to become the outstanding objectives of the teaching and learning process in all of its aspects and at all the stages.

A dynamic system of education in a nation proud of its diversities must remain ever-alert to monitoring, assessing and evaluating the learner's needs, societal aspirations and external influences. That would regularly need inputs from an alert, active and functional system of surveys, studies, evaluation and research. The quality of these needs to be monitored by independent autonomous professional bodies that have acquired professional credibility in supporting and monitoring the quality in every context.

The salient differences between general administration and management on one side and that of educational administration and management on the other must be properly understood and the appropriate structures put in place. The bureaucratization of education deserves a thorough scrutiny after an incisive analysis of the experiences of over six decades.

The agriculture sector, rural poverty and increasing rural to urban migration must impact the thinking and approach of the academics formulating curriculum, syllabi or designing textual materials. Neglect of the agriculture sector, rural production skills and crafts has contributed to avoidable unemployment and poverty.

Neglect of skill development and vocationalization must be corrected at the earliest. The spirit of entrepreneurship and self-assurance must pervade every activity in schools and colleges. It must begin prominently and effectively from teacher education institutions.

Institutional networking is a rather compulsory ingredient of quality enhancement efforts in the current times. Some of the top professional institutions of technical, management, medical and a few other areas seem to be too obsessed with collaborating with their foreign counterparts. Not many of such institutions are willing to collaborate among themselves to upgrade some of the institutions that need professional support within the country.

The 1986/92 National Policy on Education envisages the concept of a national system of education. It "implies that, up to a given level, all students, irrespective of caste, creed, location or gender have access to education of a comparable quality". It contained assurances to take effective steps to move towards the common school system recommended in the 1968 National Policy. A common educational structure and a national curriculum framework with well-defined core elements are the essential features of a national system. The common school system has never been pursued with commitment. Some of the State Boards of School Education are not yet adhering to the common structure, common curriculum and the three-language formula. These aspects have to be analyzed and suitably redefined, particularly in the light of the Right to Education Act.

The content of education requires serious transformation and the academics responsible for curriculum and textual material development shall have a tough exercise in removing the obsolescence and bringing in the new content that would help learners making effective contributions in an increasingly complex world.

Certain basic elements shall be identified which shall run across all the stages and variations of the curriculum in different states, universities and every other institution, need to be identified. Environmental issues, terrorism and also religious and regional fundamentalism, depleting natural resources, global initiatives for economic dominance and a few others shall constitute this category. Fundamental duties, disaster management, drug abuse, sex education and adolescence education, prevention of cruelty to animals, human rights, equality of sexes, age-care and provisions for the education of the handicapped, respect for democratic governance and need to strengthen democratic practices must also find a prominent place in education. Love for the culture and the country and inculcation of values of patriotism and serving others in various ways should no more remain ignored or neglected.

The concept of secularism must be interpreted in terms of experiences gained over two millennia in giving equal respect to all religions and making it an integral part of social and cultural practices. The Constitutional safeguards for minorities should be dutifully protected, but politicisation of secularism must not be permitted to enter the education sector. It has to be effectively discarded and disallowed. This can be achieved through an educational policy that takes note of the misutilisation of the concept through curricula and textual materials. Attempts to bring in ideological compulsions in the areas of social sciences and subjectivity in history teaching shall be particularly discarded

The spirit of constitutional safeguards for the weaker sections that require affirmative/additional support must be reflected in the educational policy and also in the content and process of education, which must permit additional support and inputs for those who need these. Education must contribute to preparing a generation that would sincerely strive to create an egalitarian society.

The constitutional provisions on reservations and on minorities have been grossly misutilised by intruding private players, often with the tacit support of governments with ulterior motives. These have often not been in the interest of the intended beneficiaries and have not contributed to strengthening social cohesion and communal harmony. Education must prepare young persons capable of seeing through such efforts and discarding these without any hesitation.

The deficiencies that engulf government schools are known to all. Two-third of our universities and ninety per cent of the colleges are said to be functioning at a 'below average level'. Such a situation requires a thorough probe and analysis of the root causes of this sorry state of affairs. The role of state and national level regulatory bodies, created to ensure the maintenance of norms and standards, must come under a sharp scanner.

Higher education must utilize science, technology and the information and communication technology (ICT) to the maximum. Every possible support needs to be given to enhance the quality of research and innovations in core areas.

Widespread confusion prevails in the education sector regarding the role of private players and foreign investors and international institutional collaborators. A clear-cut policy initiative is necessary on this count. The role and responsibility of state and private investments have to be clearly defined.

The issue of institutional autonomy vis-a-vis state control and coordination will emerge sharply and would require a very considered mention in the policy formulation. The increasing dependence of the State/UTs on central funding does not represent a healthy state of relationship between the two.

Optimum utilisation of available resources in higher education shall have to be ensured to achieve the maximum benefits out of the investments made. Institutional networking within the country and also with external institutions of repute, shall have to be explored, strengthened and its benefits made available to all those conducting researches in their specific areas in remote and normally considered 'distant' places.

The concept of a complete man, elaborated by Indian thinkers and philosophers, including Swami Vivekananda, Maharshi Aurobindo, Dr. Radhakrishnan, Rabindranath Tagore, Mahatma Gandhi, Dr. Zakir Husain, Maulana Azad and others must become the guiding principle of all the policy formulations, academics and the teachers. Gandhi Ji's dream of bringing out the best out of body, mind and spirit can no longer be ignored in the Indian education endeavour.

Brilliant and talented young persons, under the lure of the glamorous opportunities in multinationals, need to be exposed to appreciate the immense possibility that research opportunities could offer them to contribute to the cause of growth and development and derive tremendous personal satisfaction of contributing to the welfare of the humanity and its empathetic relationship with nature. Indian diversity demands far greater emphasis on Research and Innovations than is available at present.

The issue of man vs. market is already confronting the education systems everywhere and India is no exception. In fact there are high expectations from India as its strength in superior spiritual understanding is acknowledged globally. The nurturance of spirituality and eternal human values of Truth, Peace, Nonviolence, Righteous Conduct and Love now assumes critical significance in a world experiencing frightening erosion of values.

The significance of the role of the teacher must emerge out of policy documents and routine exhortations on certain special occasions. The need to prepare competent, committed and performing teachers must be seriously redressed. No institution of teacher preparation should be permitted to compromise on quality. India needs teachers who are "proud of being in the profession"! No system of education can succeed unless it prepares its teachers well, looks after them continuously and ensures a congenial working environment and, above all, due dignity to every teacher. Teacher preparation has suffered most during the last four decades. It would be a Herculean task to transform it in to a dynamic and professionally sound system that includes pre-service; in-service on-site professional competency development and other innovative institutional initiatives promote teacher empowerment. This one change remains the 'must' for quality and comprehensive reforms in education.

Learning opportunities must be made available through alternative modes and for everyone at any age and every stage of life. Provisions for acquiring new skills and updating skills already acquired need to be provided for on a much wider scale to make these accessible to anyone willing to utilise the same. Particular care has to be taken of the rural tribal, hilly and other 'difficult' areas and habitations.

Education was brought on the Concurrent List in the Constitution of India in 1976 through a Constitutional Amendment. Considerable experience has been gained in subsequent years in policy implementation—not all of which is really encouraging. States/UT's have become too much dependent on the fund-flow from the central government. The contours of this partnership have to be reviewed and the coherence and symphony of the efforts and initiatives need be ensured in actual practice.

The strategy of open and distance learning has, unfortunately, acquired the stigma of being the next lower alternative. This sector, including the management systems and delivery mechanisms will have to be strengthened in all its aspects.

The role of heads of institutions at each stage of education, beginning from the Head Teacher of a primary school to the Vice-Chancellors of universities and chiefs of professional institutions must be redefined. Innovations, nurturing of creativity, growth of institutional culture, networking with the outside partners can flourish only when external controls are minimised or are totally removed.

The Indian education system has become predominantly theoretical and; consequently; extremely weak on the applied and skill development side. This anomaly has to be corrected. Much could still be learnt from the emphasis that was integrated in the concept of Basic Education given by Gandhi Ji through its dynamic interpretation in the current times.

The strength of the indigenous system emerges out of the traditional school society interaction. It stands eroded after independence. Even the Panchayat Raj Acts came rather too late in the day and the symphony of the school-society is yet to be restored.

Public-private partnership is a growing necessity. It has to be worked out extensively in a dynamic mutually acceptable strategy that ensures smooth functioning and maintains quality and relevance of the education imparted. It has to be saved from being converted in to a purely commercial enterprise.

India needs to develop a sense of pride amongst its young and old alike in the National System of Education. The cognitive capital of India would be second to none once their stated objective of equality of opportunity reaches without any reservations to the last man identified by Mahatma Gandhi.

Elementary Education

A clear policy on age of admission to pre-school education and to class one in continuity should be finally evolved and firmly laid down. Coordination with the initiative in Early Childhood Care and Education (ECCE) programmes like the Bal Wadis and other public/ private initiatives, provision of preschool education and day care centres need to be extended and universalised.

Regeneration of Indian economy shall continue to remain significantly dependent on the regeneration of rural economy. This in turn would depend on levels of achievements of universal elementary education and simultaneously on the quality and relevance of the content of this education.

Issues like Infrastructural input inadequacies and non-availability of teachers need to be addressed very seriously and on a time bound basis. Responsibilities for the proper functioning of schools implementing RTE Act should be clearly delineated. The problems of teachers, particularly the lady teachers, must be attended to. In difficult areas, innovative and alternative approaches should be encouraged. A time bound programme to improve the infrastructure facilities, as also the academic inputs are essential to provide good quality education and appropriate skills to all the children. The Sarva Shiksha Abhiyan must be continued and strengthened with greater focus on quality and equality.

Education cannot progress ahead until the holistic nature of the growing up is coordinated and managed comprehensively. Special attention will have to be paid for health, nutrition and, care for the siblings.

Special incentives, like awards and generous grants, should be given to Panchayats that focus on imparting good quality education.

Child friendly, joyful education to provide practice and practical-based stress-free learning should no more be treated as a mere cliché, instead attempts shall be made to reorient the pedagogical practices to concretize these in actual school situations and settings.

Parent-teacher associations need to be made effective and supportive to both the students and the school.

While the focus on cognitive learning would grow as the child advances ahead, effective steps shall be put in place to provide skills through practice. The skill aspect has to be given its due place in schooling.

Primary school timings, vacations, and holidays shall be flexible and decided upon by the local community and the parent teacher association. Schools shall be supported through health care facilities and nutritional inputs.

People and the communities must be encouraged to strengthen schools' infrastructure, and making it a place that attracts children.

Teacher recruitment and posting should strive to ensure the non availability of adequate number of teachers in schools irrespective of their locations.

The management systems of the Mid Day Meal Scheme should be streamlined and made pilferage and corruption proof.

School dropouts shall be stopped completely. Wherever necessary, supportive measures should be taken, in consultation with the community, to bring every child to the learning center, retain him/her there for a minimum of eight years and further provide him good quality education and adequate life and learning skills.

Secondary Education

Achievements in universalizing elementary education determine the participation rates and quality of learning at the secondary and senior secondary stage. Though late, India has launched the much-needed initiative to universalise secondary education. The Policy formulations in education in India must now see universalizing elementary education to extend to achieve at least a ten-year schooling for every child.

Huge infrastructure inputs need to be organized to ensure that both boys and girls have easy access to secondary education and the supportive inputs are available to them in terms of mid day meals, hostels, scholarships, and others. Girls will have to be specifically targeted and supported. The Rastriya Madhyamik Shiksha Mission has to be reviewed and the possibility of combining it with SSA shall have to be examined.

Special care on content and pedagogy at this stage is necessary. This is the stage that shall prepare most of the children for life. They develop a sense of heritage, history and their own role in the national perspective. They see the interconnections between areas like science, social science, humanities, and arts and visualize their relevance in life.

A major issue at the secondary stage is to equip children to comprehend various aspects of the diversity that characterizes India. They have to appreciate the way Indian thought has survived and the culture of India has emerged in the historical context of changes.

Skill orientation at this stage requires a fresh look. It must be a compulsory component of the curriculum that has to be taken up and evaluated with all the seriousness it deserves.

This would be the major stage of education for most of the learners who shall be entering life. They have to acquire the skill and attitude for lifelong learning and also to upgrade their skills.

The system of assessment and evaluation at this stage becomes critical as it must extend to estimate the total personality development of the learner who would either be entering life or joining higher pursuits in education. It is the internalisation of the spirit of democratic society and the aspirations of a developing nation which require working and striving together to contribute to the national cause.

Higher Education

The force and energy that guides the nation in its march towards the knowledge society gains momentum primarily from the acceleration provided by innovations, new knowledge, and its dissemination and utilization. The quality of higher education is the lifeline for creating an inclusive egalitarian society.

The emerging roles of higher education have to be clearly defined and the educational policy formulations and programme orientations have to be re-delineated and redesigned accordingly.

Except for about five to ten per cent universities, the quality of higher education is 'pretty bad'. The process of acceleration has to be accelerated. Industry and academia have to come together to develop new structures, programmes and networking.

In the march towards progress and development, higher education can play a pivotal role. The well established role of higher education in social change, economic growth and in strengthening the roots of democratic governance require more institutions and more places for increased participation in higher education, innovations and research. India must aim at least 30 percentage-appropriate presence of the young people into institutions of higher learning.

The participation rate of the population in the age group 18-23 was only around seven per cent (2006, National Knowledge Commission). It would be around 16-17 per cent by now but remains far below the average of the developed countries and only one-half of the average for Asia. In addition, the quality of higher education is far from satisfactory. It would require a fresh perception on the extent of state support, privatisation including the role of industry and corporate and extent of access being granted to foreign players. Substantial increase of both the financial and academic resources and a change of work culture are the basic inputs needed.

Higher education aims to prepare top-level manpower for every sector. Hence, its quality and relevance will have a great multiplier effect. There has to be coordinated manpower planning for higher education.

The National Policy on Education 1986/92 had assured that "urgent steps shall be taken to protect the system from degradation". Seemingly, the degradation has spread further, unchecked and brazenly unrestricted. Far greater effort is a must to uproot it and reverse the trend and ensure quality up gradation.

Autonomy and accountability could play a critical role in improving the quality of higher education. These two together could also encourage private initiative and thus provide greater opportunities for its participation in higher education. Autonomy bereft of accountability could be disastrous.

The science of pedagogy generally remains ignored and neglected in this sector. It has to be corrected. Higher education not only provides teachers for the vital school sector, it also prepares its own teachers and researchers. With ICT and global connectivity, this aspect can play a critical role in improving the quality of higher education.

Intensive efforts are necessary to attract brilliant young people as researchers in social sciences and humanities as also in the basic areas of sciences. The acute shortage of well-equipped manpower in universities, research laboratories and institutions must not be allowed to persist further and needs to be redressed early.

The quality of existing research, particularly the research leading to the doctorate degree requires monitoring on the principle of 'sample surveys' as there are considerable apprehensions that it has deteriorated after the career advancement schemes were accepted by the universities and Ph.D became an essential qualification for entry and promotions. The implications of poor quality research could only be fearsome.

The National policy on Education 1986/92 had assured to give adequate support to Research in Indology, the humanities and social sciences. It went to the extent of stating, "To fulfill the need for the synthesis of knowledge, interdisciplinary research will be encouraged. Efforts will be made to delve into India's ancient fund of knowledge and to relate it to contemporary reality. This effort will imply the development of facilities for the intensive study of Sanskrit and other classical languages." This aspect mostly remained neglected and need to be taken up on priority basis.

A mechanism to persuade universities and colleges to treat curriculum and syllabi renewal as ongoing processes has to be put in place. That would keep them dynamic and up-to-date in their endeavours, and also motivate the faculty to remain aware of the latest developments in their own area of specialization and also in the allied disciplines.

A thorough review of colleges and other institutions conducting traditional courses unrelated to the sectors that may offer opportunities for absorption of the products shall have to be conducted. Those who prepare unskilled under prepared university graduates deserve to be ruthlessly weeded out of the system. None is to be allowed to tinker with the prescribed levels of learner attainments.

National level regulatory bodies in education have mostly played a 'big brother's' role. These must realise that their common objective is to prepare state level expertise and management mechanisms, which should function with confidence and at the optimum level of professional efficacy. An attitudinal transformation in this direction shall be positive step in morale boosting of the institutions and also of the faculty.

Higher education systems are already facing complex and complicated demands all around. Investors perceive it as an area that delivers assured dividends. With an eye on easy money, they may offer easy options to the learners also. B.Ed. correspondence courses were accredited even by the state universities as a means of generating (financial) resources. There are widespread instances of low-quality courses being offered in management and technical institutions. Issues like quality, profit, control, and autonomy are potential areas of conflict. Hence, there is a need for a consensus centered around the concerns of the future generations and nothing else.

Higher education will undergo a change of face in the years to come. Institutions shall have to be prepared and empowered to convert every curricula into a multimedia, web-based format making full utilisation of the opportunities that have emerged consequent to advances and innovations in ICT.

The advent of ICT has already opened a floodgate of programmes that can be delivered through the distance education mode or in the dual mode. It would require the formulation of new norms and standards for adherence.

Never before the need for an industry-university dialogue and collaboration was felt as intensely as of now. Policies shall have to take note of this development. The need of the times ahead would be a triangular partnership with academia, industry and the government.

There is every chance of knowledge workers and highly skilled personnel being prepared by institutions, which may not care, about the formal governmental accreditation. They may just tie-up with the private sector employers and ensure full employment for their alumni.

Functioning of Academic Staff Colleges created by the University Grants Commission to enhance the pedagogical insights of the university and college teachers is now more or less 'routinised'. These Colleges were supposed to motivate the trainees to 'become the part of the change'. Such orientations are now considered necessary in view of the pace of change both in the content and pedagogy of each discipline and its linkages to other areas.

Income generation projects should no longer remain a 'no-no' in higher education institutions. Already, a rethinking on the issue is taking place. The objectives that India identifies for itself in the global context in the coming years would depend on the importance it assigns to the three key drivers; wealth generation, social transformation and protection of indigenous knowledge. These would benefit all, academically, professionally and financially.

Demands for conducting projects the outcomes of which may be of help in industry, health of other areas of public welfare shall increase. Higher-level specialisations are now becoming necessary in several areas and universities shall have to respond to these through their own initiatives and also in conjunction with other institutions and industrial or research establishments.

Exploration, protection, preservation and utilisation of indigenous knowledge and composite culture shall become significant components of the learning processes in higher education. Teachers and students have to become lifelong learners.

Merit and suitability alone has to the consideration in locating the top functionaries of institutions of higher learning. It should not be constrained by considerations of caste, region and even religion. At present, there have been instances of ambitious academics not hesitating to cultivate the right 'connections'. It is high time to accept this reality and take corrective steps.

New universities and colleges should be opened only after it has been thoroughly ascertained that these have the necessary financial and professional resources. Norms in these respects must be strictly adhered to.

Vocational Education

The criticality of skill development and vocational education in India often projected as having the 'golden period of demographic advantage', hardly needs any reiteration or reemphasis. The mismatch between the demand and supply of skilled manpower needs urgent corrective measures. The challenge also includes how to divert the large segment of young persons pursuing routine outdated courses in higher education without much interest and purpose, vocationalisation now deserves a large push-through.

Developing interest in working with hands and acquisition of productive skills right from the beginning of schooling, existing structures will have to be strengthened and new ones created after cases VIII, particularly after Class X to provide generic vocational skills to 'every child who is interested in it'.

The process of impacting the much needed attitudinal

transformation amongst pupils and parents towards vocationalization has been painfully slow. Some change of attitude has taken place and people are not as enamored of government jobs as they were a few decades ago. A fresh countrywide initiative shall have to be launched in public education.

Work experience, working with community and vocational education provide concrete opportunities to inculcate self-help, self-assurance, character building and a sense of social responsibility and concern for others, particularly those who need support.

School and the community should decide together the area for work experience and vocationalization. In rural areas, it would generally be agriculture oriented and even that would require a vast array of possible courses.

Industry must be persuaded to play a far greater role than at present to prepare skilled manpower, which may benefit them as well. It needs to establish institutions in the newly emerging areas, within the country and also abroad.

Widening of the coverage of institutions of Open Learning like NIOS and IGNOU would be a much-needed step in the right direction. The experiences already need to be strengthened and consolidated.

Involvement of local authorities and communities in identification and organization of vocational courses is weak and needs serious efforts to revitalize it.

In the context of the 73rd and 74th Constitutional amendments, the specific roles of local body institutions such as Zila Parishads (District Councils) need to be redefined based on the experiences gained. The system of planning, management and monitoring at district level deserves support and has to be strengthened.

District level plans can no longer be permanent documents. These have to be constantly renewed and a mechanism to assist in the process has to be established. It would also ensure that vocational education programme is effectively implemented and the requisite infrastructure and other facilities are in place.

Gandhian perceptions on education and development are now being read afresh globally. The Mahatma had laid emphasis on village republics, self-sufficiency, essentiality of skill development and working with the hands. Through these, he perceived inculcation of respect for nature, self-esteem and readiness for entrepreneurship and employment. This formulation was basically an attempt to harmonise intellectual and manual work. Policy formulations must respond to these to make education directly relevant to the life of the people.

The existing courses of vocational education in universities need to be expanded, extended and their quality upgraded. New areas have to be identified. Here again, the industry must come forward in a big way and only genuine private investment is to be encouraged.

A widespread programme of preparing teachers of vocational courses has to be envisaged and universities and institutions of technical education could play a major role. It must take note of the opportunities available abroad for employment.

Young persons with formal qualifications but with inadequate knowledge and skill acquisition due to various reasons must be supported as special interest groups and provided opportunities for additional knowledge acquisitions and skill inputs so that they are ready to join the productive work force with confidence and self assurance.

The target of achieving 25 per cent enrolment in vocational courses at the secondary stage must now be achieved within five years.

A programe of training and identification of resource persons and teachers in the vocational education is necessary. There should be every encouragement to utilise community-based resources including ex-servicemen, retired teachers and functionaries with experience in various skills gathered during their years of active professional contribution.

A national system of evaluation and certification of skills acquired from the unorganised private sector is yet to become effectively functional at the district and block levels. It would enable trained young persons acquire a sense of satisfaction and achievement. It may benefit them in other ways as well.

Value Education

Value orientation is an over-arching and comprehensive area that needs conscious integration with general education at each stage, adult education, teacher education, and also the technical and management education. Education has little meaning without development, nurturance and internalisation of values.

In an increasingly complex globalised world, the erosion of values is adversely impacting the human life in practically every sector of activity and endeavour. It has resulted in alarming levels of exploitation of human beings and also of natural resources. The sensitive man-nature link has snapped rather irretrievably. Sufferings inflicted on most of the human beings by a much smaller number are immense. When values are ignored, humanity suffers; so does the man-nature synergy.

India has suffered serious consequences arising out of the increasing threat of terrorism and fundamentalism. Education, in its entirety, has to prepare persons for creating a world of peace, harmony, mutual trust and one based on values.

An acquaintance with the Indian tradition of acceptance of diversity coupled with an objective description of Indian heritage, culture and history, could lead to social cohesion and mutual trust amongst Indians even when they adhere to their respective religious faiths. The content and process of education, particularly school education has to be prepared accordingly and revised regularly.

Eternal human values: 'Truth, Peace, Non-violence, Righteous Conduct (Dharma) and Love' are acceptable to everyone. These represent five dimensions of human personality; intellectual, physical, emotional, psychological and spiritual. These must become the foundation for a value-based education in totality.

Every teacher should be prepared to internalise that apart from his professional readiness and responsibility. He must serve as role model, inculcator of values and expected to lead a value-based life.

For a proper appreciation of secularism and value education programmes, the recommendations of the Chavan Committee Report submitted to the Indian Parliament in February 1999 must be implemented in letter and spirit.

Education about the basics of religions could be helpful in understanding the living together of the people of different faiths and religions. The judgment of the Supreme Court of India delivered on September 12, 2002 is a milestone to achieve social cohesion and religious amity.

Value inculcation is essential as emphasis on equity and social justice to all is a constitutional guarantee. National integration, strengthening of the culture of acceptance and inculcation of scientific temper can be strengthened primarily through internalization of values aspects in the process of teaching and learning.

The recommendations of Justice J.S. Verma Committee Report (1999) on Teaching of Fundamental Duties to the Citizens should be implemented fully and totally as an essential step in providing education in human values.

Schools must develop key qualities like regularity and punctuality, cleanliness, self-control, industriousness and spirit of entrepreneurship, sense of duty, spirit of service, responsibility, creativity, sensitivity to greater equality, fraternity, democratic attitude and sense of obligation to environmental and earth issue.

Creating and maintaining a congenial school environment should be an essential responsibility of the teachers. Social values must be given their due importance in every act, action and activity. These shall include friendliness, cooperativeness, compassion, self-discipline, courage, concern for the rights of others and keenness to support others in genuine cases of justice and fairness.

Various alternative and innovative models of value inculcation in the country need to be studied, analysed and documented. These could be disseminated on a large scale to various organisations and schools/ institutions to let them choose their own approach and modality.

Monitoring of various value educations initiatives by an independent standing setup could be greatly helpful in up grading its quality and also to maintain the dynamic and responsive nature of the process.

The way our political leadership, the executive and judiciary function and whatever of that is witnessed and read by sensitive young minds also creates a lasting impact. This factor should be kept in mind by our decision makers so that they set a right example to others.

It needs to be emphasised before the elected representatives of the people at various levels that their conduct and behaviour impacts young persons of sensitive age groups. Icons and adorable from the field of sports and entertainment shall also be made aware of their responsibilities to the society and generations ahead.

Sports and games have to be given their due place. These must become part of the teaching-learning process in schools and colleges without any exception. Professional institutions must be seriously brought in the picture. Apart from other benefits, the aspect of value education would thus be greatly strengthened.

Technical and Management Education

The credibility of the products in this sector has suffered immensely due to the failure of the regulatory bodies in maintaining quality and skill acquisition at the desired level. In many instances, these have not succeeded in controlling various other malpractices in the sector. Institutions of engineering and management are closing down at a stage when the country needs more of them. This issue needs to be addressed with all seriousness. Strict monitoring is needed to upgrade the quality of existing institutions and to encourage only such new institutions that have the necessary inputs ready and available.

A realistic dynamic system of comprehensive manpower planning covering all possible employment and entrepreneurship avenues needs to be put in place and made active and effective. Such an exercise is most essential as its coverage now extends from farms and fields to international opportunities.

This sector must establish an organic relationship with the plans, processes and products of the vocationalization of education at the senior secondary stage. It must create avenues for the upward mobility of the products from the schools.

Facilities for continuing education, renewal and up-gradation of the skills and also for learning new skills have to be created in large numbers in these institutions.

The general impression that management practices are often borrowed from the West and lack indigenous imprint has to be professionally examined and, if necessary, changes should be suggested to meet the indigenous requirements.

Majority of institutions in these two areas need up-gradation in terms of infrastructure, academics and in introduction of ICT. The top institutions should be persuaded to bring in more and more institutions within their fold for guidance and support. The present accreditation systems have serious limitations. The approach and procedures followed by the national accreditation body need to be thoroughly reviewed.

The possibility of introducing flexibility in admission to the management courses based on field experience and contribution made while working deserves to be explored.

The quality of programmes in this sector requires intensive focus on networking with other institutions and the corporate sector and the industry.

Education of Special Groups

During the last several decades, a large number of schemes were implemented to support the education of children of SC/ST category. There are schemes and incentives for the children from OBC and minority communities and provisions to assist and support handicapped children. Most of the schemes launched after the 1986 policy and those announced after May 2004 shall have to be reviewed by a High-Power body to determine why the intended targets have generally not been achieved.

Education of children of the weaker and the deprived sections requires additional support by way of teacher availability, hostel facilities, scholarships, transport, teaching-learning materials, preparation for competitive examinations and those for recruitment to various jobs, provisions for training in vocations and other areas depending on the local and regional requirements. Formally, it is invariably claimed that practically every aspect has been taken note of at the policy and programme level. However, the lack of resources, and committed and vigorous work culture become hindrances in the transmission of the intended benefits to the learners. Such a situation needs to be corrected.

In case of handicapped children, in addition to government inputs, voluntary agencies with credibility could be persuaded to shoulder greater responsibility to give a personal touch to their education and training of such children.

The issue of the education of minorities is often submerged under political consideration. A clear-cut, transparent and professional approach within the framework of the constitutional guarantee given to the minorities to establish and administer their own educational institutions and protection of their languages and culture shall have to be evolved. These provisions have been often stretched for extraneous considerations and it has not always been in the interest of the minorities. Many consider religion based reservations, schemes and programmes as divisive steps with political intentions. This issue needs to be examined in detail and the necessary clarification given to the public in general.

Industry, big and small, must effectively extend its outreach to schools and colleges, particularly in neglected areas, and help in giving training to the handicapped children.

Single teacher schools shall remain a necessity for several mostly in rural, tribal, hilly and forest areas. These would need tremendous support from all quarters and that has to be dexterously organized. Government must create additional mobile resources in men and material to assist in such situations.

Government policies on Ashram Schools, Madarasa's, Ekal Vidyalayas, or chain of schools run by other agencies should not give any indication of discrimination in word and spirit.

Sensitive handling of language issue in tribal areas where dialects may have no script of their own is necessary in light of the experiences gained earlier in finding solutions to this problem.

It is generally accepted that the coverage of the rich cultural heritage, identity and history of certain sections and regions is not getting its due importance. The efforts to correct this anomaly have to be expedited. Institutions of higher education must support the curriculum developers in schools by giving them the necessary inputs obtained through research and studies.

Education of girls becomes very significant from amongst these groups. It requires teacher preparation from these categories and particular emphasis on preparation and recruitment of lady teachers.

It is a fact that schools in tribal, hilly, far-flung and in-habitations consisting mostly of scheduled castes and minorities remain more neglected than others. It hampers every effort to bring their education on par with that of others.

Provisions of supportive systems like day care centres, Bal Wadis, health centers, sanitation, and potable water supply have to be provided on priority basis in habitations that need special attention in education. This would also apply to several areas in metros and large towns as also places where migrants from other places come in large numbers.

Alternative Schooling and Adult Literacy

The education system just cannot ignore the presence of young and aged school drop outs and those who wish to upgrade their learning or acquire new learning at some stage of life. Experience gained through various programmes already implemented, like non-formal schooling; alternative schooling and other models shall be comprehensively scrutinised and new opportunities created.

Age can be no bar in flexible and learner-friendly system designed for those outside the school system for various reasons. Practically everywhere in the country, educated and skilled persons are available to assist in any initiative that intends to extend the outreach of education to drop outs, un-enrolled and others interested in upward mobility in knowledge and skills.

The commitment to adult literacy in the years to come must aim at total adult illiteracy eradication coupled with substantial skill development. No-holds barred approach inviting all eligible persons and organisations to come forward and participate in this mission could be the way to succeed.

Alternative schooling and adult literacy initiatives should have a major component of local elements of the curriculum, skill development and awareness.

There is no dearth of ideas and alternatives in terms of conceptualization and management. The issue is: how to bring in the desired level of sincerity, commitment and approach at the implementation stage.

Adult education probably needs to free itself from comparisons from the formal system. It has often hampered its progress and even acceptance. It deserves to develop itself as an independent entity.

Teacher Education

The education system must trust its teachers and provide them opportunities for getting necessary recurrent orientations to enable them to update and upgrade their knowledge and skills. Those without the requisite training qualifications deserve support to go back to training colleges and acquire the necessary qualifications. To keep pace with the advent of ICT and spectacular changes taking place in the field of pedagogy.

Overburdening of teachers due to vacancies, absenteeism or their being assigned non-academic tasks by the administration outside the schools, results in serious dilution of learning attainments. This has to be avoided at all costs.

The issue of non-availability of teachers in tribal, forest and hilly areas shall be tacked by making certain District Institutes of Education and Training (DIET's) fully reserved for Girls from the district concerned. In fact girls could be selected after class VIII and placed on probation with suitable stipend in a residential mode in these Institutions for 4-5 years and then be appointed as regular teachers.

A congenial and conducive learning environment cannot be created unless schools have competent, committed and performing teachers who are fully satisfied with their working conditions, career opportunities and consideration and motivation are given to them for performing a nation building job.

The prevailing conditions in many of the teacher training colleges, particularly those eligible to teach for B.Ed. degree are deplorable. The professional suitability of the products suffers because of the persistent inadequacies of the system

The issue of extended duration of secondary teacher training programmes should be resolved in the light of the experiences gained in running the innovative two year B.Ed programme in the four Regional Institutes of Education and the Gujarat Vidyapeeth. The existing four year integrated teacher preparation programmes of the NCERT and the Delhi University also deserve greater attention and acceptance.

Alternative models of pre-service teach education must be implemented to ensure quality in the system. The possibility of integrated courses of five years duration after ten-year schooling to prepare primary teachers and of 12 year schooling and five years for secondary teachers must be experimented and extended on a large scale.

In the existing models of teacher education, the possibility of separate emphasis on the extended duration of regular teaching, school based internship and distance cum electronic mode could be explored.

Those who wish to become teachers after post-graduation could be provided with an advanced diploma course of one-year duration and made eligible to teach at senior secondary schools. Those With B.Ed degrees when promoted to teach in senior secondary classes must undergo another training schedule designed specifically for serving trained teachers to prepare them to teach at the next stage.

New entrants amongst college and university teachers must undergo a course of specified duration like six-month face-to-face component and another six months for an on-line component of the one year's diploma in dual mode. Academic Staff Colleges should move away from organising programmes of a few weeks' only as is the practice at present.

Programmes shall be designed to upgrade the professional competence and commitment of teacher educators on a priority basis. The efficacy of the functioning of the teacher education institutions gets reflected in schools and subsequently even in colleges and universities. These institutions must serve as a role model for others.

Teachers' unions and associations need to be encouraged to take up academic responsibilities, and contribute effectively in curriculum development, textbook preparations and other academic tasks. Subject teacher associations need to be encouraged and supported.

The credibility and integrity of teacher recruitment procedures must be re-established. This is a very weak aspect at present.

The code of professional ethics of teachers should be an outcome of an interaction between teachers, parents, and the regulatory systems. Such a code must be strictly adhered to by all.

The issue of teachers being assigned non-academic duties has been adversely commented upon by law courts, including the Supreme Court of India. However, the problem persists and education suffers. The situation has to be promptly remedied.

A performance evaluation system for teachers must be evolved and put in place. The concept should be extended even for those who are supposed to be managing the teachers and the system.

Examination Systems and Assessment Procedures

It is a sad commentary on the functioning of school systems that the long-entrenched process of evaluation has lost its spirit and has been converted to stress-full procedure of the year-end examination that weighs heavily on the child and also the parents. The remedy adopted by no detention up to class eight and voluntary Board Examination after ten years are creating some serious problems that shall have to be examined and eliminated. Cosmetic changes and high-sounding assurances create only clichés. The systems of evaluation, assessment and examinations needs to be overhauled and, in the process, the role of remedial teaching has to be brought in seriously.

Memory has its place and significance in the process of teaching and learning. However, excessive insistence on memory leading to various types of stress and strain must be done away with.

The systems of evaluation in teacher education must change thoroughly and these should present a model of what they expect of student teachers to carry out in schools in later years.

Firm, final and implementable decisions must be taken in respect of semester system and grading versus marks. The present system of internal assessment leaves much to be scrutinized and repaired.

Instances of students committing suicide because of fear of examination should be unacceptable and steps need to be taken to avoid any occurrence in future. Though in such cases the entire blame may not lie on the examinations alone but it must introduce steps that would remove the prevalent fears amongst practically all of the examinees.

Evaluation systems, formative or summative; criterion referenced or norm-based; in whatever shape these are designed and conducted, must have sufficient transparency to earn credibility in the eyes of all the three stake holders: students, teachers and the parents.

Examining bodies must be assisted further in modernising and up-grading their set ups and also encouraged to introduce innovations.

The possibility of conducting national level proficiency examinations in specific subjects, leading to national level certification and equivalence appears necessary at this stage.

Immense hardships result to thousands of students when examination papers are leaked and other unprofessional practices creep into the system. Use of ICT to prevent such aberrations could be the right step. Failures on these fronts reduce public acceptability and reduce institutional credibility.

Educational Management

The heads of institutions are the key functionaries that make the system work with optimum efficacy and who are responsible to upgrade the quality in totality. They need professional preparedness in managing soft skills and create a result oriented work culture and spirit of working as a team. Apart from managing the system, they have to continuously evolve themselves as academic leaders who command respect by their own example. Every school or institution that creates a name and acquires credibility does so mostly because of the top leadership.

Education of tomorrow must take cognisance of the knowledge divide and the digital divide and attempt to foresee the positive components that could be absorbed to reduce these. The knowledge divide has international implications as also within the country and within societies and communities. Corrective measures to minimise it have to be planned and managed well in time.

Increasing global presence of the Indian Diaspora of over 20 million people keenly interested in India, its culture, religions, philosophy, languages and heritage necessitates an educational response from within the national education system. This group could be very helpful in strengthening the linkages and building up partnerships and international interactions including institutional networks.

Systemic management of the knowledge and skills that children bring to schools has been shabbily managed. The role of indigenous knowledge is being globally acknowledged. This aspect was well emphasized in the National Curriculum Framework of School Education—2000. It highlighted the importance of the local element of curriculum in this context and had suggested utilization of skills, expertise and knowledge that is invariably available locally. Children could learn much from the flora, fauna, historical background, practices, festivals, local crafts, local methods of growing and preserving foodstuffs and so many others. It is necessary for imbibing a sense of identity and self-esteem. UNESCO report "Towards Knowledge Societies" brought out in 2005 specifically advises each society to raise its awareness levels about the richness of the knowledge each one of these possesses but may not be aware on a large scale.

Social cohesion and learning to live together are identified as the most outstanding objectives of education in the 21st century. Simultaneously, there are the times of intense insecurity, distrust and violence in the name of religions. These factors are not conducive for creating a harmonious and peaceful world. Inter-faith harmony and culture of acceptance of diversity of every sort has to be the foundation stones of a dynamic and responsive system of education. The values of Truth, Peace, Non-violence, Righteous Conduct (*Dharma*) and Love must become integral parts of every activity concerned with teaching and learning at every stage of education. That alone would have the inherent strength to win over those gone astray and chosen the path of violence, terrorism and fundamentalism.

Increasing impact of globalisation and ever-spreading glamour of the pursuit of materialism presents the real danger of the youth getting distanced from their own culture and traditions. Knowledge of one's own culture and respect for the traditions makes people more respectful towards others. The National Policy on Education of 1986 postulates: "Efforts will be made to delve into India's ancient fund of knowledge and to relate to contemporary reality." It still remains a pious dream. It has to be converted to a reality.

There is a serious need of overhauling the functioning of the authorities and bodies entrusted with the task of maintaining norms and standards and the quality at different stages and disciplines in education. Most of these have very little credibility and are generally perceived as points of hindrance and corruption. It is a hard reality and cannot be ignored 'for want of proof'. The whole nation knows what it takes to set up a new institution. In the times of major private investments and opening of education sector to global players, an attitudinal transformation in the approach of the regulatory bodies is essential. An overarching body needs to be created to give single window directions and approvals for setting upon educational institutions and it deserves scrutiny in its various aspects.

Effective procedures of comprehensive monitoring of achievements in institutional objectives and skill acquisition of functionaries within every institution must be inbuilt in the systemic evaluation. Every institution deserves an input of new ideas and corrective measures from those who have the necessary expertise and experience. A statutory body like National Commission on Innovations could undertake such a responsibility.

Educational management is an art and cannot be improved by those who treat it as a mere craft.

Management systems must develop their own procedures of system evaluation of institutions and also that of the products. Institutions offering low quality courses are doing more damage than good to young persons.

Non-negotiable in Education

The basic purpose of education is character formation; to prepare future citizens equipped enough to lead a value-based, creative, productive and fulfilling life.

The implementation of the Right to Education Act without equipping every learner with stipulated levels of learning and skills does not fulfill the spirit of universalization of education as contained in the Constitution of India. The age group 0-6 stands rather ignored. This has now to be organically linked to the Rastriya Madhyamik Shiksha Mission.

The education system must acknowledge that Gandhian philosophy is still relevant and it implies moving ahead in accepting new developments in science, technology and ICT. At least one model school must be set up in every district on the lines of Gandhian Basic Education in which, apart from the regular curriculum, every learner will acquire vocational skills and education.

The concept of the school system must be seriously implemented, particularly in metros and urban areas. This is essential for equality of opportunity of access and success.

The policy must be very clear in respect of three-language formula, place of the mother tongue and that of Hindi as the link language.

Private investment in education is essential but unbridled commercialisation is not to be permitted. The promised allocation of six per cent of GDP must be strictly adhered to.

Regulatory bodies need to focus on quality. These may prescribe norms but should be supportive to the establishment of new institutions, while simultaneously ensuring adherence to the prescribed norms. Their suitability could be judged by the quality of their products.

Only those fully proficient in pedagogy and skills and with an aptitude for teaching should be appointed regular teachers in schools. No compromise with quality of teachers should be entertained.

Every effort should be made to provide a congenial working environment and acceptable working conditions to all the teachers. An Act of Parliament would be required to establish a National Commission on Innovations and Research.

Immediate steps need to be initiated to appoint a statutory National Commission on Education, the Report of which could lead to the formulation of New National Policy on Education that would replace the NPE-1986/92. This commission should undertake continuous envisioning of educational plans, strategies, methods, materials and researches to make India a knowledge society and develop several Indian Institutions of higher learning and research as centers of international pursuit of knowledge and learning. Capacity building could be one of its major responsibilities.

Additional Inputs

Institutional autonomy must be respected. Simultaneously, norms and standards, once agreed to, must be strictly adhered to and that must be regularly monitored.

Education absorbs what is valuable in history and culture and transmits it to the next generations for understanding its significance, to appreciate its relevance and to strengthen it further through value additions. Only those who learn from the past can create better future.

Dynamic policies always keep their doors and windows open for new ideas and inputs. These also remain steadfast in their basic pursuit of humanistic, moral and democratic values.

The education policy must specifically emphasise the continuum of learning which at present stands stratified into different stages that provide little space for interactive strategies.

No child can be ignored for any reason. Every child deserves education and skill orientation appropriate to age, environment, aptitude and interests.

Resource allocation practices in education require a thorough review—both at the union and state/UT levels. The long pending assurance of six per cent of GDP allocation to education should be implemented.

A review of the educational structure in schools is needed. Universal Secondary Education should be "Free and Compulsory" to all children till they attain sixteen years of age. This can be ensured only by strict and total implementation of the RTE.

Basics of education in finances and marketing have to find a place in the curriculum. The list of emerging areas is increasing fast. The list of obsolesced has to be dexterously prepared.

Girls' education, particularly imparting them skills and preparing for higher level jobs has to be prioritised by arranging avenues for vertical mobility.

(September, 2013)

2

Gandhian Perceptions on Education

Contemporary Relevance

The Gandhian Philosophy on education had received considerable attention during his lifetime. It, however, received only respectful references in policy documents and textbooks as India preferred to retain the inherited structure and philosophy of education. Presently, the deterioration in the quality of education is being observed all-around. It is also being realised that the concepts of common school system and the neighbourhood school practically stand ignored in a system that tends to primarily focus on the utilitarian aspects of education and has ignored the responsibility to assist in creating an egalitarian society. Value inculcation, character formation and concern for the poor appear to be almost neglected areas. This paper presents a couple of aspects which could lead to a comprehensive discussion on the relevance of the Gandhian thoughts that were dynamic and willing to accept new inputs and thus remain relevant without being overwhelmed by the materialistic trends of the times.

Context

The freedom struggle of India continues to be studied, analysed and interpreted globally for many of its unique and innovative features. Indian independence remains a rare instance in human history in which an individual led the nation in the struggle against a mighty colonial power only with the weapon of nonviolence. Under his leadership, the nation won the war. The very strategy of nonviolent struggle conceptualised and concretised by Mohandas Karamchand Gandhi not only succeeded in evicting the mighty British Empire from India but also became the leading strategy in the freedom struggles of several other countries. The man and his convictions, principles and practices are being studied with far greater interest and insight globally as the world aspires to get rid of violence, distrust and bigotry. An array of numerous luminaries, from Martin Luther King Jr. to Nelson Mandela, acknowledged that it were the principles postulated by Gandhi that inspired them in their monumental struggles and subsequent historic achievements. To Mohandas Karamchand Gandhi, the "world was but one family"! Wherever and whenever a set of people tried to establish their superiority over others on the basis of diversities like the colour of skin, race or religion, the eventual consequences were invariably disastrous. With the increased spread of literacy and the evolution of dynamic and responsive education systems, things began to change for the better. Slavery and apartheid are now only sad reminders in history. Lack of education and ignorance inflicted innumerable miseries on nations and their people. India had a very sound education system which was decimated in a well-planned manner by the alien rulers. Mahatma Gandhi realised much earlier in his life that the root cause of most of the miseries that India and Indians had suffered under the subjugation of the British was the strategic destruction of the Indian system of education and, as a consequence; the success of the British in delinking of Indians from their own culture, history and heritage. To him mere lifting of the alien yoke was not sufficient to put India on the path of progress unless India resurrected its own system of creation, generation, utilisation and transfer of knowledge to future generations. In a letter he wrote on January 22, 1922 he puts things in a rather anguished perspective: "We should remember that immediately on the attainment of freedom our people are not going to secure happiness. As we become independent, all the defects of the system of elections, injustice, the tyranny of the richer classes as also the burden of running administration are bound to come upon us. People would begin to feel that during those days, there was more justice, there was better administration, there was peace, and there was honesty to a great extent among the administrators compared to the days after independence. The only benefit of independence, however, would be that we would get rid of slavery and the blot of insult resulting therefrom." In the same letter he goes on to suggest the solution: "But there is hope, if education spreads throughout the country. From that people would develop from their childhood qualities of pure conduct, God fearing, love. Swaraj would give us happiness only when we attain success in the task. Otherwise India would become the abode for grave injustice and tyranny of the rulers." He did not leave things at that point. Based upon his personal experiences, understanding of India and its strengths and his own vision of future India, he developed his own philosophy of education and put it to implementation. Unfortunately, the policy makers and implementers in education in the post-independence era ignored these futuristic and prophetic propositions of their mentor. Probably, the inherent focus on character building in the Basic Education could not suitably impress them. India suffers painful erosion of moral ethical and humanistic values which has reached shocking levels. No one knew India better than Mahatma Gandhi and nowhere else in the freedom struggles against colonial powers, one finds such an extraordinary emphasis on evolving a country-specific model of education as in India that is rooted to culture and committed to progress.

The Basics

The post-independence education in India ignored the need to put in place an education system that aimed at mental and physical development as necessary elements and, more importantly, gave pointed attention to the training of the spirit as finally, that turns out to be the most essential ingredient that prepares young men and women committed to lead a value-based life. Training of the spirit, obviously, is more difficult task than concentrating on mental acquisitions and physical development Gandhi Ji considered it as 'a thing by itself'! He worked with children of different backgrounds at the Tolstoy farm and came to certain pragmatic conclusions which remain far more valid in the prevailing socio-cultural conditions of today: "To develop the spirit is to build character and to enable one to work towards knowledge of God and self-realization. And I held that this was an essential part of the training of the young and that all training without culture of the spirit was of no use, and might be even harmful."[1] In his autobiography he also prescribed what could be termed the pedagogy of education that would be necessary in this context: "Just as physical training was to be imparted through physical exercises, and intellectual through intellectual exercises, even so the training of spirit was possible only through the exercise of the spirit. And the exercise of the spirit entirely depended on the life and character of the teacher. The teacher has always to be mindful of his p's and q's whether he was in the midst of his boys or not."[2] The two aspects that could become the pillars of 'man-making education', thus, are the training of the spirit' and the persona of the teacher. Today, the education systems of the day are very keen to bring in the element of dynamism in the content of education that is meant primarily for making it more relevant for the 'market'. The impact of the personality of the teacher and, hence, the teacher preparation often gets relegated to background. Learning and practising manual work and acquisition of vocational skills became the prominent components of the Basic Education scheme of Gandhi Ji which was discussed in great detail in the Wardha session of 1937. What is often forgotten was the stipulation at the Tolstoy farm that no student shall be asked to 'do what the teachers did not do'! It resulted in 'learning together', 'exploring together'; 'innovating together' and 'learning to work with others'. It created the basic mindset to respect others and help others whenever such a situation arises. It extends to respect for the religions of others, their culture, traditions language and the like.

Skill Development

Gandhi Ji has written extensively in the *Hind Swaraj* and also in his autobiography on various aspects of education. His experiences and conceptualisations finally culminated in the formulation of the scheme of Basic Education in 1937. Twenty days before the conference, Mahatma Gandhi had written in an issue of *The Harijan*:[3] "I have felt an irresistible call to make good the charge that the present mode of education is radically wrong from bottom to top. And what I have been struggling to express in these columns very inadequately has come upon me like a flash, and the truth of it is daily growing upon me. I do, therefore, venture to ask the educationists of this country to study the two propositions that I have laid down, without allowing their preconceived and settled notions about the existing mode of education to interfere with the free flow of their reason...." As is well known he wanted seven years education covering all subjects except English plus a vocation that was to act as the 'vehicle for drawing out the minds of the boys and girls in all the departments of knowledge '. The second point was that such an education shall be self-supporting. When Gandhi Ji made an elaborate presentation in the Wardha Conference, it was Dr. Zakir Husain who had the stature to put up some incisive queries. He even stated that 'those who are working in the education field will not find Mahatma Ji's scheme very new'! And, he went ahead to caution that 'There may be some aspects of the subject which cannot be taught through the *Takli (a tiny tool to develop thread from cotton)*'. He expressed serious doubts about the proposed scheme becoming self-supporting. Both these points were considered relevant at that stage and remain so even today in the much changed circumstances and conditions. In May 1939 Mahatma Gandhi wrote that "a more correct though much less attractive description" of the scheme would be "Rural National Education through Village Handicraft".[4] The essence of the Basic Education proposition and its subsequent emergence as the National Basic Education were strengthened by Dr. Zakir Husain based upon his scholarship and understanding. In the contemporary context everyone points out that the existing system of education fails to provide adequate skill orientation and that eventually results in severe deficiencies in the personality development of the young. A generational demoralisation amongst the youth is a stark reality before the nation. The euphoria generated by the projected 'demographic dividend' could vanish in thin air, if India does not radically transform its education policy and the consequent content and process of education. Unfortunately, creation of national level bodies often results in a bureaucratic approach which invariably fails to bring about any attitudinal transformation in teachers and parents. This has been the bane of Indian education in the post-independence period—resulting in accumulation of certificates and degrees that have little value even in the employment market and offer no motivation and readiness for entrepreneurship or self-employment.

The 'Heart' in Learning

Gandhi Ji's most quoted words in education refer to his keenness to bring out the best in 'body, mind and spirit'. In educational parlance, it is also referred to 'Head, Hand and Heart' or 'Self, Society and Nature'. In a broader sense, this 3×3 matrix indicates the path to formulate the content and process of education that would prepare a 'complete person'. In other words, what Swami Vivekananda had visualized as the 'man-making education' that would not fructify if the concept of education is mere 'utilitarian' or even only 'opportunistic'! If education has to prepare a comprehensively developed person, its very concept has to be idealistic and also pragmatically comprehensive. That would just not be possible if the existence of diversities and their consequences are not handled carefully or are neglected on non-academic considerations. Every nation is suffering a moral crisis of one sort or the other. Practically every citizen is complaining of erosion of moral, ethical and humanistic values. Five values: Truth, Peace, Nonviolence, Righteous Conduct and Love are accepted in every civilization, faith, religion or sect. These could also claim acceptance in every religion. After a very thoughtful consideration based on widely spread consultations, it was recommended in the year 2000 that the school curriculum needs to make provisions for making all children aware of the basics of all religions. They should know the commonalities and learn to respect differences wherever these exist. The basic objective was to strengthen social cohesion and religious amity through value inculcation as "Although religion is not the only source of essential values, it certainly is a major source of value generation".[5] Value education; its inculcation, nurturance and development must become an integral part of the entire education process; within classrooms, outside on play grounds, during festivals and celebrations and every teacher becomes a teacher of values also.[6] If, in the name of secularism, the education system simply leaves it to parents and the society to achieve 'social cohesion and religious amity', it would be a great folly. Gandhi Ji wrote in *Young India* of December 6, 1928 on this aspect:[7] "To me religion means Truth and *Ahimsa* or rather Truth alone, because Truth includes *Ahimsa*, *Ahimsa* being the necessary and indisputable means for its discovery. Therefore anything that promotes the practice of these virtues is a means for imparting religious education and the best way to do this, in my opinion, is for the teachers rigorously to practise these virtues in their own person." He goes on to state that "A curriculum of religious instruction should include a study of the tenets of faiths other than one's own". Every religion and every civilization emphasises 'Pure conduct, fear of God and love' as the qualities that must be developed right from the childhood. If education in independent India had really incorporated these aspects seriously and in the requisite measure, education would have prepared young men and women of unimpeachable character and commitment. It would have strengthened the pillars of social cohesion and religious amity. Instead, Indian education gradually discarded the very presence of religions in education in the name of secularism. One of the most brilliant minds of the freedom struggle, C. Rajagopalachari, wrote in the post-independence period: "Mass education,..., which is to result not only in knowledge and mental preference of the good but in capacity and readiness to work and suffer for it, cannot, as far as I see, be organized except on a religious base, religious in a broad sense."[8] He thought that to treat religions as untouchable was one of the many unfortunate follies. India stands for righteous conduct and that accepts diversity and respects all faiths and religions on an equal footing. This perception leads to spirituality at its best and the world respects India for the same. Who could be a better secularist than Gandhi Ji? He always claimed that he was a *Sanatan Hindu* and everybody loved that. Why can Indian education not be based on this highest level of interpretation of religions and spirituality and move towards a value based life for all? There is a widespread belief that a truly religious person would invariably be a truly secular person. In its rightful interpretation no religion could discard the presence of other religions.

A teacher is viewed as the mentor who transforms the individual learner from 'a person to a personality'. This makes a very strong point: no nation could afford to neglect its teachers as they transfer the treasure of indigenous knowledge and wisdom to generations ahead. It has to be presented appropriately in the current and futuristic context. In a large country, it is the teacher who understands the local context in totality and builds up his strategy of acquainting the learner keeping the gap between school environment and home environment to a minimum. The initial lessons in values are learnt here and, as Gandhi Ji was convinced, must be encouraged to do so through 'working with the hands'. Every nation is passing through a moral crisis though its contours and elements may vary depending on various specific contexts. It has to develop its own models. Education in every country must be rooted to culture and committed to progress. No education policy could neglect the need for early emphasis on tackling the moral component of growing up. Further, there can never be finality in the content and process of education as it is an organic dynamic entity. Mahatma Gandhi once wrote[9]:

> "The real difficulty is that people have no idea of what education truly is. We assess the value of education in the same manner as we assess the value of land or of shares in the stock-exchange market. We want to provide only such education as would enable the student to earn more. We hardly give any thought to the improvement of the character of the educated." This improvement is continuous process. Learning never stops and continue to grow throughout life. Gandhi himself was a lifelong learner. His following words could motivate every person who wishes to 'grow up' in life as he grows in years:[10] "I would like to say to the diligent reader of my writings and to others who are interested in them that I am not at all concerned with appearing to be consistent. In my search after Truth I have discarded many ideas and learnt many new things. Old as I am in age, I have no feeling that I have ceased to grow inward or that my growth will stop at the dissolution of the flesh. What I am concerned with is my readiness to obey the call of Truth, my God, from moment to moment, and therefore, when anybody finds any

> inconsistency between any two writings of mine, if he has still faith in my sanity, he would do well to choose the latter of the two on the same subject."

Man-making Education

Gandhi Ji was a 'complete person', who fully and completely exemplified how a *Vaishnava* of his perception transcends all sectarian and religious boundaries. He called himself a *Sanatan Hindu* and went on to define it in a manner that would bring in every person of character, morals and principles on one platform. And that would not come in the way of anyone's religion and belief. This is real secularism that projects the best out of religion, in fact every religion, and paves the way for internalisation of the principle of 'universal unity of all human beings'. In the Sabarmati Ashram, Gandhi Ji made it compulsory to adhere to eleven vows, none of which would adversely impact any person, sect, faith or religion. In Indian tradition, all the eleven of these have been respected, accepted and practised for ages. Nonviolence, Truth, Non-stealing, non-accumulation, physical labour, respect for all religions, fearlessness are the proud possessions of Indian family tradition. He added celibacy, not eating for pleasure and use of country made articles also to this list. Finally it is Truth and Nonviolence that encompass all of these. Education policy formulation and its implementation in India, he was convinced, would find it impossible to neglect the poor, ill-fed, deprived and exploited. He wanted every act and action to examine *a priory* how far it would help the 'last man in the line'! Post-independence policies have failed on this front. It can be achieved only if desires are to be renounced, necessities reduced to the minimum and only needs are fulfilled, not of a few but of one and all. To many, it may appear utopian in the times of unbridled materialistic pursuits. The fact, however, remains that there is no other way out that could create a peaceful, harmonious world that respects man-nature mutuality and gives dignity and humane life to everyone. Further, India's USP that the world has consistently accepted and respected is its strength in spiritual understanding, its philosophy of practising equality of all human beings and its capacity to overcome and shed off aberrations like caste system and other discriminatory practices. If India is to regain its place of honour and respect, it is the Gandhian interpretation of education that would become the beacon light. Every child has to imbibe it in initial stages that the global crisis has reached disastrous proportions and the very existence of the planet earth is at stake. Prepare them to live their life around the famous Gandhian adage that nature has sufficient to meet the needs of everyone but not the greed of anyone.

Published for the first time in the *Young India* of October 22, 1925, the Seven Social Sins indicated what a prophetic insight Gandhi Ji had for the 'shape of things to come'. These could be the 'syllabus' for the young and old alike and could lead to value inculcation and internalization the lack of which engulfs the society under the debris of corruption, exploitation, tensions and turmoil. A critical appraisal, scrutiny and analysis of all these seven sectors in the contemporary context could lead to healthy insights and, may be, open up certain ways and means to rectify the state of confusion, tension and uncertainty that prevails globally at present. *Politics without Principles* was the first one and everyone would agree to its potential to inflict insurmountable damages to the system of governance. *Wealth without work* attracts all and *Commerce without Morality* has become the order of the day. The glamour of *Pleasure without Conscience* and *Commerce without Morality*, are denting the vitals of moral and ethical living. In such an environment, Religion *without sacrifice* gets unprecedented acceptance. Violence and wanton exploitation of nature and its resources are an obvious consequence the application of *Science without Humanity*. In totality, these seven sectors, if handled adequately by education in its content and process could transform human life for the better.

It is impossible to reject Gandhian philosophy of education. Education is supposed to lead every person towards 'right faith, right knowledge and right conduct'. This is what education is primarily supposed to achieve. And if it succeeds, this world would get rid of misery, poverty and sufferings of varied kinds. These can be achieved only after social evils are vanquished by the educated and through the process of universalising education. The description of Gandhi, his life and struggles and the assessment of his contributions during his lifetime need to be put up before the children right from the initial stages to highest levels of education. That would generate interest and generations ahead shall continue to incisively analyse and study these for centuries ahead. They shall take inspiration from what Albert Einstein had to say: "Generations to come will scarcely believe that such a man as this ever in flesh and blood, walked upon the earth." They would be amazed to read the concluding lines of the judgement delivered by the British Judge who convicted him on March 10, 1922 but also wrote the historic lines, "Even those who differ from you in politics look upon you as a man of noble and of saintly life." There are numerous instances that give the glimpse of the universal impact

Mahatma Gandhi created through what he once said: "My life is my message."

Challenges Ahead

In a multi-religious society, secularism has to be interpreted with sensitivity and must draw its strength from the laudable practices of the past. A society that is religious with all possible diversities, enjoins upon the adherents of every faith to accept, with respect and internal conviction, the existence of other religions. The days of religious conversions or pretention of such efforts as 'salvaging the souls of others' must become history, like slavery, apartheid and racial discrimination. Religious persons must learn to internalise that all religions are created by 'God' and He has not authorized anyone to deprecate the religions of others. Religious leaders have a far greater responsibility in this direction. Gandhiji worked all along on these lines and his message was to respect every other faith and religion on equal footing, adhering to one's own with full devotion and dedication. Religious fanaticism has no place in this world and, if it is allowed to survive on any pretext, the ruin of human race would become inevitable. The world looks towards India to provide spiritual leadership. A resurgent India must, at the earliest take a pragmatic decision on religious education or education about the religions. The existing approach of totally removing everything about religions has adversely contributed in efforts directed towards social cohesion and religious amity. Though much has changed in the context of religious education in the India-after-Gandhiji, it is relevant to recall some of his views on this critical element in education: "If India is not to declare spiritual bankruptcy, religious instruction of its youth must be held to be at least as necessary as secular instruction."[11] In the contemporary context the measure of mutual distrust and religious bigotry are on the rise. It must be acknowledged that whenever a decision not to ignore the presence of religions in the name of secularism is taken, the foremost problem would be to prepare teachers suitable to do the job with objectivity. On 24 November 1927, Gandhiji commented on this aspect also: "I have experimented with quite a number of boys in order to understand how best to impart religious instruction and whilst I have found that book instruction was somewhat of an aid, by itself it was useless. Religious instruction, I discovered, was imparted by teachers living the religion themselves. I have found that boys imbibe more from the teachers' own lives than they do from the books that they read to them or the lectures that they deliver to them with their lips."[12] The very success of an educational policy formulation shall primarily depend on the extent it pays attention to teacher preparation and professional growth. Most of the problems related to quality and comprehensive nature of education could be attributed to the absence of professionally equipped, attitudinally committed and satisfied teachers. Indian education, apart from several other demands must accept its responsibility to strengthen social cohesion and religious amity. Both of these were very close to the heart of Mahatma Gandhi. The qualities of serving the needy, caring for others and respect for diversity could be very effectively nurtured within in the classrooms and other interactive opportunities that the institutions are supposed to provide for.

Education of girls and use of mother tongue in initial stages were often commented upon by Gandhiji. The manner in which English medium is being thrust upon boys and girls right from the nursery stage of education is indeed a matter of serious concern. The nation needs to take a serious note of it. Gandhiji was very clear about it:[13] "I refuse to put the unnecessary strain of learning English upon my sisters for the sake of false pride or questionable social advantage. I would have our young men and young women with literary taste to learn as much English and otherworld languages as they like, and then expect them to give the benefits of their learning to India and to the world, like a Bose, a Roy or the Poet himself. But I would not have a single Indian to forget, neglect or be ashamed of his mother tongue, or to feel that he or she cannot think or express the best thoughts in his or her own vernacular." Unfortunately, the race towards English medium schools has been glamourised to an astonishing level and as a consequence, millions of young persons develop a low self-image purely because of inadequacies in the learning of English. They are deliberately being put to disadvantage in the job market as it is controlled by those who are proud of being 'well-versed in English'! It obviously puts the larger section of the populace to serious disadvantage. Unless government schools are brought on par with private high-fee charging schools, education would be widening, instead of reducing, the socio-economic divide; as also the digital divide. Why can India not move swiftly towards neighbourhood schools or a common school system? Probably only then the last man in the line would have a chance to realise the dream of living a decent and dignified life lighted by the 'ray of hope' that education is presumed to be.

Indian education system can no more ignore its responsibility towards the millions who have aspired for generations to lead good, healthy and dignified lives. On one side, India could rightly be proud of the recognition of its talent as evidenced by the presence of enterprising young Indians earning huge packages in NASA and Silicon Valley. It must also recognise the presence of millions of jobless young persons and another equally numerous set of those who remain unemployed or are forced to work on a pittance of some honourarium, solely due to lack of opportunities of skill orientation and job opportunities. For Gandhiji, simplification of life was the solution. But that did not mean deprivation. It meant control/renunciation of desires, reduction of necessities and fulfillment of needs. Our existing education system prefers to swim with the tide, globalised world believes in accumulating as much as possible and that too in the shortest possible time. Indian educational planners must accept the challenge to find out what is best for India and Indians, remembering that it just cannot be a copy of an alien model but must have its roots deep in the soil of India. That would include an objective view of India's culture, history, heritage and the knowledge tradition. Gandhian philosophy and pragmatism combined together provided a sound basis to harmonize ancient tradition in spirituality and quest and transfer of knowledge to the modern approach that primarily depends on advances in sciences and the support systems that have been provided by technology and particularly by the communication technology. Education is the key to human happiness. Gandhian philosophy opens up an alternative path that he considered most suitable for one and all in India to march ahead and progress ahead. So much has been written on his educational philosophy, an incisive study of which could provide an enriching opportunity to teacher-educators, teachers and all those interested in the progress and development of Indian education. It is not difficult to realise the pragmatic suitability of the emerging solutions once one internalises the essence of the Gandhian philosophy and practices which harmonise faith, philosophy, spirituality, science and reveal the path for marching ahead to knowledge society. New pedagogical alternatives and solutions to the issue of obsolesce and bringing in new in the content of education become so simple when one remembers the following words of Gandhiji: "I do not want my house to be walled in on all sides and my windows to be stuffed. I want the cultures of all the lands to be blown about my house as freely as possible. But I refuse to be blown off my feet by any." That defines his conviction on philosophical ingredients that are always coupled with pragmatism, dynamism and a futuristic vision. It could become the pivot of new education policy for India.[14]

(January 06, 2014)

Notes

1. Gandhi, M.K., *An Autobiography*, January 2005 Edition, Navjivan Publishing House, Ahmedabad.
2. *Ibid.*, p. 311.
3. Mujeeb M.; *Dr. Zakir Husain*, 1972, National Book Trust of India, New Delhi.
4. *Ibid.*, p. 107.
5. NCERT, National Curriculum Framework for School Education-2000; NCERT, New Delhi.
6. Rajput, J.S., *Human Values and Education*, 2006, Pragun Publication, New Delhi.
7. NCTE, *Gandhi on Education*, 1999, National Council for Teacher Education, New Delhi.
8. Rajagopalachari, C., *Rescue Democracy from Money Power*, 1978, Bhartiya Vidya Bhawan, Kulpati K.M. Munshi Marg, Bombay.
9. NCTE, *Gandhi on Education*, 1999, National Council for Teacher Education, New Delhi.
10. Gandhi, M.K., *Towards New Education*, 1953 Edition, Navjivan Publishing House, Ahmedabad.
11. Gandhi, M.K., *An Autobiography*, January 2005 Edition, Navjivan Publishing House.
12. NCTE, *Gandhi on Education*, 1999, National Council for Teacher Education, New Delhi.
13. *Young India*, 1-6-21. The reference here is to S.N. Bose, Prafulla Chandra Ray and Rabindranath Tagore.
14. *Ibid.*

3

Curriculum Concerns

Education is the universally acknowledged key that empowers and opens the doors to every individual to lead a dignified human life that does not suffer from dependence and subjugation. It gives everyone a chance to contribute effectively and creatively to the eternal human quest for a better tomorrow. Elementary education is a fundamental right. It is an essential and necessary ingredient to the right to life. Not everyone needs to go to higher education and hence, school education must prepare learners for life; and for living. It must be noted that education in India was never considered merely as a preparation for earning a living. It was to be a comprehensive process of 'drawing the best out of the heart, hand and head. The transformation in value-premise of education is now not only visible but impacting all of its stages. Higher education and professional education focus only on market requirement and in a highly competitive environment; every other expectation from education and learning tends to get relegated to background. The majority now accepts that 'the ultimate goal of higher education is to prepare the learner and thereby the society only to create material wealth'! According to them it is knowledge that creates wealth, so wealth creates a knowledge society! Heart and hand are losing their place in scheme of things. It is all mind power and the cliché 'future empires shall be the empires of knowledge' appears perfect fit! While the curricula of education at various levels may still contain inputs that are supposed to cater to body and spirit in addition to the 'mind', in pragmatic realty, even learner attainments are judged by the performance of the mind alone. Current global trends have greatly complicated the process of curriculum development in education at every level. The impact of LPG; liberalisation; privatisation and globalization; has drastically influenced every area of human action and activity. It has created wealth; but only for a small minority. When one acquires far more than one's legitimate due; others somewhere get deprived of their genuine share. Consequently, the world suffers injustice, deprivation, exploitation, violence and all such avoidable traits that were supposed to diminish considerably, if not completely vanish after the advent of universal education. Hence, every aspect of education including its content and process need a thorough scrutiny in specific contexts. The discussion on curriculum follows in this background.

Curriculum for Growth and Survival

Curriculum is one of the most significant of the terms in the vocabulary of the teachers, teacher educators and education policy makers. Its interpretation varies from just a specific course of study to the entire gamut of learning in the process of education that draws out the best from 'body, mind and spirit'. It is well "recognized that curriculum is a key element in the educational process. Its scope is very broad, and touches virtually everyone who is involved with teaching and learning."[1] In easily comprehensible terms, we could consider a curriculum; as encompassing general education coupled with skill development which; at secondary or post-secondary levels; must include works and experiences associated with preparation for life and living. Also, preparation for life just can never follow a uniform pattern as the same is governed by socio-economic and cultural considerations specific to communities and nations. When ninety per cent of India was living in villages, Gandhiji gave the curriculum of Basic Education that emphasized productive skills, working with hands and preparation for life in a self-sufficient village that was to offer peace, harmony and tranquility. He wanted the revival of village economic life; and hence his focus on acquiring skills related to village occupations. For him, education was primarily the process of character building and an all round development in which earning a living following a value-based path was one of many elements. In Hind Swaraj, Gandhi quoted Huxley who termed an educated person as:

"That man I think has had a liberal education who has been so trained in youth that his body is the ready servant of his will and does with ease and pleasure all the work that as a mechanism it is capable of; whose intellect is clear, cold, logic engine with all its parts of equal strength and in smooth working order... whose mind is stored with a knowledge of the fundamental truths of nature... whose passions are trained to come to heel by a vigorous will, the servant of a tender conscience... who has learnt to hate all vileness and to respect others as himself. Such a one and no other, I conceive, has had a liberal education, for he is in harmony with nature. He will make the best of her and she of him."

In whatever manner one visualises education in totality; the basic remains the same preparing a liberal, open minded, broad hearted, committed and sincere person. With changing times, it is only necessary to reframe the strategies in the current terminology.

Presiding over the Session of the Indian Science Congress held in Pune in January 2000, the eminent scientist Dr. R.A. Mashelkar[2] presented a five-point strategy for growth, development and advancement of India and the Indian society as:

- Women centered Family
- Child centered education
- Human centered Development
- Community centered society
- Innovation centered India

These five elements comprehensively articulate the guidelines for practically every sector of governance. These have the potential to become the key components of deliberations and concretization amongst those entrusted with the task of formulating policies and design schemes and programmes for proper implementation. The most important component would be the quality of manpower in specific fields, specified sectors and specialised vocations. This quality would depend on the quality of education they receive and, hence, the criticality of a dynamic curriculum. One of the most important achievements of the 20th century was the global acceptance of the responsibility to extend elementary education to every child on planet earth irrespective of any conceivable diversity of any dimension.[3] Millions of children the world over are still outside the pale of elementary education in spite of sincere and active global efforts to achieve the already-delayed target. While the developed countries were already experiencing the advantages of universal education on which they had developed the edifice of higher, professional and technical education, the newly independent countries faced many problems in persuading communities and diverse sections of their society to appreciate the need for education; both for boys and girls. Today, this situation has changed drastically in the positive direction. People from every strata of the society now demand not only education for both boys and girls but they insist on "quality education coupled with skill acquisition" that may prepare them to lead dignified, creative and value-enriched lives. Ever-changing human aspirations and expectations from education were very comprehensively summarised in the 'Report to UNESCO of the International Commission on Education for the Twenty-first Century'[4] which was released in 1996 and retains its validity on the strength of its sheer clarity and foresight to envision the future and relate it pragmatically to the existing global realities including the fast-evolving potential of ICT in the global village: "In confronting the many challenges that the future holds in store, humankind sees in education an indispensible asset in its attempt to attain the ideals of peace, freedom and social justice... education has a fundamental role to play in personal and social development. The commission does not see education as a miracle cure or a magic formula opening the door to a world in which all ideals will be achieved, but as a one principal means available to foster a deeper and more harmonious form of human development and thereby to reduce poverty, exclusion, ignorance and war."

The apprehensions and doubts associated with the new techniques and technologies relevant to educational expansion, learner attainments and skill acquisition no longer deter people from accepting and adopting change. The shape of the classroom has changed. Self-learning and learning by choice and not in rigidly prescribed formats of time, place and content. There is another aspect that has emerged very prominently and is now a known cause of concern to nations, communities and individuals. The sensitive thread between man and nature stands snapped. From Ozone hole, the world has moved to the situation in which even a common citizen appreciates the import of the query: the survival of the planet earth is at stake!

In the national context everyone knows with rather personal familiarity that our rivers and forests are vanishing, mining and extraction of mineral resources are playing havoc with the routine lives of people. The glare and glamour of materialistic pursuits have relegated spiritual quests to some isolated corners. The expectation was that expansion of educational access would result in advancement of human values that are common to every civilization, region, faith and religion. In principle, no one questions the universality of Truth, Peace, Nonviolence, Righteous conduct; and Love.[5] In practice, there was never so much of violence, distrust, bigotry, hunger, poverty, preparation for war in the name of strategic readiness! Nations with millions of their hungry citizens living inhuman lives spend beyond their capacity on deterrent readiness against a possible attack from outside! On the other side even a ten-year old is now told by all around him that we are living in a global village! It is also well known that never before human beings had gained so much knowledge of the forces of nature as now. This knowledge and the techniques and technologies derived out of it by human beings through their own endeavour and ingenuity have all the potential to ensure a dignified life to every human being irrespective of any conceivable diversity. Why this is not happening is the most pertinent question before education of today and tomorrow.

Equality, Human Dignity and Justice

One of the most outstanding of the features of the Indian freedom struggle was its excessive emphasis; for genuine reasons; on universalising elementary education. Gandhi had realized it when he was in South Africa and he realised it through inflictions of insults and humiliations on his physical self and mental makeup. He was a visionary and instead of limiting these to himself, an individual, he extended it to all his countrymen and then to the deprived and depressed everywhere on the globe. He realized how simply because of illiteracy and ignorance, a vast majority of human beings is deprived of its basic natural and fundamental rights and how because of it, injustice and exploitation takes shape as inhuman cruelties that billions have suffered for ages. When he was in the thick and thin of the freedom struggle, he became more concerned about education and its content. He wrote on January 24, 1922:

> "We should remember that immediately on the attainment of freedom our people are not going to secure happiness. As we become independent, all the defects of the system of elections, injustice, the tyranny of the richer classes as also the burden of running administration are bound to come upon us. People would begin to feel that during those days, there was more justice, there was better administration, there was peace, and there was honesty to a great extent among the administrators compared to the days after independence. The only benefit of independence, however, would be that we would get rid of slavery and the blot of insult resulting therefrom."
>
> "But there is hope, if education spreads throughout the country. From that people would develop from their childhood qualities of pure conduct, God fearing, love. Swaraj would give us happiness only when we attain success in the task. Otherwise India would become the abode for grave injustice and tyranny of the rulers."

As the world became a global village, strangely enough, the complexities of life and human relationships have experienced far more tension and turmoil than ever before. The expansion of education did not result in proportionate acceptance and internalization of the values of brotherhood and eternal human unity. Articulation of these complexities has to be matched with the advances in sciences and consequent technologies—to establish a balance between limitations of human endeavour and aspirations that often become limitless in the absence of reason and logic. While education passes on the essence of knowledge gained over centuries by various civilizations, its main task is to prepare citizens of tomorrow who would care for the future of the planet earth and towards that end would realise how essential it is to maintain cordiality of human existence on one hand and prevent any further deterioration of the bonds between man and nature, on the other. It is a challenging task to develop the content and process of education that would respond to current requirements and, more importantly, create a future worth living, living in peace, religious harmony and brotherhood. The curriculum of education has to remain ever-dynamic and responsive.

Curriculum Development and Transaction

Young people are told that the "World is Flat".[6] India, in eyes of external demographers is passing through a golden period of demographic advantage as the ageing nations of the world are waiting for young Indian who would constitute over 65 per cent of its population to look after the country's manpower needs. Consequently, the curriculum of education at every stage has to encompass these and related challenges prominently in its ambit and ensure its extension to the process and pedagogy of teaching and learning. The issues of morals, ethics and values are under debate and discussion practically on a daily basis everywhere but not much of the outcomes are really seen in practice. The process of educational expansion has faced several problems which could be analyzed to find out why the deterioration in quality has become a matter of concern why the 'only ray of hope' has not shown the path towards peace and tranquility? Independent India had its priorities clearly cut out for governance: rehabilitation of the displaced from Pakistan; hunger, poverty, and shelter, health and all that a newly independent nation exploited and resource-squeezed for centuries would face. Education obviously lacked the requisite resource inputs and, in spite of the best intentions, delays and dilutions became inevitable. Even now, most of the schools lack basic amenities as well as the acute shortage of teachers. Declining interest amongst the bright and brilliant young persons for the teaching profession, inadequate support systems for innovations and research, exodus of the worthy to greener pastures abroad are factors relevant to the total process of teaching and learning at every stage. Clearly the curriculum transaction also requires a well-oiled support system. Even if the curriculum incorporates all that it could, its effective transaction shall always depend on available infrastructure, quality of teachers; policies and the commitment of those who formulate these policies. It is now well established that India continued with its inherited system and structure of education after independence. It was designed for a few as that alone was the requirement of the alien rulers. When such a system is universalised for all by a nation, cracks are bound to develop and systemic failures are inevitable. The diminishing credibility of government schools is one of the consequences of this 'continuity' and is known to all. Privatisation in education should normally be welcome as it indicates people's interest and willingness to contribute to the cause of education and preparing better citizens for tomorrow. This was the traditional Indian approach in establishing schools and higher education institutions. The current trend in privatisation in education is a different story. Education and health are considered the most secure areas of investment that ensure assured returns at high level. Now the anomaly in the education system at this juncture is characterized by resource squeeze, faculty shortage, commercialization and scant regard for the personality development aspects of the learner. It would be naïve to assume that a fulsome curriculum transaction would not be impacted by the presence of these debilitating factors. Curriculum developers have to take note of these factors as well. The techniques and technologies that are ever-evolving under the impact of the ICT are not necessarily reaching the teachers and teacher educators at the same pace. While some of the institutions are well-equipped and sufficiently resourceful to acquire and utilise, through proper training of the staff, all that is new and advantageous, most of the schools lag behind. Wide gaps exist in curriculum implementation at the grassroots level and this trend is on the increase. Learner attainment studies often present a dismal picture on the part of majority of the learners and it is a cause of worry for everyone. The principles of equality, equity, social justice and comparability of levels of learning get clouded under these conditions. Hence, some products of schooling are deficient as compared to others for no fault of theirs. Curriculum developers often rue that they are not in a position to take note of these extraneous factors. To some extent they may be right but a harmonious blend of the expectations and reality has to be established by the policy formulators and implementers. Curriculum developers must interact with them apart from receiving research and survey inputs of the previous cycle.

Curriculum developers of today must also realise that the relationship between teacher and learner remains powerful even in current times, when learning and knowledge can be acquired from a variety of ways. New technologies are now acknowledged as effective but the majority amongst the teachers have yet to acquire and master it. Over the last four-five decades, the terms like joyful learning, learner centered teaching, constructivist approach, learning by doing have come under public discourse prominently. All of these have contributed in efforts to make the curricula more relevant and responsive to the demands of the times. It must be acknowledged that the NCERT through its curriculum frameworks of 1975[7] and 1988[8] contributed greatly in generating awareness on critical concerns like environmental degradation, gender sensitivity, child marriages, value incuication, national integration and social cohesion. In addition, the National Curriculum Framework of School Education NCFSE-2000[9] highlighted the national goals of secularism, democracy, justice including gender justice; social cohesion and religious amity. It also aimed at developing respect for human rights and an attitude to perform fundamental duties with commitment and sincerity. The weaker sections including SC/ST, women, children with impairments and minorities, can no longer be ignored to remain underprivileged. It highlighted how education could contribute to their upliftment and empowerment. It acknowledged the need and significance of local knowledge; the knowledge that students bring with them; criticality of life skills; lifelong learning, internalisation of the need to contribute to social cohesion and religious amity. It also emphasised on value inculcation and character building. It took note of the tension between materialistic pursuits overshadowing spiritual quest that has been leading the human advancement in every civilization. The next National Curriculum Framework;[10] NCF-2005: again brought by the NCERT; highlighted the aims of education in the contemporary context and prominently included: independence of thought and action; sensitivity to other's well being; response to new situations; predisposition towards participation in the democratic process; and readiness for participation in economic process and social change. Towards this end; it emphasized the need for a curriculum that 'goes beyond the textbooks'. Essentially, the basics of curriculum framework are governed more by the external happenings and developments and hence the curriculum is a process of mutual support and assistance of what happens in the classrooms and how that and the learner interact then and in life with the externals. The ingenuity of the curriculum developer, its implementer and its evaluator depends on how far they assimilate the 'current' epistemology and put it in action.

Curriculum for Quality-in-demand Education

Essentially every cycle of curriculum development and renewal aims at enhancing the quality of education to every learner without any discrimination. In actual practice, every learner receives the curriculum as is visualized and imbibed by the individual depending upon one's interest, orientations and capabilities. The curriculum when implemented derives its efficacy from several factors that include learning environment, pedagogy adopted and the competence; commitment and professional readiness of the teacher. Further; it is significant to know that every learner brings his/her own learning. It could be derived from socio-economic and cultural factors. It could include hunger, malnutrition, traumas, absence of love and care or an excellent upbringing in the initial years. The diversity of individual learning experiences enriches the group's own knowledge and the teacher has to build upon it as delicately and in an harmonious manner as is within his/her competence. Primarily; the process; environment and the content are critical. Further; to remain pragmatic in their formulations, resources; management and administrative systems, monitoring and evaluation systems and procedures are major considerations before curriculum developers. The quality concerns could also be expressed as:

"A high quality education, therefore, implies an environment that actively seeks out learners and assists them to learn—using a wide range of modalities, recognising that the learner is linked to experience, language and cultural practices, gifts, traits and interests. Such an approach recognizes that people learn in different ways, each emphasising different senses and abilities.

A high quality education also welcomes the learner adapting to meet learning needs. It is inclusive and it strives to ensure that all learners, regardless of sex, age, language, religion and ethnicity are reached, and that they have the possibility of participating in, and learning from, organised learner activities."[11]

Every learner brings with him a large amount of learning and it becomes the learning brought by the group in which he/she participates. Huge amount of diversities in characteristics, skills, conditions and situations could be determined in understanding it. Some of these may not necessarily be conducive to learning ahead in a formalised manner. It poses a serious challenge to the ingenuity not only of the teacher but also remains a significant concern before curriculum policy makers and curriculum developers as it impacts both the content and pedagogy. It has to be pragmatically recognized that it is no longer valid to emphasise only 'one learning style' but to accept that there are 'preferred learning styles'. In developing countries it has posed serious practical concerns. Initial attempts to have a uniform syllabus or a textbook that ignores local/regional elements of curricula have contributed to the lack of interests in continuing in schools and significantly contributed to the rise in dropout rates. Such considerations obviously require professionally competent teachers who use learner-centered pedagogical strategies and skill acquisition approaches. There has to be sufficient anticipation of a learning environment—in which learners are able to express themselves; their views, thoughts and ideas; without hesitation and invariably remain active partner in the entire process of teaching and learning—resulting from the efforts of the curriculum developers.

Envisioning the Second Decade

High expectations from curriculum development and its renewal would be met, only when the strength of the process of curriculum development is articulated scientifically and has the potential to analyse and sift all the inputs that are received from all possible quarters and are related to those golden words: aspirations; expectations; progress and development. The process has to be locally/regionally appropriate and relevant; in the absence of which the subsequent development of the syllabus and learning outcomes could suffer from lack of credibility and acceptability. Curriculum change no more remains confined to educators and educational experts only. It is imperative to ensure detailed consultations with the general public and local experts and newly emerging areas which are impacting life and labour market in the globalised world. It would require considerable ingenuity to balance the priorities of various groups. It would also be equally difficult to get rid of what has become obsolete and to bring in what has become presently relevant and what would have a greater impact in the years to come. Hence, the significance of lifelong learning and acquisition of new skills are the most prominent of the challenges before curriculum developers.

Schooling of fixed years is now a process of lifelong learning. Hence, the process of curriculum development must incorporate the necessary elements to equip the learner accordingly. Certain basic elements have to be part of the process: From teaching it is now learning; it is no more transfer of facts but student's construction of knowledge. Memorization of information beyond certain initial stages is unacceptable. Instead, learning needs to be more about analysis, synthesis, evaluation and application. The world over, now the emphasis is on learner attainments—that too in terms of totality of the process of growing up. Parents and the doyens of the employment market are now asking questions about personality traits, value internalisation, capacity to face complex situations, willingness to accept new challenges and keenness to innovate even in adverse of the circumstances. Hence, curriculum is no more a mere product—but both "as process and product".[12] Now it has to be an interactive methodology that must take into account the round-the-clock presence of the ICT around the learner. The shape of the classroom has changed and one could say it extends itself beyond any definable boundaries.

In the gamut of human endeavour, activities, aspirations, complexities of living and relationships, expectations and concerns to see family advancing ahead in a world that values peace and harmony; curriculum developers must delineate certain specific aims, objectives and strategies to proceed ahead in their task. In such an articulation, the following shall certainly find a place:

1. Knowledge is to be acquired from various sources and through varying styles and strategies; thus extending the scope of curriculum far beyond the classrooms;
2. In the times of ever-increasing complexities, the skills and attitude to tackle unforeseen situations through innovative and creative capabilities must be acquired and internalized;
3. Eternal human values of Truth, Peace, Nonviolence, Righteous Conduct and Love are critical elements for a world that believes in peace and harmony;
4. Learning requires concentration and attention but it must not be made burdensome. Instead, every effort must be made to make it learner-friendly and interesting to generate interest in further learning including self-learning;
5. Respect for democratic values, the universality of 'serving and caring others who are in need' and keenness to perform

fundamental duties honestly to ensure that everyone gets his/her rights remains one of the most sought after goals;
6. A sense of pride in the national culture, heritage, literature, scriptures, contributions to world civilizations and proud moments of history must find a place in the curriculum;
7. Future generations must be prepared to make significant contributions towards the eradication of 'curses' like poverty, ignorance, ill-health, casteism; dowry; untouchabilty, violence and bigotry.
8. The citizens of tomorrow shall have an added responsibility, irrespective of their stations of work; to contribute in ensuring justice, health, community cohesion and generating awareness to shun unscientific and injurious practices;
9. The curriculum must leave enough scope for promoting and sustaining multiple talents and creativity amongst all learners in various domains of knowledge; and
10. There must be freedom, flexibility, relevance and transparency in the selection of content, transaction and procedures at each stage of education.

It is always possible to reword the above formulation, but what matters is the totality of the aims and objectives and their potential to enhance the dynamism and capacity to respond to change in education.

Specific Inputs

Curriculum policies, as also the curriculum development and renewal are ever-dynamic processes that lose their efficacy if the process of assessing the possible impact of external changes on education gets diluted for any reason at any stage. The curriculum in India must make children aware of the gaps that are being created in the society consequent to the present economic policies and various agreements pertaining to liberalisation and privatisation. The promise of social justice and equality of opportunity is just getting obliterated. In the name of economic advancements and inviting an investment, the state acquires lands of farmers at throwaway prices under some clause or the other and allocates that to money-bags and land sharks for their farm houses and commercial complexes! This is a sensitive issue, but people must get their rights and educated citizens must come to the rescue of those who may otherwise never get justice; as in this example where farmers are illegally made landless and; thereby totally resource less. How can they get justice in a system which is known for its delays and long-drawn out grievance redressal processes? The aspects of social cohesion, mutual trust and a sense of justice can come in only when education prominently focuses on high quality. "Nothing short of excellence in every aspect of school education is the first imperative for meeting the multifarious challenges of today and tomorrow. In other words, the curriculum must stand on the three pillars of relevance, equality and excellence."[13] Enriching the curriculum so that it goes beyond textbooks and connecting knowledge to life outside school were emphasized in the National Curriculum Framework prepared in 2005.[14] Biases and imbalances still exist in Indian society in spite of constitutional provisions made over the last over six decades and serious efforts made in pursuance of the same by enactment of several relevant legal provisions and Acts of Parliament. Rural-urban divide, on one hand and that between the rich and poor, on the other, is increasing. Further; caste, religion, ideology, gender, region, language, etc. continue to be unscrupulously used to favour or to seek favours on that basis. With the Right to Education RTE-Act having come in force for the last couple of years, one expects that such discriminations and biases would banish from education. The curriculum must create an awareness of the provisions of equality which, if tempered with, must be asked for as a constitutional right by the aggrieved person. The curriculum could be a strong vehicle to remove prejudices and complexes that have deprived billions of their fundamental rights for over centuries.

Equality amongst sexes is a fundamental right guaranteed under the Constitution of India. The state has been empowered to exercise positive protective discrimination in favour of the disadvantaged, deprived and deficient. The 1968 Policy on Education opened the way for teaching of science and mathematics for both boys and girls during the first ten years in school. It was a forward looking bold step which has paid rich dividends to the nation and opened up opportunities to millions and millions of girls after the NCERT curriculum framework of 1975 was made available to all the states and school boards. There was added emphasis in the National Policy on Education 1986/92 which moved to 'education for women's equality and empowerment'. The curriculum has to take note of this aspect and particularly ensure that more and more rural girls benefit from it.

India needs gender inclusive and gender sensitive curricular strategies to nurture a generation of boys and girls who are equally competent and are sensitive to one another, and grow up in a caring and sharing mode as equals. Education of learners with special needs requires special pedagogy and investigation into individual aptitudes and requirements. Similarly, specific considerations for the learners from disadvantaged groups are necessary. Likewise, no nation can ignore the responsibility of identifying the talented and nurturing them, if necessary in separate establishments and schools or institutions. Curriculum development now also comes under pressure from certain quarters which make specific demands. These may come from green activists, voluntary agencies working against drug abuse, or for children's rights; human rights; population and family life education; consumer protection; legal literacy; education of the migrants; peace education; rights of the tribal people and so many other aspects. It is a serious exercise to weigh the suitability of suggested inputs and at the same time ensure that curriculum does not become a load. Under no conditions, curriculum should be allowed to extend beyond the physical and mental capacities of the learners of each stage. One of the strategies that help is that of relating education to world of work which begins right from the initial years and could be suitably pursued further. Mahatma Gandhi's dream of 'thinking fingers' could be realised in this approach. One of the prominent outcomes would be the genuine respect for work of every level and variety. The total scheme of teaching, learning and working must also provide opportunities to the learner to 'construct knowledge'. According to the NCFSE-2000: "The acquisition of knowledge through active involvement with content and not imitation or memorisation of the material is at the root of construction of knowledge. In the constructivist setting the learners have autonomy for their own learning, opportunities for peer collaboration and support occasion for learner generated problems that drive the curriculum, time for self-observation and evaluation and also for reflection." The teacher becomes a facilitator of learning and tends to act as, ensuring availability of resources and enabling them to decide how to learn and why to learn. It is the responsibility of the curriculum developers to ensure the transactional feasibility of the key elements of cognition; emotion and action. The multiple intelligence approach offers learners opportunities to explore significant concepts and topics and to think about them on their own in many ways and to make sense of what they find or infer.

Strengthening of national identity remains relevant and pertinent as ever before even in times when certain sections are swayed away by the glare and glamour of the Western culture of materialistic accumulation and unbridled consumerism. In this effort considerable part could be played by integrating indigenous knowledge with the modern scientific advancements wherever possible. India's response to the impact of globalization would, in such a case, be more sound, logical and non-injurious. Responding to the phenomenon of globalization would lead to new scope emerging for traditional disciplines of social sciences and foreign languages. Further new approach to areas like active citizenship and human rights, environmental issues and common core of human values that would create a world imbued with social cohesion and fully prepared and equipped 'to live together' and respect diversities of all the conceivable varieties. ICT is to be appropriately infused and the curriculum of tomorrow shall give greater space and attention to linking education to life skills. The overarching umbrella of value nurturance, moral upliftment and developing aesthetic sensibilities shall always guide every action and interaction. Education in every nation must have its deep roots in the culture and heritage of the nation. Curriculum planning should ever remain conscious that the general principle of education everywhere being 'rooted to culture and committed to progress'. The secular fabric that India has successfully woven for over two thousand years in the recorded history is its most outstanding possession. Initial acquisition of knowledge and skills must also all along take cognizance of the need to connect the processes to society and life outside the learning formal education centre. Learning extends far beyond knowing and doing, essential though these two are. In life the criticality of 'learning to be' and learning to become shall have a real supportive role in 'learning to live together'.

Evaluation and Managing the Curriculum Change

It has always been stated that one single most significant reform in education is that in its evaluation system. The annual single board examination has proved ruinous to millions and millions of learners each year. Now things are changing. The class ten Board examinations have been made optional; grading system in place of marks has been introduced; and at the elementary stage no failure system has been introduced. Pedagogically correct, both of these are causing severe anxiety at the implementation stage. If teachers are not trained, system suffers from teacher absenteeism and the teacher taught ration is heavily skewed, it would be impossible to look after the individual learning needs and all the advantages of continuous and comprehensive evaluation would be lost. Same would be the fate of recommendations like laying stress on mastery learning approach by using diagnosis and remediation for weaker students and enrichment inputs for the brighter ones. Use of different methods of grading scholastic and coscholastic areas would also become non-implementable. Alternative evaluation procedures for learners with special needs, record keeping and reporting; peer evaluation and all such suggestions do require trained teachers who work in a congenial environment and have sufficient time and willingness to perform these tasks. Practically each of the curriculum frameworks emphasizes the need for reforms but mere articulation has little meaning unless the support system in right measure is in place and functional in real practice. Introduction of new pedagogy and assimilation of new technology requires huge training programmes for in-service teachers and drastic changes in the curriculum of pre-service teacher preparation programmes.

Gradually it is being realized that curriculum change and renewal suffers every time due to deficiencies that are perennially known. The impact of any curriculum change hinges mainly on the following:

1. Dynamic nature of the curriculum that offers opportunity to the inclusion of the local element of the curriculum; encourages the teacher to innovate and ensure learner participation.
2. Encouragement to the utilization of environment and community resources;
3. Strong systemic as support including availability of infrastructure, equipment, teachers in adequate numbers and arrangements for their training at regular intervals.
4. Committed immediate management support.
5. Strong political will and insight.
6. Teachers' understanding of the aims and objectives of the curricular changes.
7. Availability of adequate teaching learning materials including multimedia packages.
8. Monitoring mechanisms to provide remedial inputs to teachers
9. Institutional arrangements to keep teachers aware of relevant inferences emerging out of research and surveys.
10. Enhancing teachers' self-confidence as curriculum developers and associating some of them in the process at state/national levels.

The challenge before the Indian education system is to implement the recommendations that already exist beginning prominently from the report of the National Commission on Education of 1964-66 to the this date. While these have been rightly revisited on several occasions through policy changes and curriculum renewals; the implementation strategies have never shown desired level of keenness to ensure implementation with commitment. If that could be ensured, the outcomes in quality and learner attainment would show remarkable improvement.

(May 18, 2012)

Notes

1. Curtis R. Finch and John R. Crunkilton, *Curriculum Development in Vocational Education*, Allyn and Bacon, Inc, Boston; 1984.
2. Rajput, J.S., *Dimensions of Curricular Change*, NCERT, New Delhi, 2002.
3. UNESCO, World Conference on Education for All, Jomtien, March 1990.
4. UNESCO, Delors Commission Report, 1996, Paris.
5. Rajput, J.S., *Human Values and Education*, Pragun Publication, 2006, New Delhi.
6. Thomas L. Friedman, *The World is Flat*, Penguin Books, 2006.
7. The Curriculum Framework for the Ten-Year School, 1975, NCERT, New Delhi.
8. The National Curriculum for Elementary and Secondary Education: A Framework, 1988, NCERT, New Delhi.
9. NCFSE-2000; National Curriculum Framework for School Education, 2000; NCERT, New Delhi.
10. National Curriculum Framework; NCF-2005, NCERT, New Delhi.
11. Kenneth N. Ross and Ilona Jurgens Genevois, *Cross National Studies of the Quality of Education*, 2006, UNESCO, Paris.
12. Lucille C. Gregario, Learning and Facilitating Curriculum Change, Seminar-cum-Workshop on the Management of Curriculum Change, Workshop Report of June 7-9, Diliman, Quezone City, Philippines, 2006.
13. NCFSE-2000.
14. NCF-2005.

4

Teaching of Fundamental Duties to Students and Citizens

"I learnt from my illiterate but wise mother that all rights to be deserved and preserved come from duties well done. Thus the very right to live accrues to us when we do the duty of citizenship of the world. From this one fundamental statement, perhaps it is easy enough to define duties of man and women and correlate every right to some corresponding duty to be first performed..."

—Mahatma Gandhi

The planet earth is certainly not in good health. The man-nature relationship has been shattered by the human beings; the only thinking creation expected to know and hence, be conscious of one's own interests and define the relationship with nature accordingly. Today, man is worried about climate change, global warming, melting glaciers, and one can go on counting. Is it not really amazing that human beings just ignored their responsibilities to function as the trustees of the future generations? How could they themselves alter and damage irreparably the link that human beings are ordained to maintain to ensure the continuation of life on this planet? Nature, Mahatma Gandhi has warned much earlier, has sufficient to meet the needs of everyone and not the greed of anyone. If it were so, billions on the globe would not be sleeping hungry and thousands of children would not be dying of malnutrition every day. The rich becoming richer and poor continuing to be exploited, deprived of their legitimate due, languishing in hunger and poverty is the picture of the planet earth. It could have been so refreshing, rewarding, joyous and worth living for every human being only if human beings had learned and internalized one value: to do your duty and earn their right to live; and live really happily. If human beings understand the import of the adage: 'No one can be happy if anyone is unhappy'; then; why is the world so full of violence and bitterness, mistrust and bigotry?

The sufferings inflicted by some on many are part of human history as are the exploitation, annihilation, subjugation and avoidable infliction of cruelty and misery on the powerless by the powerful. Human evolution and growth of civilization is also expressed in terms of transition from muscle power to money power to mind power. We are witness to the transition from information society to knowledge society. Then what prevents a global upsurge for internalization of human values and why this delay in marching towards a world full of peace and tranquility? If that succeeds, then every human being could share the bounties of nature and warmth of human relationships in a congenial environment that acknowledges the eternal unity of human beings and their organic mutuality with the nature.

The answer is: it is human greed often accentuated by ignorance and overshadowed by false notions of superiority and power that have resulted in self-destroying attitude build up across the globe. It is failure of the system of transfer of knowledge and wisdom by the present generation to the next generations. It is the absence of icons that could be living examples of those 'performing their duties sincerely and with commitment'; totally bereft of greed and wish to accumulate more than others. Does the answer lies in the erosion of human values?

It is acknowledged globally that every country suffers from several crises that are common to all. Even the most developed countries are uncertain of and worried about their economic status and there is none who is not afraid either of economic slowdown or even of collapse. There is total confusion in regard of the ideology of progress suitable to a particular nation. While some do not know what they really require, others are keen to thrust their models on them and reap economic and cultural benefits. All this results in creation of human development Index, corruption index, health gradation, malnutrition index and gradation of nations on the extent of their lethal weapon power! Every country is concerned about the moral crisis. Terrorism and fundamentalism have made the world a very insecure place to live. Humanity must search for the real roots of these inhuman aberrations in human behaviour. It is not as if the causes are not known. The doubt arises as to why solutions are hard to emerge in spite of all the talk of global village and the miracle of connectivity that has brought everyone in the neighbourhood of everyone else! In any sector of human activity, it is common experience that a crisis occurs when someone fails to perform the task assigned to him. An act of seemingly small negligence could result in a catastrophe under certain conditions. Is the performance of one's duty of such a paramount importance? One does find explicit evidence in every culture of training the young person's to perform certain duties and obligations as essential to live contributing and creative life. Is the inadequacy of such practices and training that results in serious aberrations in adult human behaviour? Every citizen is a witness, participant or a sufferer in the scenario of decline in human values and the resulting degradation of human behaviour on vast and widespread scale. The need to arrest this decline is being expressed in practically every articulation that relates to building future society and providing some relief to the present generation which also suffers immensely on this count. The constitution of India explicitly provides for human rights, their preservation and protection and makes specific provisions to ensure that every section of society is protected against any infringement of these rights by any vested interests. The focus on human rights in Indian constitution which includes equality of genders is indeed unique and outstanding example of the serious concern of the nation determined to obliterate every sign that inflicts social, cultural or economic inequality because of unacceptable practices.

A question has often been raised 'why the similar elaboration of duties was not considered by the Constituent Assembly'? To the framers of the Constitution of India; all men and women of great sacrifice and those who practised what they preached, promotion of harmony, secularism and preservation of the rich heritage of India's multifaceted culture were basic and inherent values which were to be practised by each and every one and the initiation for the same was an essential part of the traditional upbringing of every child in India. In such a situation why make any provisions? Duties are an integral part of the Indian way of life. The case of Human Rights was different; everyone was convinced that these were being denied to millions on one ground or the other. This logic brings about one very pertinent point; Indian society is duty oriented society. Here, duties are assigned instinctively at the time of birth itself: the debt to parents; to the scholars and teachers; and to the nature and god! Maybe the constitution makers thought it as 'the given' and did not consider it necessary to formalize these in the Constitution. Things did change and the external influences gave rise to conditions in which the need to specifically emphasize the Duty component of life became necessary. The 42nd amendment in the Chapter IV of the Constitution was brought about and the same is now included as Article 51-A. It initially had ten clauses. Later on the eleventh one was also added. It is obvious that the absence of adherence to these aspects is primarily responsible for the steep decline in the humanistic, ethical and moral values in the personal as well as public life. As mere delineation does not meet the objective of inclusion, it is necessary to examine how these clauses could be operationalised.

It needs to be recalled that the issue of fundamental duties has to be seen comprehensively in consonance with the Fundamental Rights in Part III and Directive Principles contained in Part IV of the Constitution of India. The Supreme Court of India has in several cases relied on Fundamental Duties contained in Article 51-A to determine the duty of the State, and when necessary, given directions or frame guidelines to achieve the purpose. This has been done in several cases relating to preservation and conservation of environment, ecology, wild life, flora and fauna, etc. The Principle of sustainable development, striking a balance between development and preservation of natural resources, has been possible by reading the Fundamental Rights in Article 48-A and the Fundamental duties in Article 51-A. The Court has observed that the preservation of environment and the maintenance of ecological balance are the responsibility of the government but also the Fundamental duty of every citizen. Several other decisions in which the Article 51-A has contributed significantly in conjunction with other provisions in the Constitution could also be cited.

Article 51-A

The pedagogical implications of the eleven Fundamental Duties could be derived in a couple of ways. These could be classified in a time sequence; past, present and future. In another approach, it would be seen that certain clauses demand every citizen to look at the nation as a whole. Certain others demand duties to community. The remaining are related to individuals. In the list given below, these are indicated by N (Nation), C (Community) and I (Individual). Simultaneously there are also the indications in time sequence: P (Past); Pr (Present); and F (Future). The individual remains important in each of these.

(a) To abide by the Constitution and respect the National Flag and the National Anthem: (P, N)
(b) To cherish and follow the noble ideals which inspired our national struggle for freedom: (P, N)
(c) To uphold and protect the sovereignty, unity and integrity of India: (Pr, N)

(d) To defend the country and render national service when called upon to do so: (Pr, N)
(e) To promote harmony and the spirit of common brotherhood amongst all people of India transcending religious, linguistic and regional or sectional diversities and to renounce practices derogatory to the dignity of women: (Pr, C)
(f) To value and preserve the rich heritage of our composite culture: (Pr, C)
(g) To protect and improve the natural environment including forests, lakes, rivers and wild life and to have compassion for living creatures: (Pr, C)
(h) To develop the scientific temper, humanism and the spirit of inquiry and reform: (F, I)
(i) To safeguard public property and to abjure violence: (Pr, C)
(j) To strive towards excellence in all spheres of individual and collective activity, so that the nation constantly rises to higher levels of endeavour and achievement: (F, I)
(k) To provide opportunities for education by the parent the guardian, to his child, or a ward between the ages of 6-14 years as the case may be: (F, C; Pr)

An analysis of the expected outcomes of educational programmes on fundamental duties could also be delineated as understanding, appreciation and action. This essentially involves wide range of cognitive levels. Every curriculum and textbook must be evaluated from all of these angles and possibilities of strengthening aspects that may not have been prominently covered must be explored in each case.

Role of Education

Any attitudinal transformation on a large universal scale requires a long term strategy and planning. In the 21st century, education is the most reliable and dependable instrument available for that. It is only reasonable to examine how educational process could be strengthened to bring out the clauses of fundamental duties from the pages of the Constitution to the schools, colleges and universities and thus provide an opportunity to the young generation to internalise their obligations as common citizens each of which is dependent on and linked to others, and also to nature and its bounties, forces and furies. The subtle perception of these duties means establishing bonds with others, with humanity and nature. It implies appreciation of the gifts of God to human beings and the resulting obligation to preserve these and wherever possible and desirable, enhance the linkages.

The role of good quality education and the comprehensive nature of its content has always been emphasized by seers and saints, scholars and philosophers and also by socially-conscious and alert community leaders. Mahatma Gandhi wanted education to draw the best in the body, mind and spirit. Sri Aurobindo wanted the mind to be consulted in its own development and progress. Tagore wanted education that integrates the individual's joy and happiness with nature. Swami Vivekananda wanted 'education, education, education' for everyone. In 1922, Gandhi expressed his serious reservations on how our people will not get happiness immediately after independence. He pointed out several factors like the ills of elections, injustice, and tyranny of the rich and others that would come in the way. Then he wrote: "But there is hope, if education spreads throughout the country. From that people would develop from their childhood qualities of pure conduct, God fearing, love. Swaraj would give us happiness only when we attain success in the task. Otherwise India would become the abode for grave injustice and tyranny of the rulers."[1] The issue to be examined in considerable details is why expansion of education has not been able to check the decline of human values in amongst citizens and also in the system of governance which too is managed by educated Indian citizens! An step of real value was taken by the government of India when it appointed a committee under the Chairmanship of Former Chief Justice of India, Justice J.S. Verma to make recommendations 'to operationalise the suggestions to teach Fundamental Duties to the citizens of the country'. The Committee noted the presence of judicial decisions towards enforcement of certain clauses of Article 51A. It observed: "What is needed to be operationalised is compliance of the provisions of the various Acts. This is particularly true of clauses (a), (c), (e), (g) and (f). The remaining clauses are exhortation of basic human values and have to be developed amongst citizens in a variety of ways." The committee appreciated the role of education and remarked: "The education system has to create proper and graded curricular inputs from early years of education to the higher and professional levels of education." Essentially, there can be no finality on specific initiatives, but a continuum of efforts can certainly be identified. It is also well understood that such efforts need a constant reinforcement as the chances of unethical forces impacting the individual can never be ruled out.

Role of Teachers

Two major players emerge at this stage when one considers how to operationalise any of the steps that may be delineated in this regard. These are the teacher and the content of curriculum in educational institutions including teacher-preparing institutions. In addition, one has to consider that the recommendations apply to all citizens. While preparing the young children to become duty-conscious citizens is a national responsibility, those not in educational institutions should also have to be inducted and reminded of their role and obligations. The efforts could be aimed at the nation as a whole, the community and the individual. All citizens, including retired personnel and working professionals, must contribute their share in these nation building efforts. The first task is to internalise these duties in their performance and functioning, and then persuade others to follow suit. In view of the criticality of the task that must be performed by educational institutions, let us undertake an overview of the teachers' role be perused followed by the curriculum contents. The Report of the National Education Commission (1964-66) begins with the statement: "The destiny of India is now being shaped in her classrooms. This we believe is no mere rhetoric."[2] Obviously, the 'person' who has the key to reshaping the destiny of the country is the teacher. He requires infrastructure support and also professional and social support but nothing and none else can even think of taking over this role at the level of the teacher. Mahatma Gandhi said: "I have always felt that the true text-book for the pupil is his teacher. I remember very little that my teachers taught me from books but I have even now a clear recollection of the things they taught me independently of books...." In his autobiography under the chapter "As Schoolmaster", he talks about the culture of heart, also reworded as the building of character: ".... But I had given the first place to the culture of the heart or the building of character, and as I felt confident that moral training could be given to all alike, no matter how different their ages and upbringing. I decided to live amongst them, all the twenty four hours of the day, as their father. I regarded character-building as the proper foundation for their education and, if the foundation was properly laid, I was sure that the children could learn all the other things themselves or with the assistance of friends." When Gandhiji said that his life was his message, he was communicating a great mantra to live a decent, dignified and delightful life to everyone who could just appreciate the import of these famous words. In fact these in a way, summarise the total content of the teacher preparation curriculum. Gandhi's life was a life of renunciation and service to the people and the nation. He was a great teacher of people of all ages. He taught by example. His views and opinions; *vichar*; always followed his actions; not vice versa. A true teacher ignites the thought processes of the student to discover the 'Treasure Within'. This, as Sri Aurobindo had said, for the teacher to know that 'nothing can be taught'. The teacher must internalise his role primarily as the role-model and afterwards as a partner with the student in the process of discovering his latent talent. Sri Aurobindo elaborates the same like this: "Whose is the hand that has transmitted a useless stone into a sacred statue worshipped by many? It is the noble hand of the sculptor that has turned it into a statue and has lent an immense value to it. Similarly it is the teacher alone—verily the deft sculptor—who removes away, with deft handling, the drossness and weakness in a student and lifts him to sublime heights."

In the context of duties, why so much focus on the young? Because we love children and we love to give them a better future. The entire *world* must strive to nurture every single child who is growing up. Recall H.W. Longfellow:

> To Children
> Ye are better than all the ballads
> That ever were sung or said
> For ye are the living poems

Just to reiterate, the famous words of Socrates must reverberate in the ears of every citizen:

> "Could I climb to the highest place in Athens I would lift up my voice and shout,
> Fellow citizens, why do you turn and scrap every stone to gather wealth and so little care for your children to whom one day must you relinquish it all?"

Preparing teacher is a serious job, probably more serious than preparing doctors, engineers and architects. It requires tremendous knowledge and patience to 'consult the mind in assisting it to grow up'. Teachers have to be living embodiments of individuals who perform their duties as part of their normal approach to life. A teacher, as a role model, an icon for the young must lead a value-based life. Teaching with a healthy mind and sense of creating future is a great opportunity to fulfill the cherished goals of human existence.

Curriculum Concerns

The Basic Constitutional values identified by the Verma Committee were: Sovereignty; Socialism; Secularism; Democracy; Republican

Character; Justice; Liberty; Equality; Fraternity; Dignity of the individual and Unity and integration of the nation. These are the citizenship values and it would be apparent that once one makes a commitment to these, the issue of rights and duties ipso facto, emerges prominently before the individual. Total commitment to these values is a pre-requisite for the growth and development of the nation and success of its efforts to provide a good quality life to all of its citizens. In the Constitution of India, Article 51-A was incorporated through the 42nd Constitutional Amendment of 1976. The duties contained in the article are in consonance with Article 29(1) of "A Universal Declaration of Human Rights" which says: "everyone has duties to the community in which alone the free and full development of his personality is possible." It must be recalled that the framers of the Indian Constitution were illustrious men and women who had devoted most of their life time for performing their duties, always sacrificing the 'self' for the good of the community and the country. They knew India thoroughly well. They loved its diversity and the traditions that preserved the cohesion and religious amity for ages. There is hardly any example anywhere of an existing faith wholeheartedly welcoming other faiths one after the other faiths and providing them full support, protection and encouragement! Indian secularism, thus, is one of the most effective reminders of the duty of every individual to respect the diversity of faiths and give equal respect to the followers of other religions in the spirit of *Sarva Dharama Sambhava* (all regions are the same); which was described by Dr. Shankar Dayal Sharma in the following words: "... an approach of tolerance and understanding of the equality of all religions.... This philosophical approach of understanding, co-existence and tolerance is the very spirit of our ancient thought." This, in a way, indicates how the curricula should respond to the expectations contained in Article 51-A. For pluralistic societies, the concerns are manifold and the contents of Fundamental Duties have been delineated keeping these in consideration. These aim at propagating positive social and cultural values amongst people and make them realise that loyalties of caste, colour, regionalism and the like are never conducive to social cohesion and national progress.

One of the several essential responsibilities of the curriculum planners and developers is to integrate the basic principle that human rights cannot be treated in isolation to human duties. Indian society has traditionally given great importance to human relations and has conceived these more in terms of duties and obligations rather than rights. There are clear indications that when the universal Declaration of Human Rights was drafted, it was influenced by the Western approach to life and human relations and consequently, could not simultaneously incorporate the more essential aspect of duties and responsibilities to others.

Any exercise undertaken to examine the presence of fundamental duties in the curriculum would invariably reveal the presence of these aspects in one way or the other in the textbooks. Obviously, civics and political science shall be found to have maximum coverage, followed by the textbooks of science and environmental studies. The adult education and literacy programmes conducted by various agencies of the government, also attempt to familiarise people with these aspects; not necessarily making a technical mention of the constitutional provisions, but refreshing what is normally ignored because of several other considerations that loom large on life in its daily grind. In the formal sector, the National Council of Educational Research and Training (NCERT) and the State Councils of Educational Research and Training; (SCERT); can play a major role. These bodies can, in every cycle of curriculum renewal, impress upon their experts to remain conscious of their responsibility on this count. There is no dearth of instances and approaches that find a place in the curricula and textbooks which can be gainfully utilised to inculcate and nurture the sense of responsibility. What else is being taught when the life of a devoted and dedicated scientist is being discussed along with his achievements and contributions through hard and sustained devotion to further the cause of science? It shall depend on the ingenuity of the teacher. It is obvious to infer that while curriculum content is very significant, it is the teacher preparation aspect that becomes more significant as the quality of pedagogy of curriculum transaction is more important than the content of the curriculum. The content is the first requirement but its value depends on how effectively its spirit can be transferred to the learner.

The quality of teacher preparation has been a serious concern of the education system. It resulted in the passage of the NCTE Act by the Parliament of India in 1993. The NCTE began on a very encouraging note and succeeded in regulating the correspondence courses that were generally of unacceptable quality. The approach could not be sustained and now, with over 14000 teacher preparation institutions, the quality of teacher preparation has taken a shape which, to say the least, is alarmingly on the decline. In general it can be said that on the aspects of the duties, there is not much evidence of a focused and deliberate attempt to highlight these in the curriculum. One can, however, always find out instances and claim that one or the other aspect is being included at this or that point! This could be helpful if the approach to teacher preparation was, as desired, on development of attitude and values. Unfortunately, this is not always the case and the total emphasis is on information transfer and 'coverage of the prescribed content' for the annual examination. A major breakthrough was attempted by the NCTE when it brought out its National Curriculum Framework for Quality Teacher Education in 1998 and recommended that teacher education must equip every school teacher with capabilities to ensure internalisation of the Fundamental Duties amongst every child, both in understanding and application. It emphasised: "it may be pointed out that teacher education curricula at the elementary and secondary levels needs a thorough review from the standpoint of identifying entry points for the incorporation of Fundamental Duties."[3] It is for the consideration of the policy makers to examine whether an independent comprehensive unit on Fundamental Duties be prepared and made an integral part of the teacher preparation programmes both at the elementary and secondary stages. It could become a major unit at the Master Level programmes in the discipline of education. The same could also apply for the in-service education of teachers.

At the higher education level, the University Grants Commission has pointed out that its recommendation on foundation courses at the undergraduate level has found widespread acceptance. These courses have components of 'Indian history and culture, the freedom movement in Asia and Africa and, Gandhian thought, especially on the issue of nonviolence and peace'. Within the course of sustainable development, UGC has encouraged development of a course on interplay between human rights, women and child rights, environment and the issues of equity and distributive justice.[4] Higher education is also now emphasizing the need for focusing on various aspects of environment-related concerns, both as separate subjects and also as integral parts of various disciplines and courses. In higher education students do come across the lives and contributions of eminent personas and personalities of illustrious individuals who could be cited as role models as having worked for the welfare of others, for preserving the sensitive man-nature mutuality and for concretising the basic human value of eternal human unity. Institutions of higher learning have an additional responsibility: to conduct researches on how this transformation from rights-demanding approach to duty-first attitude could really be recreated and replicated in selected groups, areas of individuals. These institutions could also support innovative strategies by universities and spirited organisations in this sector. The success stories would interest many. Departments of women studies and adult education could be involved in a big way. Universities having departments/ cells/ units on human rights would be embarking upon a far-more challenging task by re-designating these as departments/ cells/ units for human right and duties. Those who have not yet created such wings could certainly take a new lead. The university students constitute the most dynamic, idealistic, energetic and progressive component of citizenry, a series of initiatives, aiming at moving 'their minds in the direction of compliance of fundamental duties as an integral part of their approach to life', could be launched.

Role of Professional Groups

It is often pointed out in deliberations at various levels that if those holding important positions in administration, in public life and in social hierarchy present examples of duty-conscious persons, others would be motivated to follow suit. The most prominent group, apart from teachers, is that of public representatives and 'leaders of the people'. Even a cursory glance on the freedom struggle of India would indicate how committed and self-sacrificing leadership could transform millions and millions of ordinary citizens toiling in farms; fields and factories into fighters for freedom and human dignity. Those were the times when people had developed tremendous faith in the sincerity of their leaders. That level of confidence is missing today. This needs to be restored. The only alternative is to emphasise the real meaning of taking the oath of allegiance to the constitution of India that explicitly includes the oath to preserve and adhere to the constitutional and democratic values. These persons must be reminded of the noble ideals which inspired the struggle for freedom. It is also their duty to inspire their people for self-reliance, value-based life, scientific temper and a keen desire to stay clear of petty and self-centred considerations. It is their duty to enhance social cohesion and religious harmony as practical values that are necessary for growth and development. If such representatives adopt only a positive and supportive role and do not interfere in the task-performance of those individuals and institutions which are following the right path, there would be dramatic redressal of people's grievances. It is the hurtful, unjust, arrogant and insulting behaviour of the state machinery which often results in social turbulence. It creates an environment of contradictions and complexities in which the simple, god-fearing and honest citizen gets lost. There is strong need to educate people on how and whom to elect as their representative. The responsibility to orient those who get elected follows after this. They must be regularly reminded that they are now ordained to be just and judicious; must serve others without any consideration of caste, creed, religion, family ties or any other. Now onwards, all are alike to them. This is as important for the elected members of the Panchayati Raj bodies as for the Members of Parliament.

It may be worthwhile to recall the seven principles of public life that were submitted by the Lord Nolan Committee to the British Parliament.[5] These, in fact, present, in the modern-day terminology, the totality of the approved conduct on the part of elected representatives anywhere and at any stage. These are:

1. ***Selflessness***: They should take decisions solely in terms of public interest and not in order to gain financial or other material benefits for themselves, their family, or their friends.
2. ***Integrity***: They should not place themselves under any financial or other obligation to outside individuals or that might influence them in the performance of their official duties.
3. ***Objectivity***: They should make choices on merit and on facts.
4. ***Accountability***: They are accountable for their decisions and actions to the public and must submit themselves to whatever scrutiny is appropriate to their office.
5. ***Openness***: They should be as open as possible for all the decisions and actions that they take. They should give reasons for their decisions and restrict information only when wider public interest clearly demands such a course of action.
6. ***Honesty***: They have a duty to declare any private interest relating to their public duties and to take steps to resolve any conflicts arising in a way that protects the public interest.
7. ***Leadership***: They should promote and support these principles by leadership and example.

These principles would be appropriately applicable in educational institutions and other organizations as well. If elected representatives occasionally discuss these and make a self-evaluation of their own performance, they would be highly benefitted and that would result in far more effective performance in the times ahead.

People come in contact with the official systems of governance practically on a daily basis. They have to interact with civil servants dealing with maintenance of law and order, enforcement of socially beneficial regulations and schemes, implementation of developmental programmes, maintaining the supply chain of essential requirements of varied dimensions, all on a level playing field. If civil servants sincerely apply the quintessence of Fundamental Duties to the performance of their appointed tasks, they would not only serve as worthy examples for fellow citizens but also succeed in bringing about immense improvement in the quality of their lives. There are institutions for the training and regular reorientations of civil servants. The programmes and their content needs to be regularly examined from the Fundamental Duties perspective. The performance evaluation of every public servant must give high priority to his devotion to the assigned duties and the general approach to the importance and significance of 'doing one's duty' with utmost commitment and devotion. Every public servant is supposed to project a human face of administration, supportive, responsive, and considerate yet firm in adhering to prescribed norms and standards. It is the discrimination and favour to some, particularly the influential and the resourceful, that hurts most and the sours the people-government relationship. The passing of the Right to Information Act has been a major step towards transparency in administration. It has given a huge push in the march towards greater people participation in ensuring that government machinery does not work in its own shell, but remains conscious that all its actions are being watched and overseen by the people.

Judiciary is the last resort to get justice; whatever is the rightful claim and compensation of the aggrieved people. It is one sector that has to be above suspicion and in the hallowed precincts of the halls of justice, everyone and each one of their actions have to be beyond even 'the shadow of doubt.' In this light, the Law Colleges and their teachers and students are the prime group for inculcation and nurturing of the essence of Article 51-A. The practising judges and the lawyers too have a great responsibility. The same applies to the administrative wings of the courts at all the levels. Law enforcement agencies have a great responsibility as it is their level of truthfulness and sincerity which paves the way for proper deliverance of justice by the courts.

The corporate world, the industry and the business world function under provisions of fundamental rights contained in the Constitution of India. Not all of them are willing to share their social and national responsibilities all the time. If it were so, many of our rivers, lifelines to millions, would not have been destroyed by insensitive industrial establishments—totally oblivious of their basic human duties. The way the mining mafia has exploited natural resources including siphoning off nation's mineral wealth, often denuding forests in the process, leaving the inhabitants to starve and the nation to suffer huge losses. A people's watch could on some occasions restrict the unethical forays of certain elements but much could be achieved by self-regulation by these organisations. This front is weak and needs to be encouraged to play a positive role in this regard. Small gains to some should not blind anyone to cause greater damage to many and eventually cause loss to the nation. The business community can do wonders if it discharges its duties towards the environment which includes rivers, land, forests, air and the like. Business ethos must be followed very scrupulously and there must be an independent mechanism to ensure the adherence of these with all the scruples.

One section of professionals that needs to exert a visible influence is the media; both the print and electronic. It hardly requires any elaboration how greatly it can mould public perceptions, opinions and choices. It can create national awareness on any issue if it takes it up with a missionary zeal! Unfortunately, the media tends to concentrates more on crime; indiscretions of the politicians, or other juicy items of news that would increase their viewership and the TRP in the rat race that has engulfed media! With the advent of the 24×7 channels in its own competitive world, social and developmental issues generally get relegated to background. Media, particularly the print media brings out supplements that cater to the interests of the corporate sector and the multinationals keen to market their wares and in the process, neglects its responsibility to help and educate the young on the higher and sublime aspects of life. Not to lag behind, the electronic media unhesitatingly take recourse to beam out sex and crime and it greatly distracts the younger generation. The media must assume greater responsibility to educate people and spread awareness on issues of public importance. There is a need for the media to allocate time slots with different formats to promote the skills of incisive analysis among the young of what is acceptable and what must be rejected from all that is dished out to them as news. The media must guard against the decline in its credibility when reports are made available to people on practices like 'paid news' and favour and disfavour on considerations other than objectivity. Media must protect its image and not treat young persons as the target group to which, at the instance of corporate and business, it has to transfer the message: splurge! It can disseminate a lot of information regarding the tasks being performed by the persons in various sectors of human activity. Why should the real life achievements of a primary teacher who works in a remote place, is honest to the core, find a place on the prime time TV and the front page of national dailies. The story of district collector, hones and full of energy who puts his daughter in a municipal primary school could jolt thousands of young persons in various walks of life to shift their gaze to others also! The story of a college which values every minute of the learners and in which no teacher ever misses his class dutifully could motivate many other institutions which are often accused of providing poor quality education by not insisting on rigour, just to keep the 'present batch' in good humour so that the external by-the-mouth publicity is good and more students come next year! Positivity must come in a big way in the media which must prove through its quality and content that it is among the most important institutions in the nation. It has a very important responsibility in a democracy and hence must give evidence that it adheres to fundamental constitutional duties itself and not only this, persuades others also to do so.

The Action Points

Whatever strategies and programmes and plans are devised and designed for the inculcation and spread of fundamental duties to citizens; young and old; certainly requires the presence of teachers. This task can also be sustained by parents, formal school teachers, community leaders, preachers of various sects, superannuated professionals. One may like to make a particular mention of retired defence personnel as these brave persons are held in high regard and are certainly fortunate to internalise the real; and practical import of human duties to the nation and to the fellow citizens. The practical aspect can be much better handled by those for whom there is abiding respect amongst the target groups.

Given below are some suggestive and indicative action points for inclusion on a selective basis by various institutions and organisations that prepare their target group oriented schedule of activities of training or teaching.

1. Every publication of Government of India should devote two pages exclusively to the Preamble of the Constitution on one of these and Article 51-A on the other.
2. Teacher education institutions must include modules on Fundamental Duties. Further these must make them practise the values contained in Article 51-A. The teacher educators must present a model of their own before the student teachers.
3. Elected representatives have to reorient their functioning, approach, attitude and also the extent and intensity of their dealings with people. They must always ask themselves: am I performing my duty and am I really worth the confidence reposed in me? They also have an obligation to exhort others to be dutiful wherever they are working and toiling.

4. Social pressure groups could take up issues which often infringe on the rights of others and cause them avoidable inconveniences, like, protests, marriage functions, religious processions, celebrations and the like.
5. Generating awareness is the primary requirement. Government must come in a big way. Its departments of publicity can always perform this function through the print media, electronic media and also by organising programmes in schools, colleges and universities. With a sense of creativity, this aspect can be communicated in every programme that these departments organise.
6. A thorough examination of textbooks and other supporting materials must be carried out after every revision of curricula by every school board and also by the universities in appropriate instances to examine and evaluate the extent of coverage of the fundamental duties.
7. An extensive programme of material preparation and dissemination needs to be encouraged by the concerned ministries and departments. School and college students could be encouraged to prepare materials by organising competitions and giving those rewards and even scholarships. UGC, AICTE, MCI and other similar organizations must undertake their share of responsibility in this respect.
8. Non-formal Education and Adult Education Programmes have a very special responsibility and must remain alert to it in all their functions.
9. The media can play a very positive role and its outreach could become its most effective asset in this national task.
10. Organisations, institutions and departments dealing with the environment, water resources, non-conventional energy resources, forests and land use could integrate the significance of the duty aspects in their plans and programmes and ensure proper training to their functionaries not to neglect this aspect in any of the actions and activities.
11. Co-curricular activities could be suitably reorganised in institutions to help learners realise the spirit behind each Fundamental Duty.
12. Article 51-A has a very special relevance to the Department of Women and Child Development at the Centre and also in states. Similarly, the University departments of Women Studies can also contribute through research and material production in eliminating gender bias and prevention of female infanticide.

13. Professional functionaries including civil servants, medical practitioners, academics, judges and other officers of the judiciary and also the executives of corporate houses and multinationals must undergo special orientations at regular intervals. For this each sector could design its specific plans and programmes that take note of the availability of the multi-channel input approach.
14. Particular attention needs to be paid to business and industry. Business organisations, Business Leaders and Business Management Schools have a vital and essential role to play in internalizing basic values.
15. The media, as a group, must accept its responsibility in this sector, particularly in preparing and nurturing the next generation. It must utilise its outreach for discharging its own duty towards the society.
16. Celebrations like the establishment day, founder's day, annual day and other similar occasions could be appropriate occasions to discuss and deliberate upon the implantation strategies of Fundamental Duties.
17. Interaction with achievers and contributors can have a major impact, particularly on the impressionable young minds. Schools, universities and institutions often organise such interactions. These could keep in mind how to focus on duty aspect on such occasions.
18. Value inculcation, nurturance and development are the most critical ingredient of the process of growing up. These must be highlighted in education, in-service education in various areas of human Endeavour Values of truth, peace, nonviolence; righteous conduct and love have eternal and universal acceptability.[6] Once these are internalized by the individual, duties would automatically come in.
19. Inculcation of love for the nature and the understanding of man-nature relationship at higher stages are of paramount importance in the 21st century when the very survival of the planet earth is at stake. Such knowledge leads to an approach to perform one's duty and not lag behind in the global efforts to save the earth from the apprehensions of climatic catastrophe.
20. The character formation, when assisted properly and substantially, integrates duties and responsibilities as natural corollaries of advancing ahead in the effort. This is the aim of education and also the leaning that comes to every individual throughout his life.

It would be most appropriate to recall the words of Mahatma Gandhi who gave a great message to future generations in such simple word as 'my life is my message'! Further if his premise 'that nature has sufficient to meet the needs of everyone but not the greed of any one' could be universally internalised, poverty, hunger, ill-health and exploitation could be wiped out from the face of earth. That has to be the objective and aim of every human life. It is move in that direction that this list of fundamental duties has been articulated and included in the Constitution of India. The education commission (1964-66) had stated:[7] "India has a great advantage with a great tradition of duty without self-involvement, unacquisitive temperament, tolerance and innate love of peace and reverence for all living things. It is regretted that too often these precious assets are forgotten and the tendency too often is to relapse into moods of pessimism, fears and forebodings, discard and destructive criticism. The Commission pleads that new pride and a deeper faith, expressed in living for the noble ideals of peace and freedom, truth and compassion are now needed." There can hardly be a more comprehensive guideline for the generations ahead.

(September 21, 2011)

Notes

1. Fundamental Duties of the Citizens; Report of the Committee set up by the Government of India to operationalize the suggestions to teach Fundamental duties to the citizens of the country; Government of India, Ministry of Human Resource Development; New Delhi; 31 October, 1999. In preparation of the present paper, the author, initially one of the members of the committee and later the member secretary of this committee, has liberally drawn in the preparation of this paper from the Report, now known as the J.S. Verma Committee Report.
2. Education and National development, Report of the National education commission, NCERT, 1968, New Delhi.
3. NCTE, National Curriculum Framework for Quality Teacher Education, NCTE, New Delhi, 1998.
4. Report of the J.S. Verma committee, Vol II, pp. 266-267.
5. People's Representative from Panchayat to Parliament by J. Veeraraghvan, in the J.S. Verma Committee, Volume II, Annexures; pp. 383-384.
6. Rajput; J.S., *Human Values and Education*, Pragun Publication; New Delhi, 2006.
7. Somnath Saraf, Education in Human Values: Programme Implementation, Apeejay Education Society, New Delhi, 1995.

5

Application of Swami Vivekananda's Teachings in the Present Education System

One may like to recall the prevailing conditions in the times of Swami Ji. Bengal of those days was known for intellectual discourse and reform movements. For the masses, the prevailing conditions were indeed very depressing. Literacy rate was abysmal; poverty was taken for granted, as 'fated and God-Given'! The caste system was in its full flow. Though the practices like the *Sati* were formally discarded, those who were enamaoured of these were not in small numbers. Missionaries were projecting their proselytisation endeavours as 'saving the souls' of the Indians who were otherwise condemned to eternal hell. Diseases like malaria, small pox, and plague were rampant. The worst sufferers were the women and girls. Why educate them was the common and widely accepted refrain in practically every sector of the society. Child marriage was the accepted norm. These restricted the participation of women in social and cultural life of the society, restricting them to perform certain household chores and rituals that were assigned by the male dominated family. Learned people could quote and recite from scriptures that held women in very high esteem, but the reality was far from what was preached occasionally. Indians and India together, were demoralised and had lost faith in themselves. The Impact of the aftermath of the 1857 War of Independence had greatly contributed to it.

What has indeed changed twelve decades after the departure of Swamiji? India after attaining freedom, has spent over six decades under its own rulers. There is so much to talk about in terms of progress and development. The gains, though significant, often get overshadowed by what has not been done. Illiteracy is no longer the norm, caste system stands formally and constitutionally abolished, and every citizen is entitled to equality before law, irrespective of caste, creed, language, religion and any other such diversity. The advent of electronic connectivity has reduced distances in the global village. Migration and mobility have transformed the socio-cultural context very significantly. Yet we still have dominant cultures overshadowing others as their outreach extends to the home and hearth globally. Knowledge and information are accessible at the click of a button. The list is pretty long but the concerns that have emerged on the debit side require far greater attention at this stage. Universal expansion of education has revealed its limitations against high expectations that were regularly articulated even over a hundred years ago. Educational expansion has considerably widened opportunities in access and participation but the content and process of education have yet to harmonise with the ever-expanding human aspirations. If it were so, the world would have been a far better place of social cohesion and religious harmony, it would have totally abolished exploitation of every variety and violence would have been eliminated. Corruption would have become a part of history! The manner violence and wars continue to engulf the world and the accumulation of resources remains in the grip of a select section leaving the vast majority to suffer deficiency and deprivation in basic human needs very clearly points out severe deficiencies in the content and process of education. As education outreach extends itself, the world becomes more and more conscious of the inadequacy of the education system. The search to delineate the missing elements in the process of teaching and learning, in the practices adopted in the search for new knowledge, in the utilization of new knowledge for commercial purposes, instead of human welfare are some of the questions and queries that confront those who think of the future generations! These have to be answered by all those who believe in the evolution of mankind and now know that things have reached a point where the very survival of the planet is at stake. The essence of Swami Vivekananda's thoughts; surprisingly; remain valid even today to find solutions to these critical concerns that face the humankind today in far bigger magnitude than his times. He had the foresight to visualise the emerging concerns and was fully equipped to offer solutions. Historically, India had acquired a very special place in the quest for knowledge and none had any doubts about it. Hence, it is the responsibility of India to set its own house in order, before taking up its global role! Character building and value inculcation and nurturance are yet to become the prime objectives of education. Education is rather solely for jobs; and better jobs. Even entrepreneurship finds only a casual reference and if at all some enthusiastic individuals achieve outstanding successes later in life, not much of the credit can be given to their formal education.

When Indian culture comprehended and conceptualised the thought of "*Vasudhaiv Kutumbakam*", it had laid a very solid foundation for the global village! If you don't believe in it how could you address an alien audience as "Brothers and Sisters of America"? If it was not coming from your heart and your conviction, it would never have moved everyone in the audience who had never ever even dreamt of such a world! The enlightenment that was sudden and resulted in that historic standing ovation and heartfelt appreciation from the audience: what a bond one person could create and what an impact that transformed the inner souls of the audience. This is being emphasised just to highlight how strong was the tradition of knowledge transfer in India, how it was crushed and made subservient to an alien transplanted system and how it was kept alive in certain places, transforming a Narendra Nath to the one and only one Swami Vivekananda. Our concern is: is it possible to delineate elements that have an eternal presence in the generational transfer of knowledge, which make it dynamic in nature and bestow the capability to absorb the changes and, at the same time respond to the emerging changes and challenges. How clearly had Swamiji realized this dynamic nature of education is very clearly articulated by him when he said: "True education, however, is not yet conceived of amongst us." One finds it greatly encouraging, expanding and evolving. None could ever claim to have found true education; one could only attempt to move ahead in search of it. It is this realisation in our institutions, universities, colleges and teacher preparation centers that has the potential to achieve an attitudinal transformation which, otherwise, is a very tough proposition. As a wondering monk, Vivekananda acquired first-hand knowledge of all that comprehensively constitutes India and distinguishes it from others and, at the same time, enjoins upon it the responsibility to practise a world view of humanity. He realized that every element of human existence and endeavour must be primarily directed towards ameliorating the sufferings of human beings, who are deprived of their due. The essence that continuously flows in thoughts and ideas, is best summarised in '*sarvabhutahite ratah*'; being devoted to the welfare of all beings. Education is the process that prepares and equips the individual way to plunge in the service of man and the mankind. He elevates the 'man' from humanity to divinity when he declared that "education the manifestation of perfection already in man".

Tasks before Educational Institutions

The general talk about institutions revolves around inadequate resources, lack of commitment within the system as a whole, erosion of traditional values amongst teachers, poor professional preparation of teachers, non-availability of teachers for various reasons and an environment that is not conducive to create an empathetic bond between the teacher and the taught. Practically, the most sought after objective of education is to get good marks/grades that would lead to a cozy job and, still better, a 'package'. It has resulted in total focus shifting on performance in written examination results and, in its shadow, every other component of education is lost. The consequences are grave; the man-nature mutuality is at a breaking point, materialistic pursuits have drowned the initiatives to inculcate moral, ethical and humanistic values amongst learners. There are no role models to spurt up the quest for higher pursuits in life, which has been the traditional objective in the Indian tradition: to understand life on the planet and also to explore the after-life! Yes, the Indian education system needs to reset its vision, goals, objectives and the outcomes expected of education. It has a very rich resource in the philosophy of education propounded by Swami Vivekananda. It is essentially the sum and substance of whatever has been visualised and philosophised in the Indian tradition, its scriptures and practices in institutions for ages before him. He put these in comprehensible and pragmatic terms. His philosophy, if viewed without pre-conceived notions and prejudices, is global in nature and purely; what in the modern terminology is called; secular!

Those entrusted with the responsibility to 'educate' the young need a thorough self-evaluation of their own readiness to perform the task. It has to be a continuous process as the 'teaching and learning' proceeds ahead. The giver must be convinced that 'knowledge is inherent in man, no knowledge comes from outside, it is all inside' and that his job is only to let the learner realize that he learns what he "discovers by taking the cover off his own soul, which is a mine of infinite knowledge". It may be worthwhile to recall the title of the UNESCO's Independent Commission on Education; popularly known as Delores Commission, that analysed the hopes and aspirations of the people from education in the 21st century. The report submitted in 1996 is titled "*Education: the Treasure Within*". It says it all. All the modern pedagogical terminology, often mentioned in the context of education; like learning by doing, discovery approach, constructivist approach and others need to examine the essence of education contained in the following words: "The falling of the apple gave the suggestion to Newton and he studied his own mind. He rearranged all the previous links of thought in his mind and discovered a new link among them, which we call the law of gravitation. It was not in the apple nor in anything in the centre of the earth." He further illustrates it: "Man manifests knowledge, discovers it within himself, which is pre-existing, through eternity." Imagine a situation when in every centre of education, every teacher is aware and convinced of this philosophical foundation of education and transforms himself into a researcher of his own 'self'. It would create a culture of search and research, resulting in the generation of new knowledge and countless arrays of innovations. All that stressful cramming and learning by rote would become a nullity. The issue of 'examination-oriented teaching and learning' would vanish and life would indeed become joyful and playful to the young learners in schools! There could be a revolution in curriculum development; every teacher could be a partner in learning and discovering with the child or the group of children. Another phenomenon would also emerge: every teacher would become a curriculum developer and in the process, his own 'growing up' would never be in doubt.

Educated and enlightened persons must consistently examine the relevance of whatever model is in place. Swamiji did it: "The education which does not help the common mass of people to equip themselves for the struggle of life, which does not bring out strength of character, a spirit of philanthropy, and the courage of a lion—is it worth the name? Real education is that which enables one to stand on one's own legs." The concept of self-reliance in education has to be reinterpreted: education must help prepare the learner to realise the gains of using the 'head, hand and heart' in the right mix and manner. It would nurture his self-confidence; give him skills and knowledge; and his dependence would vanish without any extra effort. Self reliance has to be the goal. In following words Swamiji gave a great lesson to educational planners and implementers: "All the wealth of the world cannot help one little Indian village if the people are not taught to help themselves." He wanted people to be educated to become self-reliant and frugal. It was exactly this spirit that was reflected in the '*Hind Swaraj*' (1909) of Mahatma Gandhi and later in his formulation of the model of Basic Education. It was also equally and strongly necessary that people realize their responsibility not to accumulate far beyond their needs and requirements. His famous statement fully matches the concept of frugality propounded by the Swamiji: "The world has a sufficient resource to meet the needs of everyone but not the greed of anyone." Taken together, this philosophical perception clearly indicate in no uncertain terms what India could include it in developing its own approach to education and a model of education that is rooted to India's soil.

Major Educational Concerns

The Idea of India

The Englishmen ruled India because they could, through conscious efforts, delink Indians from India. They demeaned India to such an extent that Sri Aurobindo's family did not permit him to interact with Indian children in his childhood in India and when he went to England aged seven years, he and his brother were left with a clergy man with instructions that he should be kept away from Indians! He spent fourteen years in England and became a fierce rebel against the British occupation of India. Even in such an upbringing, the love for the motherland blossomed. Globalization and being an international citizen is fine but none could ignore one's own mother and motherland. Take the case of religions: the rational person shall respect all religions on par but to him, his own would remain the refuge in thick and thin, in guiding him and in elevating him to higher levels of humanism and spirituality. Love for the country and countrymen needs to be nurtured to instill a sense of genuine and respectful pride that motivates people and nations to march ahead and contribute in the civilizational growth. Young people must realise their responsibility to their motherland and that would be incomplete and impossible if they do not internalise the 'ideals of India': "O India! With this mere echoing of others, with the base imitation of others, the slavish weakness, this vile detestable cruelty—wouldst thou, with these provisions, scale the highest pinnacle of civilization and greatness...forget not that the lower classes, the ignorant, the poor, the illiterate, the cobbler, the sweeper, are thy flesh and blood, thy brothers. Thou brave one, be bold, take courage, be proud that thou art an Indian, and proudly proclaim, 'I am an Indian, and every Indian is my brother.... The soil of India is my highest heaven; the good of India is my good'." Education needs to instill the criticality of love for the county and what better motivational ideas one could fall back upon than the comprehensive and forceful articulations of Swamiji. He was conscious that the fact of India being subjugated for centuries together often demoralises sensitive young persons. How beautifully he presented the rationale to extricate them out of any hesitation that may impede their motivation and enthusiasm:

"There have been periods of decay and degradation. I do not attach much importance to them; we all know that. Such periods have been necessary. A mighty tree produces a beautiful ripe fruit. That fruit falls on the ground, it decays and rots. And out of that decay, springs the root and the future tree, perhaps mightier than the first one. The period of decay through which we have passed was all the more necessary. Out of this decay, is coming the India of the future; it is sprouting, its first leaves are already out;...." This is the level of faith our educational enterprise and the institutions imparting education have to instill amongst the young of India. It has to be a vibrant India; proud of its diversities of every conceivable dimension; of its spirit of *Vasudhaiv Kutumbakam*; of *Sarvabhutahite ratah*. It is necessary to revive this legacy as many in the emerging India have neglected the eternal ideals India has perfected and followed for ages; reducing itself as an appendage of the ever-growing materialistic pursuits.

Philosophy of Education

First of all, it is the teacher who needs to internalise the import of "Knowledge is inherent in man, no knowledge comes from outside; it is all inside". It would change the pedagogy, redefine teacher-learner relations, lead to more innovative efforts on the part of the teacher along with the learner and eventually, contribute far more effectively to the process of knowledge pursuit. "The external world is simply the suggestion, the occasion, which sets you to study your own mind." The current interpreters of the philosophy in the context of teaching and learning are often amazed to find that all of their 'innovations' like the discovery approach, learning by doing, constructivist approach and others are already so clearly delineated in the Indian philosophy of the process of transfer of knowledge when interpreted as removing the veil that covers the treasure already gifted to every soul. The great Indian tradition of articulating even the most complex elements of philosophical attainments in the language of the common man is present in the words of Swami Vivekananda in its full glory: he addressed even the last man in the line of awareness, education and understanding. What better guidance a teacher could get from numerous books and treatises than what is contained in the words: "You cannot teach a child more than you can grow a plant. The plant develops its own nature. The child teaches itself. But you can help it to grow forward in its own way." The teacher, who does not internalise this aspect of teaching and learning "spoils everything by thinking that he is teaching". The Swami delineates the job of the teacher: "Within man is all knowledge, and it requires only an awakening, that much is the work of the teacher. We have only to do so much for the boys that they may learn to apply their own intellect to the proper use of their hands, legs, ears and eyes."

No negative ideas have any place in the education of a child—no matter whether these come from parents or from the teacher. "If you speak kind words to them and encourage them, they are bound to improve in time. If you can give them positive ideas, people will grow up to be men and learn to stand on their own legs." The scholars and academics of today need to seriously examine the import of the Swami's thoughts on how the external influences were; in fact; dwarfing Indian academia; "Getting by heart the thoughts of others in a foreign language and stuffing your brain with them and taking some university degrees, you consider yourself educated. Is this education? What is the goal of your education?... What good will it do you or your country? Every school, every college and university, and every institution that claims to be a centre of excellence must pose this question to itself. Sincere efforts to find an answer shall definitely contribute in enhancing the quality and make education more comprehensive and 'man making'. The all-pervasive spirit of being contributors in the task of rebuilding the nation through education and preparing lion-hearted young persons, imbued with values and commitment to serve others, particularly those who need it most, could enliven the environment of each and every institution. This was, and remains, the vision of Swami Vivekananda, and needs to be accepted and internalised by every existing institution without any hesitation. Once these young and women take over the reins of the country, the nature of governance would change and meet the expectations of the times.

Education of the Masses and Women

His was the heart that consistently suffered the pangs of the pain resulting out of the misery of the multitudes of his fellow citizens; and those of the global fraternity. The inherent idealism of the young deserves opportunities to develop critical and analytical skills to understand the disastrous trend of vested interests created by a handful of men disturbs not only the man to man relationship, but also damages the man-nature mutuality through unbridled exploitation of the natural resources. It may materially uplifts some but throws billions in the category of deprived and deficient who suffer ill health, illiteracy, and also poverty and hunger! India which; once again; hopes to lead the world in matters of spirituality languishes in the venom of ill-treating and humiliating its women and girls rather helplessly! Those under the blind influence of the West may not relish it, but the fact remains that this suffering and shame could have been vanquished fully and totally if we had trained and our young persons to realize that: "To the ordinary man in India, the whole force of womanhood is concentrated in motherhood. In the Western home, the wife rules, in an Indian home, the mother rules." He was sad and once asked, "How many schools have been started on our national lines?" He was very clear that India's future would be shaped appropriately only after women get education: "The uplift of women, the awakening of masses must come first, and then only any real good can come about for the country, for India." He had also stated: "In India there are two great evils, trampling on the women, and grinding the poor through caste restrictions." He poses a very relevant query: "It is very difficult to understand why, in this country, so much difference is made between men and women, whereas the Vedanta declares that one and the same conscious Self is present in all beings. You always criticise the women, but say what have you done for their uplift?"

In the current context, major institutions of education have a challenge before them: Are they widening the social gap by pandering to only the economically better off by barring the entry to their premises to the resourceless and focusing only on the resourceful irrespective the considerations of merit and talent? Will that not irreparably weaken the nation's effort to proceed on the path of progress and development? "A nation is advanced in proportion as education and intelligence spread among masses. The chief cause of India's ruin has been the monopolising of the whole education and intelligence of the land among a handful of men. If we were to rise again, we shall have to do it by spreading education among masses." Intelligence and awareness cannot spread amongst the masses if the education system, right from the initial years to higher education, does not realise this responsibility and works as a comprehensive unit to achieve this goal. Indian society sustains itself against all odds only through the strength of spirituality that percolated from the saints and seers for ages. The process of transmission was disturbed on a couple of occasions. It has to be restored and strengthened.

Character Building

The term is loved and liked by all, but not necessarily understood in its true meaning and import. "The character of any man is but the aggregate of his tendencies, the sum total of the bent of his mind. As pleasure and pain pass before the soul, they leave upon it different pictures, and the result of these combined impressions is what is called a man's character." Who has not gone through moments of utter happiness, joy and bliss; who has not suffered pains, travails and turmoil in life? Each one of these impacts our body and mind. This change takes place continuously in everyone. One cannot resist mentioning that the most effective teacher training was given to the student teachers after the Bhopal Gas Tragedy in the intervening night of December 2-3, 1984. It was also an occasion to witness men of character and men of clay. "Good and evil have an equal share in moulding character and in some cases misery is a greater teacher than happiness. In studying the great characters the world has produced, I dare say, in the vast majority of cases, it would be found that it was misery that taught more than happiness, it was poverty that taught more than wealth, and it was blows that brought out their inner fire more than praise." In the contemporary context India, in all its glory and misery, was never before understood so thoroughly and completely as by Swami Vivekananda. Apart from his guru-given and God-bestowed attainments in spirituality, he had travelled far and wide throughout the country, had stayed in royal palaces and in the homes of the destitute with equal ease and comfort. I recall how Mohandas Karamchand Gandhi was advised by Gopal Krishna Gokhale to travel throughout the undivided India as that was the only way to understand India and appreciate what India could mean to its own people and also to the world. Gandhi followed the advice totally and with commitment. In return he got the insight and also the foresight. On the issues of education of girls and the need to bring in the Indian ethos, Gandhi practically reiterated all that Swami Vivekananda had earlier stated. Education remains the ray of hope for all, and particularly for the suffering masses. Swami Vivekananda was ridiculed in India and abroad, Gandhiji was insulted and attacked in South Africa. What was their strength that sustained them? And one cites several other examples like Nelson Mandela, Martin Luther King Jr, Ho Chi Minh, Subhash Chandra Bose, and several of our revolutionaries. All of them had good experiences and also bad and bitter experiences. But the good ones prevailed and uplifted them to great heights on the scale of humanity. "Every work that we do, every movement of the body, every thought that we think, leaves such an impression on the mind stuff, and even when such impressions are not obvious on the surface, they are sufficiently strong to work beneath the surface, subconsciously. What we are every moment is determined by the sum total of these impressions on the mind... Each man's character is determined by the sum total of these impressions."

Educationists evaluate learner attainments; as they must; to find the gaps in the learning attainments and to provide remedial inputs. The current examination patterns just cannot lay any claim to reach anywhere near the total comprehensive development of the person and his personality. How could one be sure of the character development? No one knows the answer. Here are the guidelines: "If you really want to judge the character of a man, look not at his great performances. Watch a man do his most common actions; these are indeed the things which will tell you the real character of the great man. Great occasions rouse even the lowest of human beings to some kind of a greatness, but he alone is really great whose character is great always—the same wherever he be." It may appear rather strange to some, but it is the desire to be good and do good that can mould the character of the man in the right magnitude and direction. "What is the cause of evolution? Desire! The animal wants to do something but does not find the environment favourable, and therefore develops a new body. Who develops it? The animal itself; its 'Will'. Continue to exercise your will and it will take you higher. The will is almighty, you may say; why cannot I do everything? But you are thinking only of your little self. Look back on yourself from the state of amoeba to the human being; who made all that? Your own 'Will'. Can you deny that it is almighty? That which has made you come up so high, can make you go higher still. What you want is character, strengthening of the will." He articulated in very clear terms that the 'the road to the God is roughest and steepest in the universe'. And finally; "Character has to be established through a thousand failures."

The Teacher and the Taught

The *Guru* is supposed to lead the *Shishya* (disciple) from 'humanity to divinity'; '*Gurur Gurutamodhamah*'. The issue at the current juncture is: are our teachers fully equipped and prepared to inculcate and nurture humanistic, moral and ethical values amongst our children and young persons put under their charge in their formative years? Swami Vivekananda was an advocate of the learner, 'living' under the constant watch of the Guru, who should be 'one whose character is a blazing fire' and the learner should have before him a living example of the highest teaching. He delineates certain essentials for the learner and also the teacher. The prerequisites for the learner are purity of thought, speech and act, a real thirst after knowledge, and perseverance. For the teacher, it is character and personality, imbued with the purity of the soul. A teacher who only reads many books and all the scriptures may not necessarily be ready for the job. "The teacher who deals too much in words and allows the mind to be carried away by the forces of word loses the spirit. It is the knowledge of the spirit of the scriptures alone that constitutes the true teacher" Once the teacher is ready, fully equipped and empowered, he would himself visualize the path to be traversed: "The function of the teacher is indeed an affair of transference of something and not one of mere stimulation of existing intellectual or other faculties in the taught. Something real and appreciable as an influence comes from the teacher and goes to the taught. Therefore the teacher must be pure. Teaching has to be without any selfish motive." The necessity of external support and motivation in moving towards spirituality is highlighted in very simple terms: "Whatever we are now is the result of our acts and thoughts in the past; and whatever we shall be in the future will be the result of what we think and do now. But this, the shaping of our own destinies, does not preclude our receiving help from outside; nay, in the vast majority of cases such help is absolutely necessary. When it comes, the higher powers and possibilities of the soul are quickened, spiritual life is awakened, growth is animated, and man becomes holy and perfect." He elaborates it further: "This quickening impulse cannot be derived from books. The soul can only receive impulses from another soul." And then he visualizes the benefactor: "This person from whose soul such impulse comes is called the *Guru*—the teacher; and he person to whose soul the impulse is conveyed is called *Shishya*—the student."

This spirit of the teacher-taught relationship is eternal and, while physical environs may change with times, the principles of the generational transfer of knowledge remain the same. Self-learning is essential, it helps in many ways but it just cannot replace the personal, emotional and spiritual bond that develops between the *Guru* and the *Shishya*. "We may study books all our lives, we may become very intellectual, but, in the end, we find that we have not developed at all spiritually. It is not true that a high order of intellectual development always goes hand in hand with the proportionate development of the spiritual side in man. In studying books we are sometimes deluded into thinking that thereby we are being spiritually helped; but if we analyze the effect of the study of books on ourselves, we shall find that at the utmost it is only our intellect that derives profits from such studies, and not our inner spirit. This inadequacy of books to quicken spiritual growth is the reason why almost every one of us can speak most wonderfully on spiritual matters, when it comes to action and living of a truly spiritual life, we find ourselves so awfully deficient. To quicken the spirit, the impulse must come from another soul." In the current times, the focus in teacher preparation is constrained by several stipulations and many of these are controlled by the new advances in science and technology and; particularly; the ever-increasing presence of the ICT. The role of the face-to-face interaction, dialogue and discussion acquires far greater importance than ever before.

The Ends and the Means

As already indicated, everyone is willing to articulate his expectations from education and educational institutions. Their task and performance has to remain dynamic in nature and consequently, the institutional culture must remain alert and ready to receive all that is new in ideas, innovations and pedagogy. It, however, must retain the basics of its culture and values. In times of unbridled materialistic pursuits, it is but natural on the part of the young persons to get attracted towards glare and glitz that uncontrolled commercialisation has spread all around. Very often, young people set their eyes on the goals, which some have achieved in their materialistic pursuits, without caring or knowing what unacceptable means these would require to be followed. It is enjoined upon the educational institutions to let the learner assimilate to pay as 'much attention to the means as to its ends'. When failure occurs, one often blames a number of factors but 'in ninety per cent cases we shall find that it was because we did not pay attention to the means'. In familiar terms, how could educational institutions permit upward movement of children unless they have acquired the prescribed levels of learning? Why should any university survive if it cannot control the abhorrent practices like ragging and copying in examination? What justification could be there for an academic, who, instead of focusing on the learners assigned to him, prefers to sell his expertise in coaching institutions?

Action Points

Institutions that have acquired expertise in understanding Swamiji's vision, philosophy, thoughts, ideas, concerns, approaches, and strategies could take a lead to establish a world of peace, harmony and symphony with nature, develop detailed suggested action plans for schools, colleges, universities, institutions of management and technologies and; most importantly; the institutions of teacher preparation. These would be followed by preparation of teaching-learning packages and self-study materials appropriate to the specific learning centre. Further, Open and Distance Learning; ODL; coupled with on-line learning, could be utilised extensively. These initiatives have to be motivational and persuasive. His writings, on their own, elevate the thought process, widen its scope. Can any institution dealing with education ignore these soul-impacting words: "The education that does not help the common mass of the people to equip themselves for the struggle for life, which does not bring out strength of character, a spirit of philanthropy and the courage of a lion—is it worth the name?" These motivate and invigorate the individual to act. If appropriate guidance is available, the urge to contribute and serve could be directed in the right direction. The strategy could be built, depending upon the institutional capabilities and its readiness to bring about a tangible change in the education system within the institution and also to set up a model strategy for others.

1. *Institutional Vision and Mission Statement*: Imagine the extent of attitudinal change amongst the stake holders if every institution of education, from primary school to a university, displays its mission statement every day to everyone who enters the premises, particularly the teachers and the learners! These could emanate from the philosophy of Swami Vivekananda. After all, each one of these institutions is engrossed in man-making and what better and lasting conceptualisation of its criticality and significance could be articulated than what is already given by Swamiji. One would like to visualise the annual report of the institution to mention how far it has planned and executed its activities in accordance with their stated mission and vision! Swami Vivekananda's ideal of eternal unity of all human beings could be the foundation stone to build a strong edifice of social cohesion and religious amity, a prime need not only of India but the entire globe. This is the first step towards initiatives to develop a model of education that would be Indian in thought, action and outcomes. This could one of the many possible approaches to achieve the much-sought-after 'eternal unity of all human beings'.

2. *Approach to Learning: Role of Concentration*: Experts in pedagogy often, very rightly, point out the difference in training and education. Swamiji repeatedly emphasised on 'concentration'. Though the importance of focused attention and pursuit is universally accepted as the first requirement in the pursuit of knowledge and in efforts to create new knowledge, not many teachers and researchers indeed focus on it to the desired extent. There are indications that schools which let their young children acquire the skill of silent sitting and concentration are able to nurture talent to far higher levels than that who follow the routine pedagogy no matter how much and many modern gadgets they may extensively use. If educational institutions could deliberate on issues of concentration and the role of Yoga in it, the entire environment would undergo a sea change. It would lead to a better, worthwhile and comprehensive learning. This again would require extensive motivational support from institutions like the Ramakrishna Mission to approach the institutions and offer to orient their teachers and decision makers in these quality-enhancing measures.

3. ***Value Inculcation and Character Formation***: Character formation has always been one of the most significant objectives of education in every civilization. Inculcation of moral, ethical and humanistic values is a major component of this process. Role of institutional culture and presence of role models needs to be emphasized in this context. Teachers have traditionally inculcated value 'by example'! Swamiji's preference for the '*Gurugriha-vasa*' clearly visualises a very close relationship between the teacher and the taught. Teachers have to be prepared to realise how distinctive their role is in shaping the future not only of the learners under their charge but of the nation! It requires greater interaction with men and women who have distinguished themselves by living a value-based life, even in these days of unbridled materialistic pursuits. Further, every teacher is to be reminded all along that he, apart from being a teacher of his allocated subject, is also an inculcator and developer of values no matter what action or activity he is performing. Those who wish to provide separate time slots for value inculcation could do so as an alternative model. The widely supported proposition insists that every teacher, whatever be his area of expertise or assignment of activities, also remains a teacher, facilitator and developer of values. Towards this end, every teacher needs initial support in internalising his role as a role model, as a value inculcator-cum-developer and teacher of his assigned area of prescribed syllabus.

4. ***Education of the Masses***: It needs no reiteration that the progress and growth of a nation in current times is a consequence of the extent of spread of information, knowledge and wisdom amongst masses. Traditionally, the essence of even the highest level of wisdom was transferred to masses and its ruminants could still be seen in rural India where even an illiterate farmer may be following the values of truth, non-violence and righteous conduct in his life with commendable commitment. Why can the schools and universities establish Cells assigned to augment the process of knowledge transfer to those who may not be in a position to get it through formal education or formal systems? Children and young persons, with suitable guidance would love it. In a fast changing world, not everyone is equipped to keep pace with the times. Educational institutions could design and make an effective contribution. Even in its seventh decade after independence, India counts over 800 million of its population are officially counted to get subsidized food grains and on the other side, the number of Indian billionaires is rising steadily. Why should people not know about the exploitation that is being formally and officially inflicted upon them through land acquisitions and change of land use, unbridled urbanization, neglect of the agriculture sector and above all, the great knowledge deprivation inflicted upon the masses through a poorly equipped, inadequately staffed school system that is supposed to cater to around seventy per cent of the children? There are no problems to the thirty per cent children of the upper echelons of the society who have prestigious public schools and other especially created schools for them. Mass education of rights and duties is a critical factor that must be taken up by educational centers.

5. *Teacher Preparation*: It is indeed ironic that the traditional respect and regard for the teacher has declined to shocking levels! Decline on the part of teachers in their professional development and commitment to excellence is also no more an exception. No society can think of progress, development or the march towards a knowledge society if its teachers are not fully competent, committed and perform their tasks with genuine sincerity. The first action point is the overhauling of the teacher preparation institutions. It is a sad commentary on the system that teacher training and education is in a very bad shape and everyone knows about it. While schools can assist by getting associated with training institutions, universities could, on their own, interact with teacher education colleges and impress upon them that their main task is to prepare motivated, self-assured, willing-to-learn-more individuals who internalise the importance of their man-making role and know the implications of its multiplier effect in the long run. To achieve an attitudinal transformation amongst student-teachers and also serving teachers, there can be no better source for such motivational educational initiative than the philosophy and educational ideas of Swami Vivekananda? A very specific paper/credit course on Swami Vivekananda's perceptions on education could be a compulsory part of every teacher training course. Online courses/credits could also be planned and made available to serving teachers. Practical component on community education could be a compulsory component of such an initiative.

6. *Understanding India*: Special programmes need to be designed and conducted in educational institutions to emphatically link Indian youth to India's culture; history, contributions to global civilizations and how all this prompted Swami Vivekananda to present such a deep insight and understanding of India's glorious past before the world. What more one could do in developing communication skills and keeping the audience spell-bound than citing and elaborating how he did it. Institutions of mass communication and journalism could derive significant inputs from Swamiji's life and his works. The young of India, who are interacting internationally and have established a distinguished place not only for themselves, but also for the nation, do not wish to be found deficient on their acquaintance with their own culture and heritage. It applies equally well to those who serve their own people in India. Wherever such attempts have been made by, say, foundation courses and the like, these have received a good response from the learners. Such efforts could get strengthened by deriving sustenance from the life and works of Swamiji. The root cause of India's misery could be solely traced to the successful alien efforts to 'delink Indians from India'. The most potent instrument ever created to destroy any culture or people is to segregate them from 'whatever was their own' and make them feel deficient and low with nothing to be proud of! Who else but institutions and universities could take the lead in this direction?

7. ***Education about Religions***: Indian society has traditionally been respectful to all religions and sects. It includes those which emerged in the East and also the Abrahamic religions. The strength of Indian culture was historically witnessed when Christianity, Islam, Zoroastrianism and others came to India as the persecuted and even as refugees. There is no other example of the type of welcome they received in Indian society. This was, and is, the real secularism in theory and in practice. When Swamiji spoke those ever-reverberating words; "Brothers and sisters of America," every pore and every cell of his body and soul meant it. It was no formality; it came from his Soul and that was the strength of the culture that had nurtured him. It is the spiritual content of religion that elevates the person into one who welcomes diversity and otherness with an all-embracing approach. He aims at welfare of one and all. "For our national welfare, we must seek out at the present day all the spiritual forces of the race, as was done in the days of yore and will be done in all times to come. National union in India must be a gathering up of its scattered spiritual forces. A nation in India must be a union of those whose hearts beat to the same spiritual tune." He goes on to elaborate how the adherents of different religions could indeed 'live together': "The Christian is not to become a Hindu or a Buddhist, nor a Hindu or a Buddhist to become a Christian. But each must assimilate the spirit of the others and yet preserves his individuality and grows according to his own

law of growth." It is such an approach that shall strengthen secularism. It is imperative on the part of the educational institutions to appropriately familiarise all the children with the basics of all the religions. They must know the commonalities and learn to respect differences wherever these exist. The educational endeavour must not go into rituals and dogmas but must attempt bring out the common threads of spirituality which sustains the concept of essential unity of all human beings.

8. *Work Culture*: No nation can rise and march ahead, unless all its citizens have learnt 'to live together, work together and progress together'. It includes every section of society, which takes note of every weakness that is to be removed and strength that is to put to the good of others. Imagine a situation in which everyone, working at any level and any sector of human activity gets convinced that he is working for the great cause: serving human beings and humanity through his efforts. Our young people identify certain goal that appears glamorous and enchanting; they lose sight of the details. Very often, such goals are set with narrow vision and half-baked considerations. Then, in the single minded pursuit, 'means' could easily escape consideration and failures are not far away. Often one gets stuck up in fruitless pursuits. Swamiji puts this situation in simple and comprehensible terms: "We know that it is hurting us, that any further clinging to it is simply bringing misery on us; still, we cannot tear ourselves away from it. The bee came to sip the honey, but its feet stuck to the honey-pot and it could not get away. Again and again we are finding ourselves in that state. That is the whole secret of existence.... We came here to sip the honey, and we find our hands and feet sticking to it. ... That is the cause of misery: we are attached, we are being caught. Therefore says the Gita: work constantly; work but be not attached; be not caught." All this can be achieved only by the mentally strong, emotionally equipped, physically strong and intellectually sound individuals. Where do young learners get their first lessons that develop and nurture their inherent tendencies to observe, explore, analyse and infer? It all begins in the first school constituted by parents and family members and then extends to the formal schooling, constantly intervened by the community. In a slightly different context, take the case of a country like Japan which suffered the maximum humiliation, cruelty and loss of civilian lives during the Second World War. It could rise from ashes to become a strong economic power by sheer dint of preparing its citizens to work hard. The objectives and goals may be perceived differently, but work culture is an essential ingredient in every move ahead, whether it is economic affluence or the traditional Indian spiritual quest for exploring the Truth.

Educational institutions generate manpower and create levels of quality depending on their own work culture. The first requirement that enjoins upon the institutional leadership is: present a model of faultless work culture in an environment of congeniality and cohesion that permits unhindered and uncontrolled pursuit of innovations and deep involvement in academic pursuits

9. *Meditation, Concentration and Yoga*: Whatever task one takes up, achievement of excellence primarily depends on one factor: concentration. It is the lack of concentration that leads to innumerable failures. "There is only one method by which to attain knowledge, that which is called concentration. The very essence of education is concentration of the mind. From the lowest man to the highest yogi, all have to use the same method to attain knowledge". The illiterate farmer, who harmonises the quality of the soil and the seed, moisture, temperature, the weather and couple of other factors, succeeds only because of the knowledge acquired dexterously. A great painting or a great sculpture is a creative contribution arising out of the concentration achieved by their creators. "High achievements in arts, music, etc., are the result of concentration. When the mind is concentrated and turned back on itself, all within us will be our servants, not our masters. The Greeks applied their concentration to the external world and the result was perfection in art, literature, etc. The Hindu concentrated on the internal world, upon the unseen realms in the self and developed the science of Yoga." The harmoniously balanced development of the person is Yoga—the union. "To the worker, it is union between men and the whole humanity; to the mystic, between his lower and higher self; to the lover, union between himself and God of love; and to the philosopher; it is the union of all existence. This is what is meant by Yoga." His articulation of the four types of Yogas is as masterly as his other interpretations. It is relevant to understand the inclination to become a Yogi! "If you want to be a Yogi, you must be free, and free from all anxiety. He who desires a comfortable and nice life, and at the same time, wants to realise the self is like the fool who, wanting to cross the river, caught hold of a crocodile, mistaking it for a log of wood."

In this context, Swamiji always laid stress on the relevance of meditation. "The greatest help to spiritual life is meditation (*Dhyana*). In meditation, we divest ourselves of all material conditions and feel our divine nature. We do not depend on any external help in meditation.... The less the thought of the body, the better, for it is the body that drags us down. It is attachment, identification, which makes us miserable. That is the secret: To think that I am the spirit and not the body, and that whole of the universe with all its relations, with all its good and all its evil, is but a series of paintings—seen on a canvas, of which I am the witness." Yoga, meditation and concentration are essential elements that constitute the soul of every worthwhile centre of learning. Such a place would become a lively laboratory for experimentation and intuition, motivation and rejuvenation.

Swami Vivekananda's ideas on education and also on religions and spirituality impact and attract academics and intellectuals who retain their objectivity and are not constrained by ideological compulsions. His thoughts and ideas could change the world. These need to be universalised. In the present times, erosion of human, ethical and moral values have resulted in evils like exploitation, economic dominance, insecurity, and violence, the world over. The world must accept the reality of existence of different religions, these being different paths to the one and only goal: the search of Truth. The path shown, and repeatedly articulated by Swami Vivekananda, clearly reveals the essential unity of all religions and lightens the path through that divine boon; the spirituality. Let educational institutions aim at preparing everyone under their charge to become an active, alert, equipped, committed and spirited person who understands himself and his duties and responsibilities. He could transform the world. And that transformation is the need of the times.

(November 7, 2013)

References

The Complete Works of Swami Vivekananda, Mayavati Memorial Edition, 1999, Advaita Ashrama, 5, Dehi Entally Road, Calcutta.

Avinashilingam, T.S., *Education, Swami Vivekananda*, 2005; Sri Ramakrishna Math, Mylapore, Madras.

I am a Voice without a Form Swami Vivekananda; concept and compilation: Swami Srikantananda; October 2005; Kala Jyothi Process Pvt. Ltd, Hyderabad.

My Idea of Education; *Swami Vivekananda*; Compiled by Kiran Walia; Published on the occasion of 150th Birth Anniversary of Swami Vivekananda.; November 2011; Ramakrishna Math and Ramakrishna Mission, Belur Math, Howrah District. West Bengal.

My India; The India Eternal; Swami Vivekananda; July 2000; The Secretary, The Ramakrishna Mission Institute of Culture; Calcutta-700 029, India.

The Teachings of Swami Vivekananda, 1997; Advaita Ashrama; 5 Dehi Entally Road, Calcutta.

The Life of Vivekananda and the Universal Gospel, Romain Rolland, 2004, Advaita Ashrama; 5 Delhi Road; Kolkata-700 014.

Learning: The Treasure Within, Report to UNESCO of the International Commission on Education for the Twenty-first Century, Delores Report, 1996, Published by UNESCO, Paris.

Increasing Relevance of Swami Vivekananda and Sri Aurobindo; article by L.N. Jhunjhunwala in the edited volume *Human Society at Crossroads*, by Dr. S.N. Mohnot, 2012, Concept Publishing Company Pvt. Ltd., New Delhi-110059.

Rajput, J.S., *Human Values and Education*, Pragun Publication, 2006, New Delhi.

6

Basic Essentials of Education in Ancient India

All living beings on earth derive support and sustenance from innumerable sources and resources. It is impossible to locate an individual human being who does not owe debt and obligation to nature, family and the society; and also to some divine and unseen forces. The internalisation of this sense of 'gratitude' deserves to become an important ingredient of the process of growing up, and later, of the 'righteous conduct' that sustains the individual in living his/her life. Even the very coming to earth is not because of one's own individual choice or effort. Some supernatural power; perceives in different ways; gives life and imparts skills and resources to sustain it. The resulting sense of gratitude manifests itself in different ways and forms in practically every civilization and every religion and sect. The *Vedas* are considered as the eternal and earliest known source of 'knowledge' by those who strive sincerely to understand these in detail and depth. These very clearly envisage that knowledge must be continuously acquired, transferred to next generations and enhanced, all in the welfare of humankind. To maintain this chain of acquisition, creation, transfer and utilization of knowledge, the *Vedas* enjoin upon every individual to discharge three pious obligations. These are *Devarina*, *Pitrarina* and *Rishirina*, for an initial understanding these could be put as debt to gods, debt to parents and debt to rishis/ teachers/learned ones. In the Mahabharata, the fourth element; *Manavarina*; debt to humanity was also added. In the present context, one may like to confine oneself to *Rishirina*, the debt/obligation to the learned and learning. The intent is very clear: everyone must acquire knowledge from the learned ones, strengthen it with one's own efforts, and give it back to society for the welfare of the people; to secure happiness for them. The basic fundamentals of education in ancient India derived their conceptualization from these principles. In pragmatic terms, education is the process in which the existing knowledge is transferred to the raw individual by the learned one in a manner that enables him to upgrade and enhance his acquisitions through research and experience acquired during its utilization in transferring to others for the larger benefit of people. Knowledge cannot be purchased, hired, stolen or achieved by any devious means. The only means for its acquisition is self-effort, supported by the 'learned one'; the teacher. It becomes a pious obligation of society to create conditions that are conducive to contribute in the growth of every individual, equipping him or her to discharge his other debts. These considerations gave birth to a system of creating and transferring knowledge and skills from one generation to another and resulted in the *Guru-Shisya Parampara* (preceptor-pupil tradition) which remains a great asset in understanding the eastern civilization.

Education Liberates

The level of importance given to education has been highlighted in India's ancient and later scriptures. As an example, one may quote this verse composed by great Sanskrit poet Bhartuhari over two thousand years ago:

Education is the special manifestation of man:

> Education is the treasure which can be preserved without any fear of loss;
> Education secures material pleasure, happiness and fame;
> Education is the teacher of the teacher;
> Education is the friend when on goes abroad;
> Education is God incarnate;
> Education secures honour at the hand of the State; not money;
> A man without education is equal to an animal.

The importance of education and the consequent obligations of the parents and teachers to impart education to the young ones are highlighted in numerous texts in Sanskrit and other Indian languages. The nature of education was also fully comprehended and put forth in various texts. The following could be an illustrative example contained in the Hitopadesha which eulogises education[1]

> "Education imparts intellectual culture;
> Intellectual culture secures capacity and stability;
> Capacity and stability enable one to secure wealth;

> Wealth so secured enables one to conform to Dharma;
> This in turn secures happiness."

Everyone wants happiness. "And what is happiness" is very comprehensively articulated in *Shikshavalli in Taittiriya Upanishd*. Happiness is this: youth should be of good character, learned, resolute and strong (morally and physically). Then only the earth will be full of prosperity and wealth. This is the measure of human happiness." Looking at these formulations it is clear that intellectual culture imbued with moral and ethical orientations resulting in capacity, resoluteness and determination to follow the righteous path are the learning outcomes of the totality of efforts involved in transferring and receiving *Vidya*. This is also perceived as moulding of the character of the growing individual who in the process acquires "*Samskaras*", which as Adi Sankaracharya defined, 'is the process by which good qualities are imparted and defects are removed."[2]

One could cite umpteen such verses highlighting various aspects of education, learning and the process of growing up. These also highlight the criticality of the continuity of the eternal search for knowledge or, how to become a part of the human search for the ultimate truth. When thinkers say that a true teacher is a learner for life, they also indicate that it applies universally to everyone who continues growing up in his chosen area of human endeavour. In the current terminology, a doctor just cannot rest on his knowledge acquired in the medical college or an engineer in a technical institution. They have to continuously upgrade and update their earlier acquisitions of knowledge. This is equally true for every profession and each area of human endeavour that attract human pursuit. Not only this they are supposed to create and generate new knowledge through their own research and innovations. Knowledge is characterised as 'the third eye of the man, which gives him insight in to all affairs and teaches him how to act'. Nothing gives us such an unfailing insight as education, says the Mahabharata'.[3] It is also the only acquisition that 'liberates'. That could be interpreted at different levels; liberation from worldly evils, ill effects or; spiritually speaking, leading to the attainment of *Moksha*, the ultimate salvation.

Education Prepares

Even a cursory perusal of various known aspects of education in ancient times clearly reveals that this was considered as the most important source of illumination. It could prepare one to live a fulsome life and could serve as a beacon whenever one felt the need to resolve issue at various stages of life in diverse situations and conditions. The Mahabharata clearly indicates that there is no other 'unfailing insight' as education. It provides opportunities to attain greater and higher levels in understanding, efficiency, intelligence, skills, strength and power. That the 'wisest is the mightiest' was realised in ancient India. The process of human advancement on social, cultural and economic fronts remains ever dependent on the nature and quality of education. It is education that refines man's nature and helps him move towards more refined social behaviour. From a stage when colour prejudice and slavery were officially allowed, we now stand at a very different, and more evolved level of understanding of human dignity and equality of all human beings. One could visualise that once the students learnt the premise that 'all human beings are the integral part of the same divine being', they may really take their own time to appreciate and internalise its implications on a broader and more universal scale. One could read a lot about the nature of discipline that was imposed on the learners. It aimed at saving them from undesirable experiences and prepared them to lead a disciplined life. To strengthen this aspect, focus on religious practices and spiritual pursuits was also a part of learning programmes. A lot of details of these could be seen in the literature. It has been noted that ancient Indian educators and scholars gave the prime importance to character formation. For them, character was more important than learning. A man of character and less learning was to be preferred to a highly learned person with inadequacies in character. Apart from instructions, oral or otherwise, the very environment was so constructed that character building and nurturance of values became an integral part of the entire process of education. Regular practices, religious inputs and glorification of national and mythical heroes contributed to the process of character building. The value of self-respect was always extolled. Social and family duties were not ignored during the stay in Gurukulas. Preservation of culture and acquaintance with social cultural and spiritual heritage were part of the curriculum.

The directive that was given to the outgoing *Shishyas* (Students) represents comprehensively not only what was expected to be accomplished during the learning stage, but also what was expected from them in the next phases of their life. This is given in the *Taittiriya Upnishad:*

> "Speak the Truth; follow the prescribed conduct
> Do not fail to pay attention to truth

Never fail to perform your duty
Do not disregard what is proper and good
Treat your mother, father and teacher as equal to God
So also treat your guest as God
Those acts that are irreproachable alone are to be
Performed, and not those that are forbidden.
This is the directive. This is the advice. This is
Discipline.

Social Context

The *Varnashrama* System of ancient India is often equated with the rightly maligned and now-discarded caste system. Those devoted to creation, generation, interpretation and transfer of knowledge were the *Brahmanas*. The next in line; the *Kshatriyas* devoted to security, warfare, and governance; followed by *Vaisyas* who looked after agriculture, commerce and trade. The last in this hierarchy were those who helped the other three by serving them in various ways were called *Sudras.* Those with scholarly and with an attitude to go to higher levels of the pursuit of knowledge were given the top position in the social hierarchy and called *Brahmanas.* It is generally presumed that the Gurus—teachers—came mostly from this group. The origin of *Varnashrama* system is often explained in reference to the root '*Var*' which means 'to choose'. This could be interpreted as profession that was chosen by the individual. Ideally, such a system could have provided liberty to every individual to make a choice of his vocation or profession. It is mentioned that a Brahman continues to be a Sudra till he receives proper education. There are innumerable examples of persons from outside the Brahmanas who made singular contribution to the growth and application of knowledge in public welfare. For practical considerations, and family impacts, it probably got transformed into strict classifications and degenerated itself in to a caste system that created so many implications in the social structure. It led to severe aberrations in the great conceptualisation of 'universal equality of all human beings'. Apart from the social classification, the stages of life were also divided into four periods according to the tasks one was supposed to perform. The period of preparation for life, *Brahmacharya* was for receiving education, training and skills, followed by the performance of one's role as a householder; the *Grihasthashrama*. Having fulfilled his social and family obligations, one was supposed to retreat and observe the fruits of his endeavour in terms of impact on the next generation. It was the *Vanaprasthashrama* leading to the last stage of *Sanyas* that ensured total withdrawal from worldly pursuits and undisturbed devotion to the pursuit of the ultimate Truth. It must be mentioned that learning, though seriously confined only to the first phase, was, indeed, a lifelong process. The basic education, its content and process was to instill the idea in the mind of every learner that the learned strives to learn more and know more throughout one's life.

The system of preserving knowledge in manuscripts was a much later development. There were classifications of students and teachers depending on the stage of learning or the experience in teaching. Normally the ancient Indian system of education is visualised in terms of *Gurukulas* where the learned Guru had his *Ashrama* and the seekers were handed over to him; fully and totally for ensuring 'growing up' and maturation for life in the second phase of *Grihasthashrama*. It was a stay that nurtured and nourished the body, mind and spirit of the young child. The entry of the child was an occasion of celebration, religiously termed as *Upanayana*. The child was accepted in the *Gurukula* only after all of the prescribed rituals were completed and their implications were made known to the child. Apart from *Gurukulas*, there were other structures also that contributed to the creation and dissemination of knowledge. *Parishads* were meant for those who were always seeking more and more knowledge. These could be called the modern day academies. These were usually constituted by those who continued to pursue their search for more knowledge and wisdom even during the householder phase of life. The concept of *Goshthis* (conferences) was meant for representative and in-depth interactions of the learned on specified aspects of knowledge. These were sometimes summoned by Kings who invited the learned and provided opportunities for the exchange of ideas and new knowledge. *Brihadaranyaka* Upanishad, the *Shatapatha Brahman* and *Vayu Purana* mention one such a congress of the Rishis that was convened by King Janaka. "The king offered a special prize of great value—1000 cows with their horns covered in gold—to the scholar who was 'the best read', 'the most learned in sacred wit' and 'the wisest'. The award was at once appropriated by Yajnavalkya."[4] Such assemblies organised by Emperor Asoka and Kanishka are well known. Earlier, the Rig-Veda has several significant references to the *Sanghas* or assemblies of learned men. From the times of Asoka, another notable and innovative development was the growth of Buddhist monasteries into huge establishments. These became centres of learning, including higher learning. By then, the oral tradition had given way to written manuscripts.

Pedagogy and Evaluation

The pedagogy was woven around the tradition of oral teaching and learning by heart. That was the only means available to transfer knowledge to the future generations. The system had detailed out practically everything: how the students would come and greet the teacher; how should they sit; how should they respond if they understood or when they wanted further elaboration from the teacher. Pronunciation was the major factor and no error in it was permissible. There is ample evidence that senior students looked after the tasks of the teacher in his absence. The teacher-taught ratio invariably provided an opportunity for individual attention and interaction. The tradition of *Prashna-Pratiprashna-Pariprashna* (Question-counter question—additional questions) effectively summarises the nature of teacher-taught relationship. Much has been said and scrutinised on this aspect. The pedagogical part is very clear. That the learner became a part of the teacher's family gave him the much-needed continuity of school environment to the home environment. Participation in the specifically assigned tasks gave skill orientation in practical terms. The modern education system has failed miserably on this front. In an ideal situation, the guru guides, assigns projects and allows the learner to move ahead on his own, providing corrective and requisite inputs at appropriate points of time in the process. He has the freedom to discuss with the Guru at every stage. He is permitted to ask questions and often may be rewarded with a counter question formulated by the teacher dexterously that may implicitly contain indications to find solutions on one's own. Things move scientifically, the teacher performs his task meticulously and the learner gets the satisfaction of discovering solutions 'on his own'. Only if this one aspect is incorporated appropriately in the current-day pedagogy in its actual classroom practices, it could transform the learner attainment levels of students in majority of schools everywhere.

In Nalanda, there were nearly one thousand teachers for about nine thousand students. The monitoring of learner attainment was ensured after the end of each lesson and the new lesson began only after the previous one was fully mastered. Depending upon their progress levels, students finished their education at different times. There were no annual examinations. It was significant that teaching and learning took place in an environment governed by religion and religious practices. Offering of prayers on a daily basis and observances of religious days and festivals was a regular part of education. "The very atmosphere, in which the student lived and breathed, impressed upon him the reality of the spiritual world and made him realise that though his body may be a product of nature, his mind, intellect and soul belonged to the world of spirit, the laws of which ought to govern his conduct, mould his character and determine the ideals of his life."[5] Obviously, this was the most conducive environment for nurturing humanistic values.

The strength and scientific basis of evaluation system could also be visualised recalling an instance from Taxila. Jivak was learning under Acharya Bhadanta. At a certain point of his stay there, Jivak made a self-evaluation of his learning attainments and approached the Acharya with the request that he was convinced of the completion of his learning and would like to take leave of him. He further pleaded that the *Guru-Dakshina* he was supposed to offer may graciously be indicated to him. The Acharya was pleased to find Jivak so confident of himself and his humility. He indicated his *Guru-dakshina* like this: Identify one vegetation; herb, shrub, plant, tree or any other variety in nature that has no use for the welfare of humankind. In modern terminology, a huge project was assigned to the learner. Jivak went back, formulated his project, decided the scope of the study and procedures, conducted his experiments, analysed the data, formulated the outcomes and after completing all the steps, came back to the guru and said, "I could find none and nothing that is not of use to mankind." The Acharya was fully satisfied and permitted Jivak to go and devote himself for the welfare of the people. Acharya Jivak earned great name and fame through his learning and its utilisation for serving others. One wishes such elements are seriously examined by the policy formulators in education who are, very rightly, considerably worried about implementing reforms in evaluation systems.

Resource Mobilization

There is ample evidence to prove that education imparted through Buddhist monasteries, temples, *Mathas* and other similar establishments was totally free. There were no hidden costs as is the practice these days, particularly in private schools and colleges. Let it also be mentioned that the society was aware of the position and as such, offering of gifts to the Gurus was sanctioned even in the sacred texts. It was a relationship of mutual trust and respect. Teachers could accept gifts that parents could offer without any stress and strain of compulsion. Teachers were always reminded that transfer of learning was the sacred duty of the knowledgeable and must be performed without any expectations of material rewards. *Vidyadana* (the gift of knowledge) was considered on a much higher plane than the gifts of land. The rich and the resourceful offered support even at the time of the entry of their wards. Lands were given to Ashramas, Monasteries, Mathas and the like by the resourceful, kings and others for regular sustenance of these learning centres. The Mahabharata mentions that Bhisma paid Drona *dakshina* in advance before he started the education of the Kaurava-Pandava princes'.[6] Kings and princes also founded education centres. Often, they did it with great enthusiasm. The great seat of learning at Vikramshila was founded by the Parmar king Dharampal. The great Nalanda University received support from kings and subjects alike. Donations also came from foreign countries. Hieun-Tsang mentions that the land on which Nalanda monastery was built was a gift to the Buddha by 500 merchants. The State supported education in many ways; by offering scholarships and by arranging dialogues and discussions and giving generous rewards and awards to the winning scholars. The state support was always without any control or even an iota of interference.

The learner, known as *Brahmachari* because of certain disciplines imposed on him during the process and period of learning, was also supposed to go on daily rounds of collecting food. This is often despised in the current discourse and not found to be in consonance with the current levels of social consciousness and perceptions of human dignity. This was the process of resource generation not for the individual self, but for the establishment as a whole in which all the functionaries participated. Learners came from varied backgrounds. The King's sons could be studying along with those of a very poor Brahmin. They were treated equally and numerous instances of the same are available in the literature. It was the most pragmatic way of developing the values of empathy and humility.

The Focal Point

The growth of Indian civilization in ancient times is mainly characterised by its emphasis on *Dharma*; the Righteous Conduct. The term *Dharma* is so comprehensive and fulsome that it becomes difficult to find another equivalent term to it. It incorporates and impacts basic essentials of social, political, economic, cultural and spiritual aspects of human life. Religion, the commonly used term, provided every individual the guidance on how to live a life that would elevate him in his pursuits and brings a sense of satisfaction on that count. One was generally guided in deciding his acts, actions and pursuits within the acceptable indications of the society which, again, determined these under the umbrella of *Dharma*. This is beautifully articulated in the following passage:

> "Ancient Indian education is also to be understood as being ultimately the outcome of the Indian theory of knowledge and a part of the corresponding scheme of life and values. That scheme takes full account of the fact that life includes death and the two together forms the whole unit. This gives a particular angle of vision, a sense of perspective and proportion in which the material and the moral, the physical and the spiritual, the perishable and the permanent interests and values of life are clearly defined and strictly differentiated."[7]

One of the most outstanding aspect that needs to be noted by educational planners of the day that the interaction between the teacher and the taught was very intense, as it should be in a well-knit family that follows a moral and ethical code and is conscious of its responsibilities and duties to each other and also to the external world that exists beyond the family. This aspect was so well articulated by Swami Vivekananda, "My idea of education is *Gurugriha-vasa*. Without the personal life of the teacher, there would be no education. One should live from his boyhood with one whose character is a blazing fire and should have before him a living example of highest teaching. In our country the imparting of knowledge has always been through men of renunciation. The charge of imparting knowledge should again fall upon the shoulders of *Tyagis.*[8] It must be conceded that the increasing pressures of population on one hand, and the exponential growth of materialism and consumerism overshadowing the spiritual elements not only in life, but also in education, on the other, demand a new model. However, the essence of the teacher-taught relationship must be extricated from the debris of these two functioning as different parts of a mechanical assembly. The ancient system did not require the learner to pay and no teacher was selling education! People and the society supported the learning centres and the teachers.

In the ancient Indian tradition, the search for 'Truth' took the central stage in understanding life. This was not confined only to the life on the planet earth, but attempted to explore the life that existed before and shall continue even after the departure of the person from the earth. Knowledge was to be acquired to understand the inner self as well, apart from gaining the objective knowledge that is necessary to live a social, creative and contributing life with family and within the society. It, at the same time, guided the individual to 'merge himself in the universe to escape from the sense of change, decay, and dissolution'. The function of education was also illustrated as the means to achieve the stage when the individual is capable of discarding such acts and activities which lure him to get 'connected with the world of matter and objects'. Once this is achieved, the individual gets ready to 'achieve his expansion in to the Absolute, his self-fulfillment, for he is a potential God, a spark of the divine'. In the times of rather unbridled materialism and consumerism, it may not be easily comprehensible to many that in the ancient Indian thought, education was perceived as a process that led the individual to control his mind. One reaches a stage when the mind is not disturbed by the onslaughts of the distractions of the material world. This was the ultimate stage to be attained, but the path of pursuit—education—was open to all the seekers. The seekers' advancement depended on the education that he received, the socio-cultural environment did have an impact, but ultimately, it was the individual's own initiative, mental steadiness and strength and the keenness to rise to higher levels that counted. The focus on meditation and control of mind and emotions said it all.

Contemporary Context

There is a general tendency amongst a set of scholars and academics to ignore the very existence of a sound system of creating and generating knowledge in ancient India and to acknowledge that it had indeed successfully comprehended the secrets of nature that extended far beyond the mundane. The very structure of the universe, the very objectives of human existence on earth, and the sublime aspects of man's sojourn on the planet received their considered and sustained attention. A very sound and pragmatic system of education came in existence. Its most important characteristic was that it responded to the learners requirements in totality; that included the self, society and nature! There is another school of thought which finds that all that was in place and practice in ancient times could be brought back as that was the best and the ultimate! Sometimes these interpretations get coloured because of ideological compulsions which were never present in ancient times. It is a fact that scientific contributions of different civilizations have been overshadowed under the prominence given to 'western white' contributions. To understand this aspect it may be relevant to recall the following:[9]

"Twenty-four centuries before Isaac Newton, the Hindu Rig-

> Veda asserted that gravitation held the universe together, though the Hindu hypothesis was the less rigorous than Newton's. The Sanskrit speaking Aryans subscribed to the idea of spherical earth in an era when the Greeks believed in the flat one. The Indians of the fifth century A.D. somehow calculated the age of the earth as 4.3 billion years; scientists in nineteenth-century England were convinced it was 100 million years. The modern estimate is 4.6 billion years."
>
> "In its January 14, 2000, issue on the occasion of the beginning of the third millennium, *Science* magazine, in conjunction with the American Association for the Advancement of Science (AAAS), published a timeline, and called "Pathways of Discovery" that detailed ninety-six of the most important scientific achievements in the recorded history."
>
> "Of those ninety-six achievements, only two were attributed to non-white-non-Western scientists: the invention of zero in India in the early centuries of the Common Era and the astronomical observations of Maya and Hindus in A.D. 1000. Even these two accomplishments were muted by the editors of *Science*. The Indians were given credit only for creating the symbol of zero, rather than the concept itself. The Mayan and Hindu "sky watchers" (the word astronomer was not used) made their observations, according to the journal only "for agricultural and religious purposes".

The above illustration also indicates how India's own generation of scholars and academics has lagged behind in understanding the significant outcomes of the ancient Indian education system that created not only luminaries in spirituality and religious understanding but also produced scientists and researchers of the highest order. It is an obvious outcome that such a system just cannot be discarded altogether. Its strengths need to be examined by the present policy makers. Education for all is the present global resolve. India has yet to attain this goal effectively. It has experienced several lacunae in implementing its policies on extending the outreach of 'education to all'. Is it not possible to explore the possibility of offering locally responsive curricula that may be very different in Delhi, Koraput and Ladakh! If we had developed curricula in tribal areas that incorporated the culture and skill acquisition relevant to their specific needs, their near total exploitation would have been checked considerably. It is also well established that *Ashram Shala*s established in tribal areas, in spite of all of their functional deficiencies, have provided opportunities in education to many. Several elements of the Gurukula system could be assimilated in these Shalas to make them effectively functional.

It is accepted by modern academics and educationists that the best assessment or evaluation of learner attainments can be done only by the teacher who teaches the child. For over six decades India continued with a system in which thousands and thousands were declared 'failed' practically at every stage of education. It has now been realised that such evaluations have a disastrous impact on the young minds. Consequently; the formal examinations up to class eight have been abolished; at least in principle. However, the conditions in which remedial and assisted learning could be provided do not exist in most of the schools. The same applies to the principle of intensive interaction between the teachers and taught. Acute shortages of teachers, their unwillingness to stay full time in schools and practically the total absence of any interaction outside the school hours are indeed retarding factors. Indian universities, including the central/state universities and prestigious professional institutions are also suffering the same fate as the schools in respect of teacher shortage and infrastructure deficiencies. If a young person in the age group 22-28 years is kept in a job on a pittance of an honourarium or is asked to teach in a university on lecture basis, the critical ingredient of professional and institutional commitment just cannot be nurtured. Uncertainty and insecurity also impact the professional performance as anxiety overtakes the overall psyche.

Two of the most quoted terms in the current educational parlance are: these are the times of lifelong learning and, these are the times of mind power. Ancient Indian education had internalized both of these in its content and pedagogy. "*Yavadjeevat Adhiyate Viprah*" (The wise are lifelong learners) and "*Buddhiryasya Balam Tasya*" (One who has got intelligence, he has got power) establish the basic continuity of the conceptual formulations that are in sense eternal. In the curriculum of education, dynamism is an essential ingredient and change in it is necessary to avoid stagnation and maintain the responsive nature of learning. Only such education 'nourishes us like the mother, directs to proper path like father, and gives us delight and comfort like the wife'.[10] A person becomes more respectable and adorable only because of his mastery levels in learning. Every academic of the present times knows that to keep his reputation amongst his students, he himself has to remain an avid reader and an active learner. When computers arrived, young children attained proficiency in handling these in practically no time, but most of the experienced teachers, reluctant to learn new technology, found that they were losing their esteem. It is education that changes the nature of man. Today, if despicable social practices like slavery, apartheid and caste systems stand fully discarded and disowned, the credit must be mostly shared by education, its expansions and extended access to persons from every strata of the society.

As a tribute to the Guru of the yore, let one recall Swami Vivekananda who had an illuminating appreciation of the past and an enlightened vision of the future. He wanted the teacher to throw his whole force into the tendency of the taught. And further: "The true teacher is he who can immediately come down to the student's soul and see through and understand through his mind. Such a teacher can really teach and none else."[11]

India needs such teachers to shape its tomorrow.

(February 12, 2013)

Notes

1. Rama Jois, M., Human Rights and Indian Values; 1997, National Council for Teacher Education; New Delhi.
2. *Ibid.*, p. 35.
3. Altekar, A.S., *Education in Ancient India*, 1965, Nand Kishor and Brothers; Varanasi.
4. Lal, Makkhan, with Dixit, Rajendra, Educating to Confuse and Disrupt, 2005, India First Foundation, New Delhi.
5. *Ibid.*, p. 9.
6. *Ibid.*, p. 29.
7. Mookerji, Radha Kumud, *Ancient Indian Education* (Brahmanical and Buddhist), 1960, Motilal Banarasidas; Delhi.
8. Swami Vivekananda; *Education*; complied by T.S. Avinashlingam, 2005, Sri Ramakrishna Math, Madras.
9. Dick Teresy, *Lost Discoveries: The Ancient Roots of Modern Science*, 2002, Simon and Schuster, New York.
10. Altekar, A.S., *Education in Ancient India*, 1965, Nand Kishor and Brothers, Varanasi.
11. Swami Vivekananda; *Education*, compiled and edited by T.S. Avinashlingam, 1957 Sri Ramakrishna Mission Vidyalaya; Coimbatore.

7

Medium of Instruction in Initial Years

Several of the distinguished features of India's freedom struggle are universally acknowledged and appreciated. It is a unique instance in which education in free India was always on the minds of its political leaders. Mahatma Gandhi himself had the experience of organizing schooling for children in South Africa. When he arrived in that country, he had to arrange for the education of two of his own sons aged nine and five years and also his sister's son who was ten years of age. How to get them educated was the issue before him. From that onwards began his well known experiments in education. His interest remained alive all along and the experiences gradually developed in his well known perceptions on education and culminated into the concepts of Basic Education and *Buniyadi Talim*. Reference to Gandhian thoughts on education is inevitable in any discussion and deliberation on concerns that relate to learning in schools and higher education institutions in India. The medium of instruction and role of the mother tongue received ample articulation from him. Addressing the students of Banaras Hindu University[1] on February 6, 1916, he was very clear on the issue:

> "I am hoping that this university will see to it that the youths who come to it receive their instruction through the medium of their vernaculars. Our language is the reflection of ourselves, and if you tell me that our languages are too poor to express the best thought, then I say that sooner we are wiped out of existence the better for us. Is there a man who dreams that English can ever become the national language of the nation.... But suppose that we had been receiving during the last fifty years education through our vernaculars, what should we have today? We should have today a free India. We should have our educated men, not as if they were

> foreigners in their own land, but speaking to the heart of the nation; they should be working amongst the poorest of the poor, and whatever they would have gained during the last fifty years would be heritage for the nation."

Where are we now after over nine decades of this speech? The latest reports indicate a 150 per cent growth in the numbers of primary students in India getting their primary education in English medium schools during the period 2005-06 to 2008-09![2] Some interesting trends appear in the increase of the numbers in English medium schools on geographical spread. In the top two states of Andhra Pradesh and Tamil Nadu, almost one-fifth of the total enrolled children learnt through the English medium. The highest jump in the number of English medium students was in the state of Maharashtra, about 11 lakhs, followed by Andhra Pradesh with 9.7 lakhs, Tamil Nadu with 9.6 lakhs and Delhi with 5.5 lakhs. Haryana recorded the highest growth rate as the numbers of children in English medium schools went up by more than seven times in the four year interval. This survey also indicates that the actual numbers of those learning through the English medium right from Class One must be far higher than the estimates as there are thousands of unrecognized schools spread over throughout the country. Everywhere in the country, there is a race for opening English medium schools. Parents are desperate to get their wards admitted in English medium schools. The entrepreneurs and investors are availing of the opportunity as one that ensures high rate of returns with no possibility of any melt down. India is in the grip of a great transition. It is no longer an issue that pertains to Hindi or English or Hindi and other regional languages. Now the concern is English as the medium of instruction right from the primary stages and it is said that parents want it, the progress of the nation is dependent on it. A good and successful life awaits only those who study through English medium schools.

It also deserves to be noted that the trend amongst the young persons is to opt for jobs in the Multi National Corporations in India and abroad. There are genuine economic reasons for it. In spite of the economic meltdown, the BPO's are perceived as amongst the finest of employment options for young persons from middle class, particularly those from small towns and cities. The heads of management institutions have the major task of ensuring teaching of English that prepares their wards for interview that may enable them to impress the prospective employers through their proficiency in language and communicative skills. Other skills, they say, could be learnt later! The position is that without English, every young person faces serious disadvantages in interviews everywhere including the government jobs, admissions in higher education institutions. The panacea is said to be the English medium schools, which can help young persons overcome the disadvantage. An interaction with young persons in a district town in UP or Bihar would indicate how English elitism demoralises the young persons who did not get a chance to 'master' English language as is possible in convent schools and other Public Schools! No parent wishes to be blamed later on and, wherever possible, makes every effort to get admission in English medium schools.

Only those who have limitations of economic factors or other constraints opt for the *Sarkari* (government) School! These mostly teach through the medium of regional languages. English is now being taught in most of the state schools from Class One onwards. The Municipal Corporation of Delhi is said to be considering converting all of its 1800 schools into English Medium schools. That shows the trend and paints a picture of the emerging scenario. Those who do not study English are doomed to stray away from pursuits in higher and professional education. The situation has become critical indeed with the advent of ICT, globalisation and the notion that it is only English language that permits the dream of entering the glamorous world of corporate and multinationals. The education planning has silently favoured the class of Indians that was dear to Englishmen as it was their own creation. The barriers between the elite and the rest have assumed alarming proportions. The elite are happy with the existing arrangements. The ignored and neglected stand resigned to their fate.

At present, there are two distinct practices that are in vogue for learning English. In one, children go to English medium schools, get tuitions, coaching and all that they require to score the highest possible percentage of marks in the board examinations. In the second, children are supposed to learn English as a second language but have to do so in conditions of serious deprivation and deficiencies. They may have to make do even without qualified and competent teachers. This is bound to lead to lack of interest in school and contribute to drop out rates. The proportion of the problem is far bigger than what is being visualised. It appears that the system has not learnt its lessons that were consistently indicated by the huge dropout rates from schools during the first four to five decades after independence. These have declined but still remain a cause of great concern for the planners and the implementers of the education policies. Matriculation results in those years were invariably around 35-40 per cent. And majority of those who failed were found to be deficient in English. When most of the children enrolled were the first generation learners, compulsion of learning English played havoc not only with their education but also their hopes and aspirations that were crushed to dust in the majority of the cases. They carried the "failed' tag throughout their lives. While the system has taken note of the situation and it is possible to get a matriculation certificate without the compulsions of learning English, new forces have emerged that make schooling and education without 'English' a more or less worthless exercise. It is forcefully being argued that the prospect of India emerging as the economic superpower would squarely and totally depend on proficiency in English language and for that education must begin in English medium and not the mother tongue!

There are numerous examples of the nations which could compete with the Western world in its scientific and technological advances on an equal footing. Have China, Russia (the erstwhile USSR) or Japan lagged behind on any count because of the primacy they give to their own languages? When Russians could send their Sputniks in space ahead of US, the Americans were a greatly demoralized lot. The Russians had their own Journals of high level scientific research. The western world had to arrange to get these translated into English and publish for the benefit of the English (only!) knowing scientific community! China is often quoted in the Indian media as having launched a massive programme of learning English. No one reports that it has not discarded initial education being given through the medium of the mother tongue. Instead of planning and opening centres for learning spoken English suitable for specific assignments, the Indian system is fast discarding the basic pedagogical principle of modern education that no child should be burdened with beginning his/her education in an alien language. Children can learn more languages as they move ahead in age and the stage of education. The issue is that of the medium of initial instruction and in fact, even in higher education. Gandhiji, the exceptional communicator in several languages including English, had this to say on the subject:

> "The foreign medium has caused brain fag, put an undue strain upon the nerves of our children, made them crammers and imitators, unfitted them for original work and thoughts, and disabled them for filtrating their learning to the family or the masses. The foreign medium has made our children practically foreigners in their own land. It is the greatest tragedy of the existing system. The foreign medium has prevented the growth of our vernaculars. If I had the powers

> of a despot, I would today stop the tuition of our boys and girls through a foreign medium, and require all the teachers and professors on the pain of dismissal to introduce the change forthwith. I would not wait for the preparation of textbooks. They will follow the change. It is an evil that needs a summary remedy."[3]

The context and the current scenario indicate a very complex situation and it is almost certain that none amongst those who could make major decisions or influence the decision making process are making any attempt to scrutinise the issue comprehensively. However, Immediately after the promulgation of the Constitution of India, prominent Indians did come together to take a view that would be nationalistic, in the interest of Indian Languages and one that would give English its due. Persons of the stature of Sir C.V. Raman, H. J. Bhabha, V.K.R.V. Rao, Samuel Mathai, M.N. Srinivas, N.H. Bhagwati, R.P. Parija, Ms Hannah Sen, S.N. Sen and others wrote on August 4, 1952 to the Minster of Education in Government of India and Ministers of Education in states on the issue of language learning:[4]

> "We are prepared to accept the position that English shall be replaced by an Indian Language—national or regional—by the end of fifteen years after the commencement of the Constitution. In the meantime the question of preparing textbooks and translating a certain number of books in to Hindi or regional languages will have to be taken up right seriously. This will naturally take some time, and fifteen years should be certainly more than sufficient, provided the Government of India and the State governments are prepared to spend generously several lakhs every year for this purpose, and frame a definite ten-year scheme. But as educationists, we see no possibility of our being able to do without some good knowledge of English; for any number of translations will never completely meet the needs of all the subjects taught in our universities with the exception perhaps of subjects purely Indian in context. It follows that in the interest of higher education in India it is extremely necessary to keep up an adequate standard of English even after it ceases to be the medium of instruction."

In his brilliant exposition of the language issue in the emerging India, Professor Wadia summarised his 'Thesis' in a very pragmatic manner which is still relevant in the situation that is developing all round, particularly amongst the elite and the growing middle class that the only possible path of progress is to go in for English medium education right from the initial years:[5]

1.0 At the primary stage, the medium of instruction should be the regional language which would also be the mother tongue of the vast majority in the region concerned. Hindi may also begin in the last two years of the primary stage.

2.0 At the secondary stage, the regional language will be the medium of instruction. The study of Hindi will have to be continued but the study of English must begin compulsorily for those who aspire to university education.

3.0 At the university stage it is very desirable to maintain a common medium of instruction. It will have to be English for a few years to come, but when it has to be displaced, it should find in Hindi a natural successor. Regional languages at university stage will destroy the great unifying mission of the English language.

In this summarisation, the influence of the 'unifying force' of English clearly represents how the English speaking class, in spite of its efforts to embrace nationalistic sentiments could not perceive the potential of the regional languages that these could acquire once supported properly and adequately.

It is pertinent to recall the three language formula which was mooted some five decades ago by none other than Jawaharlal Nehru in the Parliament and was duly approved for implementation. Under this formula:

> The **First language** to be studied must be the mother tongue or the regional language:
>
> The **Second language**—
>
> (I) in Hindi speaking states will be some other modern Indian language or English, and
>
> (II) in non-Hindi speaking states will be Hindi or English.
>
> The **Third language**—
>
> (I) in Hindi speaking states will be English or modern Indian language not studied as the second language, and
>
> (II) in non-Hindi speaking states will be English or a modern Indian language not studied as the second language.

The intentions were very clear as the basic objective in conceptualizing the three language formula continues to remain unaltered even today: to achieve national unity and facilitate facile inter-state and international communications. It was expected that adherence to it would be ensured in letter and spirit by the central and state governments. Minor modifications in the formula and its implementation in complex linguistic situations, as in some North-Eastern states for example, could, however, be allowed as per the needs of these states within the overall spirit of the formula.[6] It may also be mentioned that the Kothari Commission (1964-66) had made a recommendation on second language in the following words:

> "The stage at which Hindi or English should be introduced on a compulsory basis as a second language and the period for which it should be taught will depend on local motivation and need, and should be left to the discretion of each state."

At no stage the liberty to begin education in a medium other than the mother tongue was even remotely considered. Even if it was, it would have been rejected outright as pedagogically unsound and amounting to inflicting avoidable cruelty on the tender young children. The flexibility of introducing the second language does not dilute the fact of medium being the mother tongue.

The Mother Tongue as the medium of instruction is critical to a meaningful beginning of education and also to a stress-free emotional, cognitive and social development. It alone establishes the continuity between the home and the school environment. It is essential for proper learning of other languages as well. The seeds of independent thinking, free and effective expression of opinions and logical interpretation of the present and the past events are sown only through mother tongue. The mother tongue as the medium of instruction just has no educationally sound alternative.

One could cite a large number of documentation that followed after the 1950s on the issues of national language, link language, regional languages and the medium of instructions. Each time, all these were examined in respect of English. One could recall the National Policy on Education of 1968, 1986/92 and the continuous debate on the three language formula, including the deficiencies in its implementation and even lack of interest to effectively implement it. English has remained the favourite pursuit of every educated Indian. There is nothing wrong about it. However, what India really needs to consider seriously is the place of its own languages. Will these be allowed to lapse into the background? A more pragmatic and operatically significant query that needs to be answered is; "Is it necessary to go through the English medium education as against the mother tongue to gain competitive proficiency?" Unfortunately, research evidence on the concerned issues is not available. The impressionistic view point is clear. 'Those who begin education in the medium of mother tongue and take up second language after four or five years can acquire the same levels of proficiency by the time they complete ten years of schooling.' Whatever be the real and apparent benefits of learning English, it should certainly not replace the mother tongue. This tendency must be scrutinised and its consequences studied and analysed scientifically. Multiple language learning is necessary in India and no one should have problems in learning English and making use of it.

While the author was addressing a congregation of over 500 enlightened citizens in Akola in 2006, a question was posed from the audience: "In Maharashtra, Marathi is getting neglected and English is spreading all around. If you are given all the authority and power, what would you do to stop this proliferation of English?" There was total silence in the auditorium. The response after a quiet pause, was "I would do nothing against English. I would use all my powers to strengthen Marathi in all respects and everywhere in every direction." The deafening response that followed indicated total approval of the stated approach. This is what India needs to implement with sincerity and commitment in the years ahead.

(December 09, 2009)

Notes

1. *CW* 13, pp. 211-12.
2. *Times of India*, December 5, 2009; p. 1 and 13.
3. *Young India*, 1 September 1921 (CW 21, p.40).
4. Wadia, A.R., *The Future of English in India*, Asia Publishing House, 1954, pp. 144-146.
5. *Ibid*., Preface of the book.
6. National Curriculum Framework for School Education (2000), the NCERT, New Delhi, 2000.

8

Emerging Perspectives before Teachers

In the second decade of the 21st century, the debate on various aspects of education remains as intense as ever. If some sixty years ago it focused on access, expansion and bringing children, particularly girls, to schools, the dimensions are now entirely different. It however remains a fact that millions and millions of children world over are still outside the fold of education. Not only this, serious issues of varied inadequacies regarding those in schools have also manifested themselves. There have been several attitudinal changes regarding education amongst the parents and the communities. These do not only want education, they sincerely desire to give good education to their children at any cost! In a fiercely competitive world, education has no relevance if it does not prepare young people to compete with the best, acquire life skills and be mentally prepared to learn and acquire more knowledge and new skills as these are the essential requirements of the century which is the century of the pace of change. Schools must impart quality education and also ensure a comprehensive personality development that would equip the students to face the emerging challenges on one hand and make creative and innovative contributions on the other. The country and the world needs men and women who believe in leading a value-based life, who understand the criticality of man-nature mutuality and who have internalised the requirement of celebrating diversities of all types that have been gifted to mankind. All this would be possible only when Teacher Effectiveness is achieved by the teacher preparation systems on a countrywide scale.

The task before teachers is indeed huge. While the constitution of India had directed the state to provide free and compulsory education to all children till they attain the age of fourteen years, it implemented its Right to Education Act (RTE) only in April 2010, including children in the age group of 6-14 years only. At that stage, it was roughly estimated that the taking into account the existing vacancies and the additional posts of teachers required to implement the RTE, some thirteen lakh of teachers would be needed over a period of about five years. It may be recalled that at the time of independence, the shortage of teachers was acutely felt when the expansion began and it continues even today. The only reason could be lack of pragmatic policies of teacher preparation and neglect of area specific requirements in diverse socio-cultural and economic contexts. While certain regions have unemployed teachers, there is perpetual shortage in rural, hilly and far-flung areas. Several state governments have employed unqualified and untrained teachers on the pittance of an honourarium, expecting many of them to run a full school from classes 1-5! After over six decades, the Indian school system still suffers from several bottlenecks in terms of non-availability of trained teachers, teacher vacancies and absenteeism, inadequate infrastructure support in schools, engagement of teachers in various non-teaching assignments, fear of transfers and inadequate action to redress the deficiencies under which the teachers function and to which they wish to draw the attention of the authorities. Politicization of teachers and political interference in various aspects also hinders the smooth functioning of the system as a whole. They need a thorough understanding of the components that constitute the quality of education. They need to understand the implications of change in expectations from education, not only in general terms but also in terms of the requirements of specific sectors and particularly the new avenues emerging in the globalised and ICT-dominated world. Obviously, this requires a thorough pre-induction education of teachers in teacher education institutions. There is also a need for functional dynamic systems of in-service education of teachers. It is the quality of teacher educators that conditions the professional preparedness of teachers and that in turn determines the levels of efficiency and efficacy in various sectors of human endeavour meant for progress and development aimed at improving the quality of life. In order to fulfill the expectations and to discharge their role with commitment and dedication, teachers need a sensitive and responsive system of educational administration and management. They also need a congenial environment to deliver the best of their performance.

Quality in Education

Quality of education is dynamic concept that keeps on evolving. It is no more a question of simply acquiring just mere literacy, numeracy and life skills. Peoples' perceptions are no longer confined to mere teachers, content and certificates and degrees. It would be desirable to have an overview of the elements that determine quality in totality. It defines the world before the teachers and also helps in delineating their tasks, professional needs and performance strategies. "The quality of education must recognise the past, be relevant to the present, and have a view of the future. It must also relate to knowledge building and the skillful application of all forms of knowledge by unique individuals who function both independently and in relation to others. A high quality education will always reflect the dynamic nature of culture and language, the value of the individual in relation to the larger context and the importance of living in a way that promotes equality in the present and fosters a sustainable future."[1] Education, as a fundamental right, requires that learners have to be sought after; no child, including those from deprived and deficient groups, girls; children in difficult conditions, in emergencies, with disabilities, with nomadic life styles and with any other possible deprivation must be brought to the fold of education. That would have a direct relationship to the way teachers are prepared and the manner in which they perform their functions. Every teacher needs to develop context specific competence and must ascertain the level and extent of the learning that the learner brings once he/she joins the school. The content of education is generally determined by the systems and may often be only indicative and not necessarily context specific. That is the ingenuity of the teacher to give content in a manner that would serve as the basis for further learning and acquisitions when the learner goes out in the world of work and is on his/her own. After all this come the processes which determine not only the levels of learning but also impact the levels of learner interest in furthering the learning with interest and, as is most desirable, whether the much sought-after 'enjoyable learning' could really be achieved! Essentially it is the community of teachers in a school or any institutions that creates a learning environment conducive to quality of education in its varied aspects. Thus the immediate system that matters in quality consists of understanding the learner background, content, process and the learning environment. This immediate circle is invariably dependent on five other systemic factors: resources; supportive legislative systems; pragmatic policy formulation and their committed implementation, management and administration of the system and finally, the means to measure the outcomes. This may not be the only approach towards quality of education but…

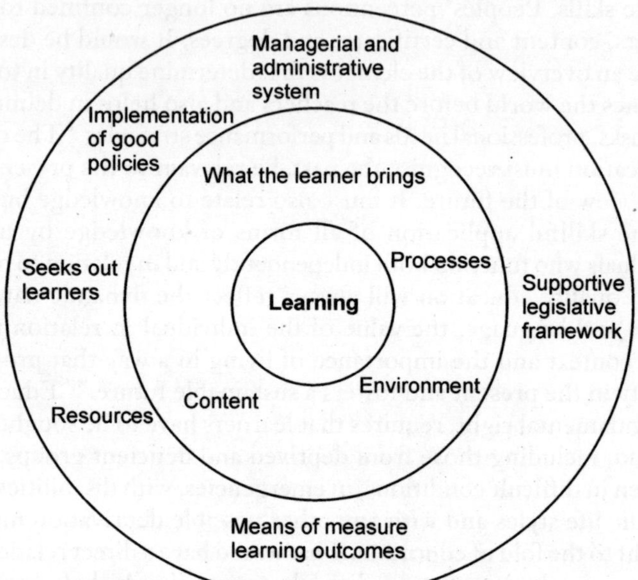

Fig. 8.1: *Source:* "Cross-national studies of the quality of education" edited by Kenneth N. Ross and IIona Jurgens Genevois, published by International Institute of Educational Planning, Paris, 2006.

…the omnibus presence of these elements would rather remain universal in nature. Depending on the context and conditions, certain aspects could be re-worded, but the approach needs to be guided by the efficacy of learning during the future life of the learner. Each of these has relevance for the teacher and teacher preparation. These also determine the width and depth of the role of teacher in the future world. Quality education, apart from other inputs, mainly and mostly depends on the competence, commitment and performance of the teachers. These teachers are supposed to know the meaning of quality, the import of learner centred education, the requisite pedagogy, learning methods, in synergy with the teaching methods and are no longer confined only to the syllabus as translated in the textbook. They know that the responsibility is 'to draw out the best out of body, mind and spirit'. These teachers must be confident on all of these aspects and quality must remain their target in the classroom, outside the class room and within the school and also outside the school. Teachers of tomorrow have to remember that they are catering to a learning society which is now deluged with shared information and has every intention to move towards a knowledge society. If the knowledge society is to develop properly, information has to be structured in such a way that it fulfills some basic conditions of interactivity, mobility, convertibility, connectivity, ubiquity and globalization, as was perceived by Toffler[2] some two decades ago. Another prime consideration in this march towards the knowledge society is the emergence of islands of prosperity and progress for limited group of global population as against the presence of continents of ignorance, poverty, hunger, illiteracy, overpopulation, backwardness and ill health. The emerging world that the teachers should prepare has to be conscious of their role in bringing about social justice and equity for one and all. The objectives of education shall change accordingly and from that the changing roles of teachers shall emerge. Husen[3] had listed these in the following terms:

- Education must prepare students to live in a pluralistic society.
- Education should not be confined to childhood or youth but should be a lifelong process.
- It should take more informal character.
- It should build and lay the groundwork for re-educability and ability to assimilate further knowledge.
- Schools must promote internationalism.
- Schools must build skills on how to deal with the torrential flow of information.

The global society, and the globalised world has travelled a long distance in educational understanding and appreciation from 1972 when the UNESCO made learning society the master concept in its well known report 'Learning to Be'[4] known as the Edgar Faure Report and then came to the much discussed Report "Learning: The Treasure Within",[5] which is called the Jacques Delors Report. The latter very precisely summarises the change and states referring to the Faure Report: "Its recommendations are still very relevant, for in the twenty first century everyone will need to exercise greater independence and judgment combined with a strong sense of personal responsibility for the attainment of common goals. Our report stresses a further imperative: none of talents which are hidden like buried treasure in every person must be left untapped. These are, to name but a few: memory, reasoning power, imagination, physical ability, aesthetic sense, the aptitude to communicate with others and the natural charisma of the group leader, which again goes to prove the need for greater self knowledge." The four pillars of education listed in the Delors Report are the key ingredients that determine the basis for the delineation of teachers' role in specific contexts that also matches the global context. Out of these four pillars it lays very special emphasis on the first: Learning to Live Together. It includes understanding and respecting otherness, rejoice diversities, be aware of the cultures, faiths, civilizations practices and every other possible difference in approach and attitude, faiths. The world of the 21st century is interlinked and is a no-distance world in which everyone has to be in one way or the other linked to everyone else! The other three pillars are: Learning to Know; Learning to do; and Learning to be. These present education in probably the totality that could not be described with such comprehension in any other manner. Teachers must be made aware of these developments and themselves delineate their roles relevant to the age and stage of learning of the child. It would be relevant to recall the definition of basic learning needs that emerged out of the World Conference on Education for All held in Jomtien city of Thailand in March 1990[6] : These needs comprise both essential learning tools (such as literacy, oral expression, numeracy, and problem solving) and the basic learning content (such as knowledge, skill, values, and attitudes) required by human beings to be able to survive, to develop their full capacities, to live and work in dignity, to participate fully in development, to improve the quality of their lives, to make informed decisions, and to continue learning."

Let it be understood fully well that a stage has been reached in which universal education has practically universal acceptance which has now grown in eagerness and keenness to impart education to both boys and girls everywhere. The latest addition to this is: the desire amongst parents is not only for education but for good quality education that is imbued with skill orientation and, still better, inculcation of an intense desire within the learner to learn more. In India this phenomenon is best illustrated by the rush for private schools as compared to government schools. It also illustrates another big challenge that has emerged before the governments: their own schools are losing credibility at a fast pace and steps must be put in place to set the house in order. Apart from other needed inputs, it has serious implications for teachers' orientation and preparation in terms of commitment and value internalisation apart from understanding their changed role.

The System

By the time one becomes a teacher, normal expectation is that he/she has undergone a programme of acquisition of knowledge and skills in the art and craft of teaching and learning. This process also acquaints the student teachers with the adequate content knowledge in the specific subjects they are supposed to teach as per the requirements of the existing system of education. The System that India follows consists of teacher education courses for young persons who pass out the examinations after twelve years of schooling, or are graduates or post-graduates from the universities and colleges. The training programmes consist of two years duration for elementary stage teachers and one year's duration for the graduates who would be teaching at the secondary stage. Based on the recommendations of the Curriculum Framework for quality teacher education, two year B.Ed courses are also being conducted by Regional Institutes of Education of the NCERT.[7] Unfortunately, innovative teacher education programmes have not been taken up on a larger scale in the country till now. The Four integrated courses initiated by the NCERT in mid-sixties for preparing quality teachers for secondary schools still remain islands of isolation in spite of researches bringing out that the products of these courses are far superior to those who undergo only one academic year of secondary teacher education courses. The introduction of the two-year Bachelor of Education in the Regional Institutes of Education was opposed by many, though not necessarily on academic grounds alone. It was a bold decision against the argument "why should anyone join a 'two-year course' when one year programmes are available in plenty?" The response from parents and student teachers proved it beyond doubt that quality is liked by every group and people are willing to walk an extra mile to acquire it. The problem, at present, is that the seriousness which teacher preparation requires is generally absent, particularly in majority of teacher preparation institutions. One of the major initiatives resulting out of the twenty years long efforts of concerned teachers, teacher educators and educationists resulted in the establishment of the National Council for Teacher Education (NCTE). It showed considerable promise in the initial years but, unfortunately, could not resist adapting the practices prevalent in other regulatory bodies. One of the suggested alternatives is to establish a National Resource Centre for Teacher Education which could function as the professional and academic light house in the field.[8]

Even in an academic and professional discussion, the existence of certain anomalies in teacher preparation just cannot be overlooked as these seriously erode the credibility of the system and quality of the products. During the last decade, teacher preparation has been converted to an investment sector in which safe and lucrative returns are guaranteed. The mushrooming of teacher education colleges has been rather shocking not because these are not needed, but the manner in which these are approved by the regulatory body and the way these function. The gap between the expectations from teacher education institutions and their real performance was never as wide and alarming as it is at present. The deterioration in the work culture and inadequacy of teacher-student teacher-school students is rampant. Not only this, teachers also face huge distractions as the recruitment procedures are still archaic and generate little hope for a free and fair inclusion in the system. Recruitment of teachers on a small honourarium could be justified in certain extreme situations, but this has been converted into regular practice by certain state governments just to 'save resources'—though they may not admit it. Services of such 'para teachers' are then regularised under various pressures and, obviously, contribute to the deterioration of the quality as most of them are untrained and under qualified.

Teacher Task

It would be interesting to recall the teachers' roles and corresponding student roles as identified by Weaver.[9]

Table 8.1: Teachers' Roles and Corresponding Students' Roles and Outcomes

Teachers' Roles	*Teaching/ Learning Process*	*Student's Roles*	*Likely Student Quality as Outcomes*
1. Appreciator	As determined by students	**1. Searcher**	Self-Determination
2. Partner	Participation	**2. Partner**	Responsibility
3. Patron	Making	**3. Designer**	Creativeness
4. Guide	Searching	**4. Explorer**	Adventurousness
5. Questioner	Experimentation	**5. Searcher**	Investigation Skill
6. Tutor	Reflection	**6. Thinker**	Understanding
7. Counsellor	Expression of feeling	**7. Client**	Insight
8. Moulder	Conditioning	**8. Subject**	Habits
9. Instructor	Transfer of information	**9. Memorizer**	Possession of Information
10. Exemplar	Imitation	**10. Trainee**	Skills

Let it be mentioned that in literature these roles are presented in different ways and it has its own justification. It must be made very explicit, in the light of above ten roles, that role of teachers as evaluator does not emerge as promptly as it should. This is one of the most important of the aspects of the teaching-learning process that impacts the growing up of the learner in all of its personality development and cognitive aspects. In India, where teachers look after a large number of children from first and second generation families, this aspect becomes far more significant. India is still struggling with examination reforms and bringing in continuous and comprehensive evaluation in its schools. Even the teacher preparation institutions are following the age old annual examination system.

Teachers also determine their task-delineation by properly understanding the expectations of the young learners. It emerged from several studies that pupils like teachers with the following attributes:[10]

- Praise pupils' ideas
- Give less direction, command or orders
- Are more indirect in their classroom behaviour
- Do less negative talk
- Ask more questions while guiding the content-oriented transaction
- Possess requisite skills to respond to pupils' ideas, talk and queries
- Integrate pupils' ideas into classroom discussions; and
- Are involved in more creative models of teaching

In India, teachers' priorities can certainly not be same throughout the country while their mission of course remains the same. Social cohesion and learning to live together are universally accepted as the most outstanding of the objectives of education in the present century. Teachers in rural areas have many additional tasks that may not be the priority for a well-funded school in a metro. It is always possible to delineate the quality attributes that would be put to proper application in differing measures depending on the contextual factors:[11]

- Love and affection
- Openness to criticism
- Truthfulness
- Sensitivity to students' emotional needs
- Perseverance
- Humility and modesty
- A positive self image

Tolerance for mistakes and mischiefs
Sense of social justice and equity

The centrality of the role of teacher requires all of them to continuously ponder over their own personality traits and the refinements that they have achieved to ensure more comprehensive contribution to the process of growing up. This growing up is not only important for the learner, but is equally, if not more, relevant to the teacher. It has been emphasized from time immemorial that only one who, it is being highlighted as 'lifelong learning' for both the learner and the teacher. It is also clear that no teacher unwilling to acquire new knowledge and skills can survive in the esteem of his/her learners and also the parents and the community. Hence, the promotion of self-empowerment becomes one of the prime tasks of the teacher. An active and alert teacher should always be ready to receive new ideas and willing to make attempts to incorporate the relevant ones in the process of teaching and learning. The process of self-learning and intellectual humility are organically linked and this could be best appreciated by recalling the immortal lines of T.S. Elliot.[12]

The only wisdom we can hope to acquire
Is the wisdom of humility: humility is endless?

The teacher who internalises the import of self-learning and humility is sure to succeed in building teacher-student rapport at the optimum level and extend it to parents and the community as well. Such teachers are most suited for group performance and enhancing institutional quality levels. They 'nourish and nurture each other' and 'empower each other'! The skill and appreciation of 'Learning to live together' follow when such attributes are visible amongst teachers and impact the learners as well. While cognitive development and individual's all-round personality development are still important and essential, the focus also includes social and economic dimensions of education in the globalised world. In a world that is struggling to sustain itself in the unbridled pursuits of materialism and unchecked consumerism, it is education that is expected to bring back the balance between human needs and human greed! That requires priority focus on value inculcation. Obviously, this can be achieved only when every teacher is trained and educated to become a teacher and nurturer of human values also.

Conclusion

The task before the policy makers and the implementers responsible for teacher preparation is far more complex now than in the past. Dynamic, responsive, comprehensive and effective education primarily depends on the availability of 'effective teachers'. All those who join the teacher preparation courses are neither necessarily motivated enough to become teachers or have come because of their priority? As jobs are always scarce in the country, personal preference often takes a back seat as against financial security and related factors. It is a given condition. It becomes the responsibility of the system and the teacher educators to try and achieve an attitudinal transformation amongst these young boys and girls who could be teaching in the system for the next four to five decades and impacting the life of thousands and thousands. This paper has discussed only some of the aspects, which the author feels are relevant for individual teacher to delineate his/her own objectives in life and in profession. The roles, within the broad frame work of educational excellence, also vary depending on the specific expertise and interest that a particular teacher may be proficient in. However, the individual excellence and interests must merge into the identified institutional goals that are determined within the broad policy framework. The teacher performance could also be seen in terms of technical effectiveness and competencies acquired for subject matter transaction that would include planning and developing curricular materials, classroom organisation, and management.[13] The Human component in building relationships should augment technical efforts. No teacher can escape situations in which conflict management techniques come to the rescue and there may be occasions when social power has to come into play. The cultural effectiveness of the teacher should be evidenced by the manner in which students are motivated to develop shared goals and imbibe values, including respect for diversity. No teacher can ignore the value of renewal as it emanates from the continuous striving for learning new and more. Systems of teacher preparation have no other alternative but to wake up.[14] It requires specific future oriented overhauling of the institutions preparing teachers and teacher educators.

In these times of widespread concern on the quality, relevance and advancement in teacher education, it may be worthwhile to emphasise that the individual teacher educator must highlight to him/herself the leadership role that stands assigned to each one of them by the society and the future. To those who become part of establishment of new institutions one would like to say.[15]

True Leader is one
Who accepts little
But gives away in Abundance

The first step in teacher education improvement is to be initiated at the individual level by teacher educators, heads of teacher education institutions and university departments. Most of them (I would like to use 'us' which some may not relish!) have known everything, but have not come forward energetically and actively to be part of the solution. With the advent of globalisation and liberalisation, coupled with privatisation, the sector of teacher education stands crowded with entrepreneurs who consider education as the safest system that promises uninterrupted returns with rather minimal investment. As most of them have market on their mind, not the man, they have lost sight of the responsibilities and social obligations that have been tagged to education for ages. The consequences are before every genuine teacher and teacher educator, who, along with those specifically assigned to regulate the system, has participated in the consequential deteriorations in quality and also the norms and standards as were stipulated by the regulatory bodies. Others have kept quiet. Neither of these is acceptable. It is a real war-like situation: the beholders of values and those blinded in the glare and glamour of materialism! The systems that create the future and are responsible for the advancement of human civilization are primarily managed by teachers. Hence far greater responsibility dwells upon teacher educators. Globally, no society can ignore its teachers and no teachers can shun their social and generational obligations; even if they have to function in difficult and tough conditions. Many may like to reassess their approach and attitude in the light of the ever-changing expectations from teachers. None of them can afford to remain as fence-sitters. In this context, it would be worthwhile to recall for them, and all the teacher educators, the following poem of Ralph Chaplin written after World War I:[16]

Mourn not the dead who in the soft earth lie
Dust unto dust
The coo, sweet earth who mothers all those who die
As all men must
Mourn not your captive comrades who must dwell in his
Steel-bound coffin of a cell
Buried alive
But rather mourn the apathetic throng
The cowed and the meek

Who see the world's great anguish and its wrong
But dare not speak

No people, it is universally admitted, can rise above the level of their teachers. The nation must never ignore this truth as it alone promises a bright future for generations ahead.

(May 10, 2010)

Notes

1. UNESCO, 2006, Cross-national studies of the quality of education, edited by Kenneth N. Ross and Ilona Jurgens Genevois, International Institute for Educational Planning, 7-9 Eugene Delacroix, 75116, Paris.
2. Toffler, Alvin. 1990. *Power Shift*, New York, Bantam Books.
3. Husen, Torsten, 1974, *The Learning Society*, Penguin Books.
4. UNESCO, 1972, Learning to Be, UNESCO, Paris.
5. Delors, J., 1996, *Learning: the Treasure within*, Paris, UNESCO.
6. UNESCO 1990, World Declaration on Education for All: meeting basic learning needs, New York, UNESCO.
7. National Council for Teacher Education (NCTE), 1998, Curriculum Framework for Quality Teacher Education, New Delhi.
8. Singh R.P.; 2010; *Dialogue with Teacher Educators*; *Teaching Content, Modes and its Nature*; pp. 78-79, Shipra Publications, Delhi.
9. Weaver, T.R., 1970. *Unity and diversity in education*, UK, London, Department of Education and Science.
10. Rajput J.S., 1994, *Experiences and Expectations in Elementary Education*, pp. 104-5, Anamika Publications, New Delhi.
11. Rajput, J.S. and Walia, K., 2002, *Teacher Education in India*, pp. 132-133, Sterling Publishers Private Limited, New Delhi.
12. Eliot, T.S., 1954, *Selected Poems*, Faber and Faber, London.
13. Yin Cheong, Cheng, 2005, New paradigm for Re-engineering Education, Globalization, Localization and Individualization, Springer.
14. Rajput, J.S., *Contemporary Concerns in Education*, 2009, Yash Publications; Delhi.
15. Rajput, J.S., *Oyster of Knowledge*, 2010, Yash Publications; New Delhi.
16. Nayantara Sahgal, *Jawaharlal Nehru: Civilizing a Savage World*, 2010, Penguin Books India, New Delhi.

9

Harnessing the Education Systems

For Comprehensive Learning

Education sustains eternal human hope of achieving prosperity, happiness and ultimately knowledge and awareness, bliss. It now stands firmly established that education can provide maximum empowerment to all human beings to strive towards a better and higher quality of life. The 1990s witnessed a global upsurge in efforts to universalise education by extending the outreach of elementary education to every child. These efforts were to be supplemented and augmented by programmes of adult literacy and alternative schooling including open and distance learning initiatives. *The World Conference on Education for All* held in Jomtien, Thailand, in March 1990, was a historic landmark in the global educational scenario. In this conference, 176 countries resolved to eliminate illiteracy by the end of the 20th century. Though still elusive, sincere efforts were launched practically around the globe to eliminate illiteracy and non-schooling.

In the present century, everyone has to strive to create a knowledge society and, simultaneously, learn to survive in it. The challenges before the education system are enormous. Even a cursory glance of the available statistics on literacy and universal elementary education would indicate large gaps that are yet to be filled. National and International support systems have been put in place in a bid to move towards the goal. Inadequacy of economic and human resources, cultural barriers and population increases are hindering the pace of progress. High expectations from education combined with intense competition at various levels and the fast pace of change are enhancing the complexities of the educational endeavour. Education systems are no longer simple monolithic ones which can be managed at the grassroots' level of implementation. Now, these are complex networked systems that are under severe stress and strain because of the new responsibilities thrust upon them. These have to universalise access to education to the last segment of people who are still deprived of that and, simultaneously, open the gates of higher and professional education to each and every eligible young person, irrespective of any possible diversity in which he/she may be placed.

Further, the still tougher challenge is to provide the equality of opportunity of success as well. There are certain sections in the society who need additional support because of various historical, social or cultural contexts. The system needs to be empowered seriously to meet the new challenges. Practically every new challenge in education quietly becomes a part of the bagful of issues and problems for which, according to the parents, the teacher is supposed to provide answers and solutions. The fact, however, is that every player in the education system, from the home, family, community to the highest levels of policy formulators, has to internalise the new role and perform it at the highest level of sincerity and commitment. That requires an attitudinal transformation which is a Herculean task. The challenge has to be accepted. There is no other alternative.

Learning to Live Together with Values

The most outstanding objectives of education in 21st century could be stated as 'Learning to live together' and to 'achieve social cohesion'. In times of unprecedented civilizational, cultural and economic interaction, the global village needs to learn, and learn fast, the essentials of celebrating diversities of every conceivable kind. Worldwide efforts made in the 20th century to universalise elementary education could be of great help in this regard. While every human being now stands connected to everyone else, what one observes all around is violence, terrorism, ethnic clashes, disproportionate distribution of the benefits of progress and development, the ever widening gap between affluence and poverty, distrust, bigotry and hatred. Millions of people, and children included, sleep hungry, live in misery and are deprived of the basic human rights to health, food, nutrition, shelter, drinking water and safety.

The major factor appears to be the mounting tension between materialistic pursuits and the spiritual quest. Human beings endeavour to accumulate unlimited worldly possessions at the cost of the real spiritual treasure that is within every individual soul, waiting to be unearthed. That alone could generate peace, fellow-feelings, ideals of service to mankind and concern for one's neighbours. As long there is exploitation, deprivation, hunger, misery and unbridled consumerism, the decline in eternal human values shall continue unabated. Erosion of values is the rule all around and adherence to values comes in exceptions only. Human civilization has produced Saints and Sages; Sufis and Fakirs; Monks and Preachers who have made successful attempts at different junctures of human history to reverse this tide. They have focused on the higher objectives of life. There are several initiatives and efforts by individuals and organisations to check the decline of values that could be cited in the contemporary context. Prominent amongst these are the initiatives of the Ramakrishna Mission, Sri Sri Ravi Shankar, Jeevan Vigyan of Acharya Mahaprajna, DAV Trusts school initiatives, Education in Human Values programmes of Sri Sathya Sai of Puttaparthi and several others.

All these have essentially common goals: teach the world how to live a blissful value based life determined to follow the path that cares for the welfare of others, values social obligations and follows the path of truthfulness and causes no harm to any living being or the gifts of nature and God. Human values could be articulated in different ways. One of these is to list Truth, Peace, Non-violence, Righteous Conduct and Love as inclusive of every aspect of human values. Everyone agrees that these five are essential values, are linked to each other and none of the five has an independent identity without the remaining four. There is an organic linkage amongst these five. Some could call it peace only; others may use other nomenclature, instead of these five. Everyone knows that eternal human values are common across the barriers of diverse civilizations, religions, sects, languages, regions or any other conceivable diversity. Inclusion of these will enhance the spiritual content in the teaching learning process. And there comes the key element of the process of teaching and learning: the Teacher.

Everyone looks towards education systems as the panacea against all that is wrong in the world. The expectation is certainly not far off the mark. Though education alone cannot create a value based society, it certainly can play the most significant and all-embracing role in creating a caring, loving, peaceful, non-violent society that attempts to be truthful and follow the path of righteous conduct. The five eternal human values articulated above: Truth, Peace, Nonviolence, Righteous Conduct and Love; when properly integrated in the comprehensive educational endeavour at the early stages could help children internalise these at an impressionable young age. Every nation needs a system of education that is 'rooted to its culture and committed to progress'; that draws out the best out of the 'body, mind and spirit'. In a world torn by strife, violence, fanaticism, fundamentalism, terrorism, greed and, exploitation of both man and nature, the education systems need to redefine their objectives. These can no longer ignore the real world around the child. Who is not suffering because of the erosion of values? And who is not a party to this deterioration of eternal human values? There is no alternative, but to redesign the education systems to acquire a dynamic nature and remain alert to incorporate the changing demands and aspirations and the new discoveries and gadgets and techniques that are available to them within the classrooms and also which make the world a global village. Hence, education must consider value inculcation, value nurturance, value development, and value internalisation as integral parts of every activity and action that takes place within the classroom, within the school and outside the school in the family and the community.

The Canvas of Education

Education acculturates. It prepares the young ones to make a distinction between the sublime and the mundane. It equips them in their pursuit of excellence in life. Pursuance of excellence and the search for truth requires a world that values peace and tranquility. The objective can be best achieved when education systems primarily aim at achieving the symphony of "self, society and nature'. Great Indian thinkers have given ample consideration to the 'education that India needs'. Gandhi's basic education was one of such attempt. Working with the hands, acquisition of skills and, once again, the harmony of the 'head, hand and heart' could be considered as outstanding core elements of his thoughts.

Earlier, Swami Vivekananda had the foresight to project the role of education when India was to become free. Dr. Radhakrishnan pleaded for a system of education that would bring in skills of conflict resolution and give spirituality its due importance. According to him; "The aim of education in India has been initiation into the higher life of spirit. The student is wayfarer in spirit *(brahmacari)* and the period of studentship is life in spirit *(Brahmacarya)*. Education should be an abiding witness to the things of the spirit".[1] This difference is best illustrated when in the Chhandogya Upanishad, Narada says to Sanat Kumara that though he knows all the branches of learning, he is yet sorrowful. "I am merely a knower of texts (*mantravid*) not a knower of self (*atmavid)*. Sorrowful I am Sir, do you kindly make me cross over to the other side of sorrow."[2] Do our teachers really realise the significance of the transition that Narada aspires? Are we really preparing our teachers equipped enough to articulate, elaborate and nurture the meaning and import of the education of the spirit? This is the challenge before the education systems, the teachers and all those responsible for policy formulations in education.

In the world of today, development stands equated rather totally with economic development. Its impact is clearly visible in the education sector and the areas that are receiving priority in institutions and in establishment of new institutes that are coming up in large numbers. What happens to the vision of comprehensive education when a young person gets admitted to a medical college after paying a huge capitation fees? Could such a commercial establishment really care to inculcate values and ethics? It is worthwhile to recall the Preamble of the Report 'Learning to be', brought out by UNESCO in 1972. It expressed the fear the world would be dehumanised as a result of technical change. The fear has been accentuated in the recent past. One of its essential messages was that education must enable ever person 'to solve his own problems, make his own decisions, and shoulder his own responsibilities'. In the "Report to UNESCO of the International Commission on Education for the Twenty-First Century", it has been pointed out that in its very first meeting:

> "The Commission firmly restated the fundamental principle that education must contribute to the all round development of each individual—mind, body, intelligence, sensitivity, aesthetic sense, personal responsibility and spiritual values. All human beings must be enabled to develop independent critical thinking and form their own judgment. What was stated in the Learning to Be in 1972 has been restated in this Report for 21st century as well: "The aim of development is the complete fulfillment of man, in all the richness of his personality, the complexity of his form of expression and his various commitments—as individual, member of a family and of a community, citizen and producer, inventor of techniques and a creative dreamer."[3]

Out of the four pillars of education identified in the UNESCO Report of 1996, the systems of education at present focus primarily on *learning to know* and, in isolated instances, on *learning to do*. The other two: *Learning to live together* and *Learning to be* are practically ignored. How could one expect to build the edifice of sound education without paying equal attention to all the four pillars of education that are now acknowledged and accepted in principle by every one?

The current day policies, in actual implementation, limit education to what actually transpires within the 'school classroom' or, at the most, 'within the school'. In Indian tradition, education was an inter-generational obligation. It could be best understood by recalling a highly meaningful passage from *Patanjali's Mahabhasya*, which delineates four stages of education and learning:

- Acquire education/knowledge from your parents and teachers;
- Study on your own and improve your knowledge
- Impart value-added knowledge to other individuals, i.e., to your own children as parents and to others as a teacher or in any other capacity; and
- Use that knowledge for family benefit, as also for the benefit of society through your profession, avocation or employment.

The above appears so relevant even in current times. "Learning to learn" was always a pre-requisite for every 'learned' one: "*Yavadjivat Adhiyate Viprah*" (The wise are lifelong learners). One wonders how thoughtful, well considered and comprehensive were the traditions of teaching, pedagogy and learning. The above ideas also present a broad canvas before the teacher and the learner on which they could together paint their individual and group perspectives. It needs to be observed how, in a clear subtle manner, the concept of life-long learning has been put before not only teachers, but also all the other stakeholders in the process. Everyone has to transmit knowledge and, hence, is obliged to acquire knowledge throughout one's active life. Knowledge or the skills acquired are futile, if these are not used for the benefit of others and also, simultaneously, transmitted to the next generation. What is the basic goal before education emerges so comprehensively in the following words of Swami Vivekananda:

> "The ideal of all education, all training should be man-making. Education is not the amount of information that is put into your brain and runs riot there, undigested, all your life. We must have life-building, man-making, character-making assimilation of ideas."[4]

This criticality of education in shaping the individual and thereby the future of the society, was ever-present in the thoughts and deeds of Gandhiji. He articulated the 'real education' very clearly as: "Real education has to draw out the best from boys and girls to be educated. This can never be done by packing ill-assorted and unwanted information into the heads of the pupils."[5] In practical terms, he elaborated his idea in the following terms:

> "I hold that true education of the intellect can only come through a proper exercise and training of bodily organs, e.g., hands, feet, eyes, ears, nose, etc. In other words, an intelligent use of the bodily organs in a child provides the best and quickest way of developing his intellect. But unless the development of the mind and body goes hand in hand with a corresponding awakening of the soul, the former alone would prove to be a lop-sided affair. By spiritual training I mean education of the heart."[6]

The following from his letter to Ramdas Gandhi may be relevant to recall:

> "True education lies in serving others; oblige them without the least feeling of one-uppishness. The more mature you grow, the more you will realise this. Great deals of religious obligations on us are fulfilled when we nurse the sick. I am not worried about your bookish learning so long as you perform your duties and observe solemn ethical conduct. For me carrying out the fundamentals of ethics is duty."[7]

In the current times, education for development and progress appears to be the key theme. However, the relevance of a comprehensive approach to the process of teaching and learning remains as relevant as ever. What Gandhiji wrote, in fact, gives indications on what education needs to aim at. The ideas and perceptions of Gandhiji and Swami Vivekananda find reflection in the UNESCO's Report of the International Commission on Education for the Twenty-first Century in the following words:

> "One of education's principal functions is therefore that of fitting humanity to take control of its own development. It must enable all people without exception to take their destiny into their own hands so that they can contribute to the progress of the society in which they live, founding development upon the responsible participation of individual and communities."[8]

The popular perception concerning education amongst the parents rarely goes beyond three important components: schools, teachers and Board examinations. In the fiercely competitive times, how many parents or those concerned with the education systems are in a position to sincerely assess all the significant aspects of teaching and learning that contribute to the total personality development of the student? Information is available in abundance, the knowledge explosion is before everyone but the focus in schooling stands entirely overshadowed by the examinations and percentage of marks obtained in the year-end examination. This certainly is a big challenge before the educational policy implementers and finally it just passes on to the teacher. Just to emphasise the point, let the following from the National Policy on Education-1986/92 be recalled:

> "In our culturally plural society, education should foster universal and eternal values, oriented towards the unity and integration of our people. Such value education should help eliminate obscurantism, religious fanaticism, violence, superstition and fatalism. Apart from this combative role, value education has a profound positive content, based on our heritage, national goals and universal perceptions. It should lay primary emphasis on this aspect."

The major aspect for consideration is that education has been seen intensively by philosophers and thinkers in India at both in its conceptual aspects as also the pragmatic translations of these concepts. Obviously, teaching, learning and education, in their holistic perceptions, constitute a dynamic entity that must retain its character but not necessarily the content, which must change and change continuously. Education expresses its global concerns when it presents concepts like "*Sarve Bhavantu Sukhinah*"; "*Vasudhaiv Kutumbakam*"; "*Tamso Ma Jyotirgamaya*" and the like. However, it shall always retain the local context of its curriculum and content. It is the diversity that makes the world afar more beautiful place. It is through education that this bounty of diversity in terms of languages, region, faiths, religions, and so many other aspects could lead everyone to realize how necessary it is to develop respect and appreciation for 'otherness'.

Indian tradition has always accepted 'otherness'. This acceptance is far too different from the concept of 'tolerance'. It is this strength of Indian civilization that prompted famous historian Arnold Toynbee to state:

> "At this supremely dangerous moment in human history, the only way of salvation for mankind is the Indian way—Emperor Asoka's and Mahatma Gandhi's principle of non-violence and Sri Ramakrishna's testimony to the harmony of religions. Here, we have an attitude and spirit that can make it possible for the human race to grow together in to a single family—and, in the Atomic Age, this is the only alternative to destroying ourselves."[9]

A strife-torn world is looking towards India once again—to get spiritual, ethical and moral leadership. India's unique position in these aspects is universally acknowledged and respected. All this enjoins upon the education system of India certain far greater responsibilities apart from the routine expectations from education.

The Current trends

Education policies in India need to acknowledge that a major change is required in their re-formulation. From the local community, the world is now moving towards a world society. Common people everywhere are now realising the reality of the global village. When a small farmer in a remote village of Uttar Pradesh, who produces potatoes and sells these at Rs. 2 per kg, and purchases 'Uncle Chips' at Rs. 15 per 45 gm (i.e., Rs. 333 per kg), he should be equipped to understand what is happening in between! The global village now presents before the education systems everywhere new challenges of commercialisation, consumerism and materialism. Capacity building and empowerment of persons and professionals at various levels would be necessary to observe the changes, analyse the change and sift what is relevant, acceptable and useful to the nation. Opportunities now exist for global sharing of knowledge, skills, and intellectual assets that are necessary for the multiple developments of individuals. These are the times of promotion of collaborations, understanding, harmony and acceptance and appreciation of cultural, linguistic and regional diversities within the country and across international borders. There is a debit side also. The widening digital divide hinders efforts towards equality of opportunity for progress not only between the individuals but also amongst the nations. Issues of cultural dominance and linguistic hegemony are becoming increasingly prominent. Exploitation of local resources and loss of indigenous, skills, knowledge, and culture is already a reality in many cases.

There are traditional role-expectations from teachers that emerge out of the discourse on Indian education indicated above. These cannot be seen in isolation to the phenomenon of globalisation and the visible impacts of Information and communication technologies all around. Teachers now have to redefine their role perception in the light of the two ends of the spectrum, which must necessarily coalesce to achieve the futuristic goals of education. It is now globally acknowledged that education the world over must be 'rooted to culture and committed to progress'. The dominant cultures and the economic giants would prefer what is euphemistically now referred to as the "Macdonalized" world! Same language, same Cola, same chips and same culture; they would like to stretch as far as possible. They have succeeded considerably.

Which Indian is not interested in sending her or his children to English medium schools if the same is available and affordable? All the talk and rationale for providing initial education through the mother tongue cuts little ice with most parents. Of all the States, even Bihar is now going to make English a compulsory subject from Class one onwards! People are in a hurry to become world citizens without clearly understanding and appreciating how essential it still remains to first belong to their own roots, family and the community. The traditional practices and modern allurements are resulting in a situation of tensions and consequent tensions. One of the basic assurances given to every citizen in democratic setups is that of social justice, equality of opportunity of access and success. It is a tall order and a daunting challenge before education systems the world over and India is struggling seriously on this count. Unfortunately, the divide in education available to haves and have-nots is increasing and concepts like that of common school system and neighbourhood schools are getting relegated to background though the systems are unwilling to accept the reality. The inequality inflicted on the child during the initial years is rather impossible to be bridged at later stages of life even if the best of the conditions are then made available. Lakhs of schools, without basic facilities of buildings, drinking water, teachers, etc., are 'functioning' in India. Even after the enactment of the right to education Act, there are no strong indications that things would really change effectively and within a short time. Everyone knows that in the 21st century, it is the pace of change that matters.

Let us revert back to the mundane happenings in education today. It is all examinations, examinations and examinations. If you wish to be more precise, it is percentage of marks in the board examination. Higher the better! Why this single minded one-track race? The answer is simple: it is a competitive world. It is a world that puts a premium on entry to Indian Institutes of Managements, Indian Institutes of Technology, and a Green Card. Still better, a seat in an US university or even in an Australian university of dubious credentials that assures a degree and a subsequent entry to US! One must hasten to add that there are visible numbers of those who prefer to serve their country and countrymen after duly and profoundly equipping themselves with the requisite knowledge skills, values and goals. The phenomenon is not new. Its magnitude has grown to dangerous proportions as education remained confined to a few and in its expansion phase, materialism overtook the spiritual enlightenment. Rabindranath Tagore had the foresight to perceive the following:

> "Mind, when long deprived of its natural food of truth and freedom of growth, develops an unnatural carving for success and our students have fallen victim to the mania for success in examinations. Success consists in obtaining the largest number of marks with the strictest economy of knowledge. It is a deliberate cultivation of disloyalty to truth, of intellectual dishonesty, of a foolish imposition by which the mind is encouraged to rob itself".[10]

The first decade of the 21st century has awakened the world to the dangers of fundamentalism, terrorism and fanaticism in proportions that were unimaginable a couple of decades ago. It has focused, as always, on education to find ways and means to prepare young persons to find a solution. As a first step, the content of education must aim at creating a cohesive society that celebrates diversity and values it. It should prepare people who firmly believe that a cohesive society is just not possible unless and until the man-nature relationships is brought back on the rails. Any society or community that ignores the adage given by Gandhiji that 'Nature has sufficient to meet the needs of everyone but not the greed of anyone' can never attain peace, tranquility and cohesion. Greed and its numerous manifestations arise out of lack of awareness or lack of a strong desire to adhere to values in life. Education can play a significant part in making the young ones realise the organic relationship of rights and duties.

The Fundamental Duties enshrined in Article 51-A of the Constitution of India pragmatically indicates the line of action that must penetrate every action and process that takes place in every educational campus. These indicate what the country expects of its citizens and, as such, are guidelines to the curriculum developers, textbook writers and all those who are expected to transact the curriculum. As a comprehensive endeavour, the teaching-learning process must enable the learner to develop concepts and inculcate values commensurate with social, cultural, economic and environmental realities at the national and international levels. Let it be remembered that in an environment of erosion of values all around, schools cannot remain isolated islands untouched by the prevailing mood of indifference and even disregard for the entire value system.

However, the potential of the educational process for transforming the very psyche can never be questioned and need not be underestimated. It may be worthwhile to quote from the recommendations made for school education in the year 2000:

> "School can, and must strive to restore and sustain the universal and eternal values oriented towards the unity and integration of the people, their moral and spiritual growth enabling them to realise the 'treasure within'. People must realise who they are and what the ultimate purpose of human life is. Self-recognition would come to them through proper value education and that would facilitate their spiritual march from the level of sub-consciousness to that of super consciousness through the different intermediary stages. Value based education would help the nation fight against all kinds of fanaticism, ill will, violence, fatalism, dishonesty, avarice, corruption, exploitation and even vices like drug abuse. It is impossible to reject these contentions."[11]

The existing conditions require a focused attention on another significant factor that merits much more attention than it is receiving at present. Religions are not the only source of values; these certainly are the major sources of value inculcation. In a secular society, education cannot be burdened with religious education. That religion has a role even in the world of science and technology was best articulated by none other than Albert Einstein who considered science without religions as lame and religion without science as blind. As human beings move under ever increasing influence of science, technology and information and communication technology, the social, cultural and human aspects of life acquire far greater significance than ever before. Hence, every effort needs to be put in action to harness every source that could be helpful in value education. The Indian state is secular; people of India are religious. There is no contradiction between the two. Only a truly religious person, exceptions apart, is capable of being a true secularist because he/she would treat all other faiths with equal respect and understanding. To know about the basics of any religion is very different from religious learning. It is recorded history that India practised secularism—equal respect for every one's faith—even over 2000 years ago. Christianity and later, Zoroastrians, Jews and Muslims were all welcome and had received all support to practice their own religion. In such a country, the interpretation of secularism need not be left to the motivated and vested interests. It is, therefore, for the consideration of the people of India whether making all children aware of the basics of all the religions of the people of India 'is in anyway against the basic premises of secularism?' To be on the safe side and remove all possible non-political apprehensions, it could be safely stated that the recommendation is not for religious education, but 'education about the religions'! No rituals, no dogmas, no practices should be brought into the educational process. Teachers must be suitably prepared to take an objective view of the contents in each case. Children must know the commonalities and learn to respect differences, wherever these exist. Every religion, faith or denomination accepts the five eternal values of Truth, Peace, Nonviolence, Righteous Conduct and Love. Familiarity and awareness could work wonders in achieving social cohesion and in moving towards a value-based society—and eventually a global order. Delivering the Convocation address at the Punjab University, Chandigarh on 28 December 2001, N.R. Narayana Murthy, the modern management giant and an achiever in the most modern sense and pioneer in the use of information and communication technology, said:

> "Consequently, teaching in schools and colleges must encompass all major religions, with the syllabi updated to include such discussions. His teaching must be started at the elementary school stage rather than being restricted to higher education."

Let the existing Indian system of education system be transformed accordingly.

Letter from a Concentration Camp Survivor

Dear Teacher,

I am a survivor of a concentration camp. My eyes saw what no man should witness:

- Gas chambers built by LEARNED engineers.
- Children poisoned by EDUCATED physicians.
- Infants killed by TRAINED nurses.
- Women and babies shot and burned by HIGH SCHOOL and COLLEGE graduates.

So I am suspicious of education.

My request is: Help your students become human. Your efforts must never produce learned monsters, skilled psychopaths, educated Eichmanns. Reading, writing and arithmetic are important only if they serve to make our children more human.

(September, 2009)

References

1. Radhakrishnan, S., 1990, *Radhakrishnan Reader: An Anthology*, pp. 504-505, Bhartiya Vidya Bhavan, Bombay.
2. Chandogya Upanishad.
3. Jacques Delors, 1996, *Learning: The Treasure Within*, p. 94, UNESCO, Paris.
4. Swami Vivekananda, *The Complete Works of*; Published by Advaita Ashram, 1962 and afterwards, II-15; II-490.
5. *Mahatma Gandhi, The Collected Works*, p. 295 or NCTE, 1999, Gandhi on Education, p. 17; New Delhi.
6. NCTE, 1999, Gandhi on Education, p. 19, *Harijan*, 8 May, 1937, p. 104.
7. NCTE, 1999, Gandhi on Education, p. 3, The Making of the Mahatma, p. 97.
8. Jacques Delors, 1996, *Learning: The Treasure Within*, pp. 78-79, UNESCO. Paris.
9. Palkhivala, N.A., 1990, (reprinted 2003), *Essential Unity of All Religions*, Bharti Vidya Bhavan, Mumbai.
10. *Quotes from Tagore*, 2005, Rupa and Company, New Delhi, pp 32-33.
11. National Curriculum Framework for School Education, NCERT, New Delhi.
12. Narayana Murthy, N.R., *A Better India: A Better World*, 2009, Penguin Books India, p. 44.

10

Philosophy in Education and the New School Classroom

Progress and development emerged as the sweetest sounding words to the developing countries at the mid-point of the 20th century. In most of the cases, the policies that were accepted for implementation by the newly born nations were, sadly enough, mere continuations of the earlier policies. Rulers had changed, but not the approach and the system. The education system in India is one of the most glaring examples of this continuity. In many instances, things did move slowly and sparsely in the right direction. Benefits did accrue, sometimes at the devastating cost of long-term consequences. Rich dividends have been harvested by large numbers but their 'gains' have also left behind huge populace to continue to suffer poverty, hunger, ill health and insecurity. The new phraseology around globalisation, information and communication technology, liberalisation, free market and the like has not presented a picture of equality of opportunity of access and success to all alike. The greatest hope for the downtrodden, deprived, and destitute did build up around education and its universalisation. A large chunk is still out of the fold of even elementary education, though the sincerity of efforts to bring them within the fold deserves to be acknowledged and appreciated. On the other side, major issues are appearing on various aspects related to the content and pedagogy of education that is being imparted at this juncture. The capacity of the education system to respond to the fast changing emerging demands is also under scrutiny as these systems are known to be too slow to respond to the change. What is the relationship between progress and education? It would be interesting to recall Herbert Spencer "Law of all progress is the same, the evolution of the simple in to the complex by successive differentiation." It may not draw universal acceptability but does make a point that is significant for countries like India which are struggling to alleviate poverty, hunger and ill health, on one hand, and, at the same time, competing to become global economic powers within the decade. Obviously, the extent of ideas being generated, strengthening of the philosophical base and extent of absorption of scientific temper amongst the masses would make tremendous difference. From simple to complex may be inevitable but a nation can not permit itself to get bewildered in complexities of its own creation.

Bertrand Russell, in his famous treatise 'Education and the Good Life' pointed out that 'before considering how to educate, it is well to be clear as to the sort of result which we wish to achieve.' It remains the perpetual concern even today before the policy makers, parents and the academics. In the contemporary context, educational concerns have been comprehensively addressed by luminaries of the level of Swami Vivekananda, Sri Aurobindo, Rabindranath Tagore, Mahatma Gandhi and several others. Man-making education, integral education, character forming education and other similar phrases are often repeated in the corridors of educational institutions. In totality, education just cannot be same for everyone. We need philosophers, we need workers in the farms and factories as well; we need poets and writers; we need translators and typists as well. What is good and desirable for one may not be suitable for the other. Designing a system that encompasses commonalities essential for everyone and also provides for the specific requirements of individual interest and social needs requires considerable thinking, a strong philosophical base and capability to be part of the change. I often mention the symphony of the 3x3 matrix that represents educational thinking rather comprehensively and in pragmatic terms; Self, Society and Nature; Head, Hand and Heart and the last one; Body Mind and Spirit!

The continuity of the process of education; transfer of knowledge and skills from one generation to the next could be analysed amongst different civilizations and commonalities would emerge without much effort. The Indian tradition broadly classifies education in to *Paravidya* and *Aparavidya*, remains very relevant in the present day context. Obviously, the content and skills involved have changed, so has the pedagogy. The other major change is the total shift to *Aparavidya* in the current times of materialism and consumerism. Education is now mostly considered as the path way to material well-being and to earn a 'decent' livelihood. Not many may really know what is being missed when education is viewed in such a limited sense. Emphatically rejecting that education is book-learning or diverse knowledge, Swami Vivekananda puts it in these words; "The training by which the current and expression of will are brought under control and become fruitful, is called education...True education may be described as a development of faculty, not an accumulation of words, or, as a training of individuals to will rightly and efficiently."[1] It may be relevant to recall what Patanjali said about education in his *Mahabhasya*. There are four steps and stages through which knowledge is acquired and becomes fruitful, these are:[2]

(1) Acquire knowledge/education from your parents and teachers;
(2) Make your own study and improve the knowledge
(3) Impart value added knowledge to other individuals. That is, to your own children as parent and to others as teacher or in any other capacity; and
(4) Use that knowledge for family benefit, as also for the benefit of the society through your profession, avocation or employment etc.

These four aspects remain ever fresh and relevant in education and its pedagogy even today. Gandhi had his own in-depth thinking on education that independent India would need and on how it should be universalised. Philosophy and pragmatism were considered to be the two sides of the same coin which, one may like to say, were the corner stones of the Basic Education that Gandhi had experimented with and presented it for implementation in independent India. The policy makers just ignored it. If one studies the Chinese model, one finds the basics of Gandhian ideas being implemented there in villages and primary schools! May be independent India could not formulate an educational policy based on sound philosophy; the significance of which is evident in the words of Daisaku Ikeda: "the absence of a leading philosophy renders human beings incapable of discovering deep values and makes them the rootless preys of idleness and depravity."[3] Ikeda also found education diverting itself to utilitarianism that overemphasizes intellectual knowledge and technological skills; resulting in two major negative consequences. "First, by making learning a tool of politics and economics, it has robbed learning of its inherent dignity and independence. Second, people engaged in learning and education becomes the slaves of intellectual knowledge and technological skills, which are the only aspects of learning prized today. As an outcome of this trend, respect for humanity declines. In short, today people are compelled to serve intellectual knowledge and technological skill, which are in turn controlled by politics and economics."[4] Ikeda made it very clear when he emphasised the importance of 'dialogue and inner search for truth'. Education must scrutinize whether it is promoting greed and turning people in to purveyors of widespread destruction? And the destruction of the natural environment that we see all around has manifold imports for the survival of not only the humanity but of the planet earth itself! The way people conduct themselves, their lives and their interactions requires a dynamic orientation through constant reappraisal and dialogue. It is the welfare of the inclusive future than the affluence of the exclusive individual that would count in the long run. The essence of the 'welfare of and happiness for all' remains the same: from Patanjali to Ikeda. And who can forget Gandhi who presented the most pragmatic of the philosophy enriched model for the welfare of the last man in the line?

Gandhi put it in his own words, very clearly indicating: "As we become independent, all the defects of the system of elections, injustice, the tyranny of the richer classes as also the burden of running the administration are bound to come upon us. People would begin to feel that during those days, there was more justice, there was better administration, there was peace, and there was honesty to a great extent among the administrators compared to the days after independence. The only benefit of independence, however, would be that we would get rid of slavery and the blot of insult resulting there from." These words are from a letter Gandhiji wrote in 1922![5] Then he, like others, puts his faith in education and practically defined what type of persons education must prepare: "But there is hope, if education spreads throughout the country. From that people would develop from their childhood qualities of pure conduct, God fearing, love, Swaraj would give us happiness only when we attain success in the task. Otherwise, India would become the abode of grave injustice and tyranny of the rulers." The words, truly prophetic, put the educational concerns very succinctly before everyone. When the philosophical base gets weak, situations like the present day arise and the comprehension of education becomes only limited.

Advances in science and technology have invariably given rise to efforts that aim at determining linkages and relationships of these developments to philosophy, religion and spirituality. It had become the major staple of the intellectual discourse particularly during the last century. When Robert Oppenheimer recalls the Gita after witnessing the first Atomic Explosion; the existence of this pursuit became clear to all. Because of the skeptics and the great visible divide between the approaches to science and to religion, it was only logical to expect even in the early stages that there would be great conflicts in attempts to reconcile the two. It all began as a big conflict and even today, when one thinks of the relationship between science and religion, it is the conflict aspect that occasionally emerges prominently in the interactive processes. However, it is also well appreciated that sincere efforts have been made by those devoted to scientific pursuits and those having full faith in their religious philosophies to understand each other better and establish the possible links. These initiatives and efforts have resulted in encouraging dividends in the shape of better appreciation of the other's viewpoint. The possibilities of developing a continuum at some stage in the future are no longer mere myths. An acceptable escape from severe and contrasting disagreements of the past now seems to be a real possibility to both the sides. Initially, the hold of moral values resulted in several controversies as to whether certain scientific discoveries or facts were really 'good' for humanity.[6] However the march of science remained uninterrupted and everyone realized that science was value neutral. Once this is understood, queries like 'is science the only overriding force that is driving the society to its doom?' shall no longer remain valid! Today, the situation has reached a point that could be summarised in one of the recent scientific advancement which is captured in the statement:[7] "This is the first self-replicating cell we've had on the planet whose parent is a computer." Once again, one hears what has been heard even before: "should man be allowed to play God?" It may still require huge effort in future to let the scientific and religious/spiritual philosophies coalesce. B.D. Josephson; Nobel Laureate Physicist summarised the developments in 1984: "nature is not mechanical but rather alive, mind-like and intelligent." This radically contrasts the mere physical view of nature by some scientists. Only those who understand the philosophy of science and scientific pursuits, on one hand, and that of religion, on the other, can really attempt to visualise the direction in which to seek harmony between the two. Much is likely to happen in future.

The Philosophy

To the common man, philosophy 'is the most abstract and theoretical of man's pursuits'. It may not really be so. In science, they perform experiments and interpret the results, based on concrete evidence. In religion, what one generally observes in practice, is all faith, experience, reverence, adherence and acceptance! There, however, is much more and beyond what is visible and apparent. Religious philosophy paves the way for achieving much more than the rituals alone. Philosophy, including religious philosophy, focuses on vision, the vision of the possible; of the probable and of the dream that motivates and invigorates the philosopher. Every great scientist is also a genuine philosopher in his own way. Think of James Watt, Michael Faraday, Enrico Fermi and host of the other scientists who made singular contributions in the advancement of knowledge. Were they not visionaries who strived to give a concrete shape to their interpretations, vision, presumed probabilities and all that? It is impossible to think of sciences in isolation to philosophy. Philosophy prepares human beings in pursuing their natural instinct to know more about themselves, about all that is around them; and to raise questions and seek answers to the eternal quest: what for all this creation and what lies beyond? In the process, philosophy makes one learn how to tackle problems and ask how to project these on a larger canvas and how to formulate and articulate the thinking processes and the sum and substance of the outcomes. Philosophy can make young ones analyse better, reflect better and synthesise better. Its study develops critical thinking and ethical values amongst young learners. Philosophy deserves a significant place in the growing process of children and young persons. It must become a part of the total process of teaching and learning in schools; and hence, a place in textbooks and other reading materials as well.

There could be some counter arguments. Violence, terrorism, wars, hunger, poverty, deprivation, exploitation are some of the concrete realities that humans have to deal with on daily basis. Where is the time for philosophical deliberations and pursuits in a world that makes millions of its inhabitants sleep hungry, insecure and sick? It was possible in ancient times to stay in a forest abode which fulfilled all the requirements of maintaining the soul and the body together, teach children and get all the respect and regard in this world; and be confident of nirvana in the next. Will even the most celebrated of the philosophers of the contemporary times be willing to choose Dantewada or Koraput as their abode for philosophical pursuits? Times have changed; and these are changing much faster than ever before. One must concede before taking the argument any further that human civilization has flourished on the basis of values that emerged from philosophical advancements and greater understanding of the 'why and for what' of human existence on the planet earth. But for philosophical basis, one wonders whether there could really have been any science at all! To me; scientific advancement owes its origin to philosophy, to spirituality and to the eternal human search for more knowledge and better understanding of the forces of nature that was imitated by saints, sages and men of intellect and devotion. Every genuine scientist becomes a part of this group!

New Pedagogy

A person coming from the education sector must take due precautions before attempting to understand the new age philosophy. What can be seen as an obvious reality is the new pedagogy: ICT (Information and Communication Technology) has invaded the classrooms and the clamour on the other side is becoming louder: it is the age of the machine dominating the man; it is the age of most serious tension between the materialistic pursuits and spiritual quest; and like that. Ask any educator or a school teacher 'what is the new pedagogy'; and you may find an expression of bewilderment and curiosity on his/her face. Things are yet to take a shape. Perhaps, at some later stage, a comprehensive picture would emerge that would be generally acceptable. Sure enough, it would not be mere use of more and more gadgets and equipments. One finds numerous schools publicising claims of establishing new classrooms and projecting the availability of more gadgets, more equipment and more teaching aids to substantiate their claim. What I know is the practical reality in education: Children must learn (and remember till the exams are over) all that is likely to decide their grades in the final examinations. Everything else can wait; it has no relevance in getting a place in top-level institutions of higher and professional education and it does not open up new vistas to materialistic prosperity and affluence! It is in education, its content, pedagogy and transaction that we see the amazing impact of the materialistic pursuits at the cost of spiritual inputs. Eternal human values, cultures, ethics and all that are needed in 'man making education' appears a thing of the past, the preachings of the earlier generations are hardly of any relevance in the world that is not only globalised but essentially corporatises and de-humanized. Humans are just a resource, like other material resources that are needed to run a huge establishment or a refinery or a ship building yard! It is the world that priorities machine over the man, and attributes it to the growth of science and technology; or you may say, the information technology. Today, it is the technologically dominated human enterprises that are destroying rivers, forests, land and much more. It needs to be analysed how humanity has reached such a stage? Is it the absence of adequate and appropriate philosophical understanding and appreciation that has led to such a situation in which the very existence of the planet earth is in jeopardy? Where do science and technology stand in this situation?

To find an answer, let a reference be made to Aristotle, one of the greatest of philosophers. He visualised science on a much broader canvas than is being done even today. According to him, science represents any ordered body of knowledge through causes and reasons.[8] Aristotle proposed productive sciences what we call today the technology; farming, surgery shipbuilding etc. in those times and could include aviation, electrical engineering and all that in current times. The practical science referred to how to do things: practice things. Aristotle included ethics and politics in this category. The third of sciences he included was the theoretical or speculative/contemplative. Knowledge, even if sought only for knowledge sake, shall have its practical applications and contributions in gaining further knowledge.

The Gap

Where is the missing link? One of the major crises being faced globally is "some sort of a moral crisis".[9] Every country is facing the erosion of moral values and ethical norms and is concerned about it. For every such concern of apparently insurmountable magnitude which evades a solution, everyone looks towards the system of education. That is why the 20th century accepted the urgency of universal elementary education. Humanity reposes its faith in "education for peace" and is convinced that education shall contribute significantly in establishing a society that would utilise science and technology for human welfare and, not for global destruction. Education alone has the potential to prepare people to accept the modern scientific findings and not to repeat the way Galileo was treated by the powers that be of those times. Acceptable modern philosophy must internalise and effectively project the eternal unity of all human beings. Equality of opportunity, irrespective of race, colour, caste or any other diversity, can no longer be denied to anyone. Religious beliefs, practices and rituals have to show internal strength to project a strong element of dynamism that enables them to absorb the contemporary context and remain relevant. Religions may appear to differ on several premises but spirituality could provide a common ground to come together; and then attempt an in-depth understanding of religions. Philosophy shall have to play a major role in this transition. Only such an effort can lighten up the link between spirituality and scientific advancement. Only then the real value of sciences for the benefit of humanity would emerge as an unchallenged realty. Most encouraging and ambitious would be a situation in which tradition, religion, spirituality, science, modernity and the state would move in tandem for the advancement of human understanding of the forces of nature and finding answers to that eternal query: what for are we here; and what and where of the beyond. Plato visualise the concept of a philosopher king. Unfortunately, it has generally remained just a utopian idea. A rare exception was almost materialising in the contemporary history when Einstein was offered the position of the President of Israel—A Scientist-Philosopher-King could have become realty! As a true scientist and philosopher of the highest order, he declined without explicitly stating that the very basis of the offer was unacceptable—he was the most celebrated Jew of the times! Only a philosopher of his stature could do it, could think of its broader implications and historical imperatives. History would appreciate it far more than several of his scientific contributions. It would help future generations to learn how great decisions are taken in the right spirit and with a comprehensive perspective.

After accepting the coveted Bharata Ratna Award, J.R.D. Tata said; "I do not want India to be a superpower. I want India to be a happy nation." This would be possible only when a sound philosophical base is provided to education that imbibes scientific temper and absorbs the fruits of science with a single minded focus on the welfare and happiness of all, not a few only. Here again, religion has to accept the presence and essentiality of science and technology as necessary tools to fructify the concept of universal brotherhood and happiness. A lot of battles have already been won. Scientific facts are accepted. It now enjoins upon the religions how to bring in dynamism and incorporate what is irrefutable. Can anyone now reject instant universal connectivity that is so easily accessible? Who would be harmed if gender equality is still not accepted?

The Curriculum Aspect

The Kothari Commission (1964-66) Report[10] that resulted in the formation of the National Policy on Education 1968 had clearly visualised that science has to be the common core in everyone's life and hence must become the common core of the educational curriculum during the first ten years in schools. It may appear amusing to some young persons today, it was considered a very bold recommendation that this applies to both boys and girls! At the same time, the Report also emphasised the criticality of value inculcation and internalisation of eternal human values. Emphasising the need to study religions and religious thought under 'education about the religions', it acknowledges the necessity "for a multi-religious democratic state to promote a tolerant study of all religions so that its citizens can understand each other better and live amicably together." It also asserts: "There will be natural points of correlation between the moral values sought to be inculcated and the teachings of the great religions." Pleading for a specifically designed syllabus, the report recommends common course and common textbooks on the subject. "It should highlight the fundamental similarities in the great religions of the world and the emphasis they place on the cultivation of certain broadly comparable moral and spiritual values." In the same vein, the Kothari Commission Report brings in science and pleads for "A vitalized study of science, with its emphasis on open-mindedness, tolerance and objectivity, would inevitably lead to the development of a more secular outlook, in the sense in which we use the word, amongst those who profess different religions." This issue has remained under discussion and debate for decades together. One of the most significant of the recommendations was made by the Department related Parliamentary Standing Committee on Human Resource Development in 1999 on this aspect:[11] "The process of making students acquainted with the basics of all religions, the values inherent therein and also a comparative study of the philosophy all religions should begin at the middle stage in schools and continue up to the university level. Students have to be made aware that the basic concept in every religion is common, only the practices differ. Even if there are differences of opinion in certain areas, people have to learn to coexist and carry no hatred against any religion." This is essential and in fact critically necessary to let a truly secular society emerge in which every religion is given equal respect by every other. It is necessary because one of the most outstanding objectives of education is to achieve social cohesion and 'learning to live together'. These cannot be achieved unless education inculcates scientific temper, on one hand, and also makes every child realise that religions and religious diversity is a historical reality and has often caused conflicts between the religions and also between science and religions. This conflict aspect has hindered the progress of sciences on one hand, and that of dynamism amongst the religions, on the other. Well, in spite of it, it is an encouraging fact that both religion and science have been in a continual state of development. This can be illustrated by numerous instances like the condemnation of the motion of the earth in 17th century and that of the doctrine of evolution even till the 20th century. Even science is always willing to consider new ideas and reinterpretations. It was in this light that developments from Newtonian mechanics to Max Plank to Einstein could be analysed. This is the strength of science. It has to become equally strongly the strength of the religions also.

How to overcome the contradictions? As time passes and new knowledge is unearthed, what was accepted as gospel truth earlier may appear to be inconsistent with the new facts and interpretations! Science provides a way out as within its own realm, sometimes it permits two different interpretations simultaneously; lives with both and paves the way for further in-depth work on the problem! A very fine illustration of this is given by Alfred N. Whitehead in his article "Science and Religion":[12]

"Again I will give you an example taken from the state of modern physical science. Since the time of Newton and Huygens in the seventeenth century there have been two theories as to the physical nature of light. Newton's theory was that a beam of light consists of a stream of very minute particles, or corpuscles, and that we have the sensation of light when these corpuscles strike the retina of our eyes. Huygens' theory was that light consists of very minute waves of trembling in all pervading ether, and that these are travelling along a beam of light. The two theories are contradictory. In the eighteenth century, Newton's theory was believed. In the nineteenth century, Huygens' theory gained greater acceptance. Today, there is one large group of phenomenon which can be explained only on the basis of the wave theory, and another large group which can be explained only by taking recourse to on the basis of the corpuscular theory. Scientists have to leave it at that, and wait for the future, in the hope of attaining some wider vision which reconciles both." Without going into the details what followed later, it certainly points out to the possibility of differing views amongst religions could be co-existing together and open up brighter possibilities of social cohesion. The same could apply equally well to the differences that exist between region and science. There should hardly be any difficulty in building such a premise on a sound philosophical basis which already exists. After all, which philosophy does not believe in the universal unity of the human kind; universal brotherhood, truth, peace, nonviolence or love?

The shape of the classroom has changed; and it continues to change fast. The content and pedagogy are responding primarily to the demands of the ICT and the globalized world. It is gadgets all around. The ethical and moral concerns often get ignored, in spite of the ever-growing insecurity, mistrust and the very threat to human existence. It is materialism and machine all around. Curriculum developers ought to have strived dexterously put in human effort to bring in philosophies that guide human beings towards adherence to eternal human values. That is not happening to the desired degree. Search for solutions has begun earnestly amongst enlightened individuals and organisations. Education should be the key once again to reverse the tide from materialistic pursuits alone to pragmatic spiritual quest once again. Once again let the class room be the place for learning the basics of philosophies and also of the sciences. Let the relationship of the two become the core of discussions and queries.

(June, 2010)

Notes

1. Rama Jois; M.; Justice Human Rights and Indian Values; National Council for Teacher Education (NCTE); 1998; New Delhi.
2. *Ibid.*
3. Daisaku Ikeda, *A Lasting Peace*, Vol. 2, New York and Tokyo, 1987, p. 169.
4. Daisaku Ikeda and Arnold Toynbee, *Choose Life: A Dialogue*, ed. Richard L. Gage, Oxford: Oxford University Press, 1976, p. 65.
5. Letter; written by Gandhiji on 24-01-22. Republished in the *Hindustan Times* of August 15, 1965.
6. Kaw, M.K., Science and Non-violence; Shri Kamalanayan Bajaj Memorial Lecture: 8, 2000, Ahimsa Shodh Sansthan, Gujarat Vidyapeeth, Ahmedabad.
7. Craig Venter, J., Geneticist, on creating the world's first synthetic living cell; *Times of India*; May 26; 2010.
8. Padmavathi, V., "Need to introduce philosophy in School and Higher Education", in *Bhartiya Pragna*, May; 2010, Hyderabad.
9. UNESCO, *Learning: The Treasure Within*, 1996, UNESCO Publications, Geneva.
10. Government of India (1966), Report of the National Commission on Education, Education and National Development, Ministry of Education, New Delhi.
11. Rajya Sabha Secretariat, 1999, Department-Related Parliamentary Standing Committee on Human Resource Development: Eighty-First Report on Value Education.
12. Whitehead, Alan N., Science and Religion; in *A Modern Reader, Essays on present day life and culture* edited by Walter Lippmann and Allan Nevins; D.C. Heath and Company; 1946.

11

Millennium Development Goals

Achieving Universal Primary Education—The Road Travelled by India so Far

"I will give you a Talisman. Whenever you are in doubt or when the self becomes too much with you, apply the following test: Recall the face of the poorest and the weakest man whom you may have seen and ask yourself if the step you contemplate is going to be of any use to him. Will he gain anything by it? Will it restore him to a control over his own life and destiny? In other words, will it lead to Swaraj for the hungry and spiritually starving millions? Then you will find your doubts and your self that emerged out of the courage of conviction and firm belief in the melting away."

—Mahatma Gandhi

It was in April 26-28 at Dakar Senegal where the World Education Forum was organized. It issued the 'Dakar Framework for Action'; 'Education for All, Meeting our Collective Commitments'. All 191 United Nations Member states pledged to meet by the year 2015 the following goals. It would be worthwhile to have a glance at the identified goals.

1.0 Eradicate extreme poverty and hunger
Halve, between 1990 and 2015 the proportion of people whose income is less than $1 a day; reduce by half the proportion of people who suffer from hunger

2.0 Achieve universal primary education:
Ensure that all boys and girls complete a full course of primary schooling.

3.0 Promote gender equality and empower women:
Eliminate gender disparity in primary and secondary education preferably by 2005, and at all levels by 2015.

4.0 Reduce child mortality:
Reduce by two thirds the mortality rate among children less than five years of age.

5.0 Improve maternal health;
Reduce by three quarters the maternal mortality ratio.

6.0 Combat HIV/AIDS, malaria and other disease:
Halt and begin to reverse the spread of HIV/AIDS;
Halt and begin to reverse the incidence of malaria and other major disease.

7.0 Ensure environmental sustainability:
Integrate the principles of sustainable development into country policies and programmes;
Reverse loss of environmental resources;
Reduce by half the proportion of people without sustainable access to safe drinking water;
Achieve significant improvements in lives of at least 100 million slum dwellers by 2020.

8.0 Develop a global partnership for development:

- Develop further an open trading and financial support system that is rule based, predictable and non-discriminatory, includes a commitment to good governance, development and poverty reduction—nationally and internationally.
- Address the least developed countries' special needs. This includes tariff and quota-free access for their exports; enhanced debt relief for heavily indebted poor countries, cancellation of official bilateral debt, and more generous official development assistance for countries committed to poverty reduction.
- Address the special needs of landlocked and small island developing states.
- Deal comprehensively with developing countries debt problems through national and international measures to make debt sustainable in the long run.
- In cooperation with the developing countries develop decent and productive work for youth.
- In cooperation with pharmaceutical companies, provide access to affordable essential drugs in developing countries.
- In cooperation with the private sector make available the benefit of new technologies—especially information and communication technologies.

The genesis of the goals identified above and the targets fixed with pragmatism, precision and urgency becomes evident when one takes a comprehensive look on all of the eight MDG's as a one complete lot. These centre on the child, mother, nutrition, health care, and all such other inputs that are necessary towards the preparation of children and young persons for a creative and the contributing adult life. Every child has inherent natural right to a healthy pre-natal care, a healthy birth and proper infant health care. To support his/her growth, the country requires certain level of resources and functional support systems nationally and internationally. Developing and least developed countries are mostly those which were exploited in one or the other in the colonial era. It is now well established that as long as ignorance, illiteracy, exploitation and deprivation remain present in any part of the world, no nation can really remain aloof and secure. The international community had realised it and the Jomtien Declaration arising out of the 'World Conference on Education for All', gave a very concrete realisation of this critical need for global mutuality. When a child grows up in any part of the world, he/ she deserve to get good quality education and skill orientation during the initial years. As young persons, they need work places to be able to live a decent life on their own and contribute effectively in the national and international efforts to march ahead and achieve the goals of growth and development. Individual development is the key to the social and national development. All the eight MDG's could be seen as centred on the 'Child'. And that is how it should be.

In his foreword to "The Millennium development Goals Report 2010" of the United Nations, the Secretary-General Ban Ki Moon summarised these goals very comprehensively:

> "The Goals represent human needs and basic rights that every individual around the world should be able to enjoy—freedom from extreme poverty and hunger, quality education, good health and shelter, the right of women to give birth without risking their lives, and a world where environmental sustainability is a priority, and women and men live in equality."

The secretary general recalled the commitment of leaders of all the member nations of the United Nations to 'forge a wide ranging global partnership for development to achieve these universal objectives'. While he mentioned that the 2010 Report shows how much progress has been made, 'it is clear that improvements in the lives of poor have been unacceptably slow, and some hard-won gains are being eroded by the climate, food and economic crises.' MDGs are a blueprint which, if concretised and given the right shape, could pave the way for every individual everywhere to lead a life of dignity, self respect and equality. It could illustrates the universal unity of mankind, on one hand, and establish the necessity of maintaining the sensitive and sacrosanct mutuality of man and nature, on the other. Non-achievement or even a delay would be disastrous not only for the weaker countries and sections of population, but to everyone, irrespective of the social, economic or geographical location.

Elementary Education in India

The Constitution of India has very specific provisions on universal education. The pre-independence period leadership of India knew it very well that even after independence; the greatest challenges would appear in the shape of removing illiteracy, ignorance, poverty and hunger. At a literacy rate of just around 20 per cent, India's Constitution makers inserted a very bold and courageous provision in the shape of Article 45 under the Directive Principles of State policy:

> "Provision for free and compulsory education for children— The State shall endeavour to provide; within a period of ten years from the commencement of the Constitution, for free and compulsory education for all children until they complete fourteen years of age."

As is well known, the goals indicated in this very significant provision could not be achieved within the stipulated period. These, in fact, still remain unachieved for a very large number of children in the specified age group. Serious concerns were expressed on various facets of elementary education in terms of access, participation and learner attainments at various stages of policy formulations and implementation, during the last over six decades. There was a great clamour for including the provisions of free and compulsory education under the fundamental rights guaranteed under the Constitution. The 86th Constitutional amendment was inserted in 2002 in the following format:

> "21 A. The State shall provide free and compulsory Education to all children of the age of six to fourteen years in such manner as the State may, by law, determine."

Now, the Right to Education (RTE) Act, which was passed by the Parliament of India in 2009, has been implemented with effect from April 01, 2010. The RTE Act provides the legal framework for universalisation of elementary education, as a fundamental right of children in the age group 6-14 years of age. It clarifies that 'Compulsory education' means obligation of the appropriate government to provide free elementary education and ensure compulsory admission, attendance and completion of elementary education to every child in the six to fourteen year age group. (Annual report, MHRD 2010, p. 20). It makes provision for a non-admitted child to be admitted an age-appropriate class. Only time will tell how much difference it can make in bringing around ten million children to schools and providing good quality education to them and also to those who are in schools but are getting below average quality education. Apparently, the implementation of the Right to Education Act is great achievement in the elementary education sector and it fits in very well with the spirit of the Millennium Development Goals and the global concerns articulated from time to time.

In India the term used for compulsory education for all is Universal Elementary Education (UEE). It fits in the MDG 2. As already indicated it has been part of the constitutional directives, educational policies particularly the National Policy on Education 1986 and its revised version of 1992. Now it finds a place amongst the fundamental rights. If one takes a cursory look on the remaining seven MDGs, it would be very clear that practically all are relevant to the most prominent of the Goals: good quality UEE with a strong component of skill orientation and value development and nurturance. As long as extreme poverty and hunger continue to inflict misery on billions of people, achieving UEE would remain a distant dream. The same applies to the prevailing gender discrimination practices and traditions. Child mortality and maternal health are critical components to education as well. HIV/AIDS/Malaria and other diseases leave millions of families and children in dire conditions that make survival of children tough. Innumerable children all over the globe have suffered for centuries when the traditional habitations of the tribals, forest communities and ethnic groups suffered displacement, snatching of their traditional sources of livelihood and exploitation in various forms and formats in the name of progress and development; the fruits of which have generally remained confined to a select few. Such disparities have greatly retarded the progress in achieving UEE on one hand and, on the other, have greatly emphasised the urgency of bringing every child in the fold of UEE at the earliest.

It would be relevant to recall the following from the National Policy on Education NPE-1986 as revised in 1992 which is still being implemented by the nation:

2.4 In sum, education is a unique investment in the present and the future. This cardinal principle is the key to the national policy on education.

4.1 The new policy will lay special emphasis on the removal of disparities and to equalise educational opportunities by attending to the specific needs of those who have been denied equality so far.

4.7 Education will be used as an agent of basic change in the status of women. In order to neutralize the accumulated distortions of the past, there will be a well-conceived edge in favour of women. The national system will play a positive, interventionist role in the empowerment of women.

5.5 The thrust in elementary education will emphasise three aspects: (I) universal access and enrolment, (II) universal retention of children up to 14 years of age; and (III) a substantial improvement in the quality of education to enable all children to achieve essential levels of learning.

It is evident from a mere glance on the extracts from the NPE-86/92 that it takes in to account all the pre-requisites necessary to enable children and young persons, more particularly girls and women, to know their rights and develop attitudes to ensure that no one or any of the systemic or social practice is permitted to usurp these any more. Essentially, the Indian education Policy and its regular revisions have always articulated the spirit of the constitution of India that assures equality and social justice to all irrespective of any diversity of caste, creed, religion, region, social practices or gender. At the global level the articulation and delineation of the MDG attempts the same.

Initiatives in Elementary Education

Official Details

As far as the support systems and the achievements in elementary education are concerned, the MHRD Annual Report-2010 gives details in terms of figures and achievements which indicate that 99 per cemt of the rural population has a primary school within one kilometre. 3,00,895 new schools opened till December 2009. The Gross Enrolment Ratio (GER) increased in 6-14 age group to 114.61 in 2007-08, from 96.3 in 2001-02 at the primary level and, to 77.50 in

2007-08 from 60.02 at the upper primary level. In the context of the MDG, this should be considered a big achievement. Gender parity ratio has also shown considerable positive change. From 0.83 in 2001-02 it has risen to 0.98 in 2007-08 at the primary level and from 0.77 to 0.92 at the upper primary level. For decades together, the Indian education system has struggled with the stupendous task of reducing the dropout rates particularly in the initial years in schools. It got reduced by 13.48 per cent to 25.55 in 2007-08 from 39.03 per cent in 2001-02. Dropout rates for girls declined by 15.06 points. The pupil-teacher ratio at the national level was 46.1 for primary and 35.1 for upper primary in 2007-08. Obviously it needs further improvements even in official claims.

As indicated earlier, India's achievements in terms of increase in the number of children in schools is really commendable, particularly when one examines these in the light of paucity of resources in the initial years after independence and over three fold population increase in the last six decades. Take one simple example; enrolment figures in the year 2000-2001 were 926 lakhs in primary classes (Class I to V; age group 5 to 11 years) and 342 lakhs in upper primary (Classes VI-VIII; 11 to 14 years of age). The Corresponding figures after five years in 2005-06 rose to 1308 lakhs and 511 lakhs respectively. The Scheme of Sarva Shiksha Abhiyan (SSA) was launched in 2001 and it aimed to bring all children in the age group 6-11 years to schools by 2007 and those up to 14 years of age by 2010. The goals also included universal retention and bridging of gender gap by 2010. It also aimed at providing elementary education of satisfactory quality, with emphasis on education for life. What more and better a society in a developing country with a large population below the poverty line and suffering diverse deprivation and deficiencies could ask for? 'The programme covers the entire country with special focus on educational needs of girls, SCs/STs and other children in difficult circumstances.' To ensure the achievements of these objectives, several schemes were launched to look after the needs of children in remote areas and in small habitations. Alternative intervention strategies were designed for specific categories of very deprived children, e.g., child labour, street children, migrating children, working children, children living in difficult circumstances and older children in the 9+ age group—especially adolescent girls. Two of the schemes, Education Guarantee Schema (EGS) and Alternative Innovative Education (AIE) have received special place in these efforts. The SSA has a special focus on girls and children of weaker sections. Several incentive schemes have been operationalised to bring the weakest and most deprived on par with others SSA includes computer education in villages and tribal areas also. The National Mission for the SSA is headed by the Prime Minister and the minister for the Human resources development chairs its executive committee. The Mission monitors the progress of the different components of the SSA has specially targeted low female literacy pockets and particular efforts are made to bring out-of-school girls to schools, particularly girls from disadvantaged sections of the society. Towards this end, two special programmes namely National Programme for Girls Education and Kasturba Gandhi Balika Vidyalaya, both of which are subsumed under the flagship programme SSA, have been launched (MHRD Annual Report 2010, p. 22).

The most significant intervention in the initiatives to give every child the right to basic education was in terms of the Mid-day Meal Scheme which has been revised on several occasions and has been in place for around two decades. The coverage was expanded and extended gradually and today around 120 million children are supposed to be benefiting under this scheme. The criticality of such an intervention can be judged from one single fact: over 44 per cent children in this country suffer from malnutrition! The scheme has been revised on a couple of occasions. At present, the objectives include improving the nutritional status of the children in all government, local bodies and government aided schools and also the EGS and AIE centres. It is expected to encourage children from poor families and disadvantaged groups to attend school more regularly. It also intends to provide nutritional support to children of primary stage in drought affected areas in summer vacations. Towards this end, provisions have been made to provide cooked mid-day meal, with a nutritional content of 450 calories. It also lays down the norms for protein content and micronutrients. There are elaborate monitoring mechanisms but the implementation of the scheme continues to suffer from several deficiencies and inadequacies.

The MHRD sponsors evaluation of Mid-day Meal schemes in various states by 'independent agencies'. Several of these reports and their findings are cited in the ministry's annual report of 2010. Some of the observations culled out from different state reports indicate the ground level situation in terms of achievement:

- It has made positive intervention in universalisation of primary education by increasing enrolment and attendance. This increase was particularly marked in case of girls and children from SC/ST community. It has also contributed to the reduction in teacher absenteeism and narrowing of social distances (Birbhumi, West Bengal).

- It has positively impacted enrolment and attendance of children. It has contributed to social amity as children sit together and share a common meal irrespective of caste and class (Rajasthan).
- There was a 15 per cent increase in the enrolment. It was more marked; 43 per cent in case of the SC/ST children (Madhya Pradesh).

It would be seen that this scheme has made a very tangible impact in efforts to give children their right to education. When around 12 crore children are to be covered on daily basis, the management and administration could invariably be under severe stress. It is generally acknowledged that the implementation of the scheme has shown visible signs of improvements over the years.

The Gaps

The Indian education system represents a vast and diverse canvas that extends not only in huge geographical dimensions but integrates diversities of all possible varieties. Providing UEE to all children is a tough task in India, as it is in the developing countries taken together. The UN Millenniums Development Goals Report of 2010 indicates that enrolment in primary education has continued to rise, reaching 89 per cent in the developing world. This further indicates that "But the pace of progress is insufficient to ensure that by 2015, all the girls and boys complete a full course of primary education". While numerical figures may indicate encouraging progress, people's expectations from education have now changed. They are no longer satisfied if their wards complete eight or ten years in schools and get a certificate to that effect. They want 'good quality education with sufficient orientation in skills'. There is one more very significant development that impacts quality of education in schools run by local bodies, governments and aided private schools.

Over the years, the rise of public schools that charge high fees has created two distinct groups: those who can afford to go to a private high-fee charging school try their best to get in there. The upper strata of society are gradually moving away from schools that offer free elementary education, resulting in considerable decline of the credibility of these schools. It is a well acknowledged 'fact' that private schools function better, have a superior work culture and hence provide better quality education. In the government system, teacher absenteeism, indiscipline, vacant positions and tendency to avoid rural tribal and remote areas is predominant. It results in poor functional efficacy and hence, lower levels of learner achievements. The ultimate sufferers are the children and thereby, the reduction in the overall cognitive and vocational capital of the country. As the government systems generally focus on expansion, which too is a must, the schemes and action points to improve the quality often get ignored at the implementation stage though it may find a prominent mention in the policies and programmes. Unfortunately, certain external factors are also responsible for the dilution of work culture in schools. In the long run, even if the figures of enrolment and dropout rates are encouraging, the long-term impact of education becomes suspect. It poses a big challenge in achieving the MDG-II in its real spirit. That is also the spirit of the RTE-2010. And finally, it is the spirit contained in the constitution of India that ensures equality to all in their human rights.

There are serious ambiguities on the estimates of out-of-school children. Different surveys give varying percentages which can be understood in such a vast system and large numbers. The NER, (Net Enrolment Ratio), was estimated at 94.5 per cent by the 7th All India Educational survey. Another independent survey, conducted in 2009, estimated 4.28 per cent children in the 6-14 year age group being out of the school; 3.92 per cent boys and 4.71 per cent girls (ACSR—2010). There are regional variations as well, since those amongst different groups like Muslims, SC/ST and others. 20 per cent of Indian children are grouped as being from migrant families and claims about their enrolment and retention may be suspect. Overall, 3.72 per cent children are enrolled in single teacher schools. The National PTR figure is 1:32, but it far exceeds this in a large number of schools. The most important issue is—number of children who complete eight years of education! A survey giving data for 2007-08 shows a retention rate till class V of 72 per cent only. (ACSR, 2010). The rate of transition of children from primary to upper primary education in 2006-07 was 81.13 per cent, meaning thereby that 19 out of every 100 children are lost to schools between classes V to VI. The ratio of primary to upper primary schools stood at 4.41 in 2007-08. Non-availability of upper primary schools and the facility of smooth transition also makes a negative impact, particularly for girls (ibid, p-36).

When it comes to teachers and their professional preparedness, things appear to require far more additional inputs than are available at present. The quality of teacher preparation at the pre-service stage has deteriorated and the arrangements to provide good quality in-service education are inadequate. The management systems have yet to transform their approach and style. The table below gives an idea of the challenges that lie before the planners and implementers in achieving the MDG-II.

Quality of Schooling in India: Some Insights

Schools without head teacher (but with enrolment of over 100 children)	45.1%
% Single teacher primary schools	13.25
% schools with PTR > = 60	12.96
% schools without female teachers	26.4%
% schools without drinking water	22%
% schools without common toilet	33%
% schools without girls toilet	46%
% schools without computer	86%
% schools without a ramp	60%
% schools not electrified	64%
% schools not receiving teaching learning material grant	27%
Number of districts where PTR is over 40 (all schools)	146
% Professionally trained teachers	71%
% teachers who received in-service training during previous year	35%
DISE Flash Statistics 2008-9	

Source: Millennium Development Goals in India—A Civil Society Report; 2010; Page 37.

It has often been pointed out (Rajput, 2009) that the Indian system of education needs to focus on aspects that are normally considered as matters of detail by the national level planners. Every school is unique in its requirements and motivational ingredients that could achieve the desired levels of efficiency and efficacy. For example, non-availability of a toilet or drinking water, or both, may become the deciding factor in the lives of hundreds of children. Official documents signify the criticality of these factors, but, in actual practice, these often get ignored. Over the last twenty years, considerable attention has been paid to basic facilities like classrooms, play material, teaching-learning materials, etc., but the situation has not yet been effectively and uniformly attended to.

Conclusion

Target setting, both nationally and internationally, helps in many ways, particularly in sharing of experiences, and through collaborations of varied kinds. Over the last around two decades, India has accepted international support and assistance in its elementary education programmes and also in several other of the MDGs as were articulated in Dakar. The fact also remains that several internal factors can be handled and taken care of, only when a thorough understanding of the local context is arrived at and each one of these is specifically addressed. Diversities abound in India on practically every aspect of life and education of children is no exception. It is far more complex at the elementary stage. One of the greatest achievements of the post-independence period is—there are no groups in social set up which oppose education of boys or girls. Education is only one part, though extremely necessary, of the initiatives to give human rights and dignity to every individual as promised in the Constitution of India. The challenges are many. India is home to 42 per cent of underweight children under the age of five years in the world (*The Times of India*, October 12, 2010). The Global Hunger Index-2010 for China, Pakistan and Sudan are 6.0; 19.1; and 20.9 respectively. For India, it is 24.7 (ibid)! It is only one example that establishes the necessity of a comprehensive approach. In a broader perspective, it can be stated that the world possesses enough resources and sufficient knowledge to ensure that even the weakest of the weak gets what nature has apportioned for him/her but which has not reached them because someone in between has grabbed more that his/her due share. Education, and more importantly, the universal elementary education opens up the gates to knowledge, understanding and appreciation of the heritage of a common planet that loves all its children equally and fully. Huge efforts on the part of everyone are needed to realise the dream contained in the Dakar Declaration.

(October 2010)

References

UNESCO, World Declaration on Education for All, Resolution of the World Conference on Education, Jamtien, March 1990.

UN, Dakar Framework for Action, Education for All: Meeting our collective commitments, Text adopted by the World Education Forum, Dakar, Senegal, 26-28 April 2000.

National Policy on Education-1986/92, Ministry of Human Resources Development, Department of Education, New Delhi.

UN, Millennium Development Report, 2010.

Annual Report, 2010, Ministry of Human Resources Development, New Delhi.

ACSR-2010: Millennium Development Goals in India, 2010—A Civil Society Report, *Wada Na Todo Abhiyan*, September 2010, New Delhi.

Rajput, J.S., *Contemporary Concerns in Education*; Yash Publications, New Delhi; 2009.

'More Hungry in India than in Sudan', *The Times of India*, October 12, 2010.

12

Education for Gender Equality

The 20th century realised the urgency of extending education to one and all and simultaneously also resolved to achieve it through sustained global efforts.[1] As nations proceeded to implement their policies on universalisation of initial education for those outside the realm of education, they came across acute multi-faceted social, cultural and religious hurdles in bringing children; particularly girls; to schools and to acquire education. Apprehensions, taboos, futility and unfounded apprehensions became the prominent ingredients in the arguments of those resisting endeavours to educate girls. India faced all of it as it became independent and soon specific steps were initiated to extend the outreach of education to every child as specifically mandated by the Constitution of India. The cultural history of India is full of accounts of brilliant women who were second to none in scholarship and knowledge. Indian scriptures accord a very high place to women. Unfortunately, subsequently several aberrations crept in, leading to innumerable sufferings being inflicted upon women. It is, however, globally acknowledged that it is the place, the respect and equality that women receive that indicates the levels of humanisation and civilization in that society. It also remains a fact that historical events led to confinement of girls to homes and hearth and for a vast majority. Therefore, educating them began to be considered a taboo. They suffered and India suffered. The post-independence resistance to sending girls to schools was considerable; in spite of very clear perceptions of India's luminaries, leaders and social reformers that no society could indeed march ahead on the path of progress and development with illiteracy thrust upon its women. Amongst those who understood India and its Soul, Swami Vivekananda was very clear:[2]

> "In India there are two great evils: Trampling on the women and grinding the poor through caste restrictions."
> "They (Indian women) have many and grave problems, but none that are not to be solved by that magic word 'education'."
> "Educate your women first and leave them to themselves; they will tell you what reforms are necessary for them."
> "It is very difficult to understand why in this country so much difference is made between men and women, whereas the Vedanta declares that one and the same conscious Self is present in all beings. .... Is there any sex-distinction in Atman (Self)? Out with the differentiation between man and women—all is Atman."

He often asked people 'earnestly' to 'open schools for girls in every village and try to uplift them'. He was convinced 'If the women are raised, then their children will, by their noble actions glorify the name of the country—then will culture, knowledge, power and devotion awaken in the land'.

Mahatma Gandhi gave the lead in the pre-independence days. He developed the model of Basic Education, refined it with inputs from Dr. Zakir Husain and others, got it implemented and presented the results to the nation, indicating its success and the potential to give education and skills to both boys and girls; also men and women without inflicting any stressful economic burden on them. In the oft-quoted speech at the Chatham Lines, in which Gandhiji very rightly claimed that India was far more literate before the arrival of the British, he mentioned about his plans being ready for implementation after independence: to open schools, for both boys and girls, in every village of India!

This description could only be a peripheral reflection on the huge efforts put in by both men and women in the area of women's education. So many other names could be cited and efforts and innovations recalled in this area. The change, though stressful and often painful, has indeed been very significant. In India, every parent is now convinced that both boys and girls must get education. It is now well established that girls are no more out of school because of social or parental resistance. They are still out of schools, higher education and employment market in large numbers because of several factors beyond the control of parents.

Some of the reasons are:

1. Absence of a school within the reasonable distance.
2. Lack of basic facilities like drinking water and; particularly; separate toilets.

3. Economic pressures, parental migration, insecurity about livelihood.
4. Domestic chores, looking after the siblings, absence of functional crèches.
5. Uncongenial home environment.
6. Irregular functioning of the school.
7. Absence of lady teachers.
8. Loss of credibility of government schools.
9. Child marriages.
10. Non-appreciation of their workforce participation. In farm production their participation is around 55-66 per cent which often gets ignored.
11. Apprehensions of insecurity and sexual harassment in institutions and the work place.
12. The traditional practice of saving on education to organise dowry for the girl's marriage.
13. Domestic discord, unsuitable home environment, drinking habits of males.
14. Ignorance about supportive government schemes and provisions.

There are several encouraging signs that could accelerate the march towards gender equality. As per the 2011 Census female literacy rates stand at 65.46 as against 82.14 for males and the overall 74.04. In UP and Bihar, the female literacy rates are 59.3 and 53.3 respectively. This is indeed a matter of serious concern. Certain unethical practices, known to one and all, somehow are permitted to persist and these impact the data on enrolment and literacy rates. Fall in the primary school enrolment has recently been reported, based on the data compiled by the NUEPA—the National University of Educational Planning and Administration. From 13.7 crore in 2011-12, this came down to 13.4 crore in 2012-13. This may appear marginal but points out some significant trends. This decline in Bihar is 11.6 per cent. Bihar abounds in dual enrolments at the primary level: children study in private schools but also remain enrolled in government schools to avail of the free benefits, and also to help the teachers who may otherwise get transferred! During this period, upper primary enrolment has risen from 6.19 crore to 6.49 crore. Data also shows that 92.14 lakh children in the 6-14 age groups are still out of school. The percentage of schools with separate girl's toilets has increased from 72.16 to 88.32 during this period. Girl's enrolment has increased in both primary and upper primary levels.[3] This increase has been achieved in spite of the fact that 'among children up to 15 years, there are 1.8 crore fewer girls than boys—the sex ratio at 914 girls per 1000 boys remaining the same as a decade ago'.[4] Has education not impacted the parents and young married couples to shun sex determination tests and permit no discrimination against girls on any account in homes and families? Some other numbers could give an idea of the change in numbers of girls in education. In 1950-51, the percentage of girls' enrolment to total enrolment was 28.1 per cent at primary, 16.1 per cent at upper primary, and 13.3 per cent at secondary/ senior secondary stages. The corresponding figures in 2007-08 were 47.5 per cent, 45.8 per cent and 43.4 per cent. Another interesting data could be the rise in the number of lady teachers. At the primary stage, there were only 82,000 lady teachers as against 456,000 male teachers. In 2007-08 the corresponding numbers were 12,07,000 and 23,15,000 respectively. For the Upper Primary stage, during the same period, the numbers rose from 13,000 to 717,000. At the secondary stage the rise was from a mere 20,000 to 795,000. The numbers of female teachers are rising, but this rise needs to be accelerated further. According to the 2011-12 data, presented by the District Information System for Education (DISE), around 1.28 lakh out of 10,75,407 government elementary schools across the country still do not have toilets and 61,000 lack drinking water facilities. Official claims show that of 84.68 per cent of the girls' toilets are functional as against 65.87 per cent for boys. Even these numbers are huge in the context of RTE; an analysis by NUEPA indicates that many of the schools which have toilets and drinking water facilities, the infrastructure is as good as non-existent as these are not functional. In the composite Andhra Pradesh State, it emerged that 74.6 per cent schools have separate boys' toilets but only 21.57 per cent of these were are functional. For girls, the claim is of 61.38 per cent functional toilets.

All this data that indicates substantial deficiencies in gender equality in practical terms should serve as a wakeup call for curriculum developers and text book writers.

Several schemes, focusing on girl children and their upward mobility to higher and professional education, have been launched by the Union Ministry of Human Resources Development. The launch of the National Mission for the empowerment of women generated high hopes. Its focus was on advocacy activities to fuel the demand for benefits that are stipulated for women, their economic empowerment, progressive elimination of violence against women, gender mainstreaming of programmes and policies and, their social empowerment through particular emphasis on health and education.

The issue of empowerment of women is primarily dependent on education reaching them. However several supportive measures like the ones contained amongst the objectives of the National Mission need to be undertaken to enable them to reap the benefits of education. The content of education and the extent of skills acquired can make a big difference. So much has yet to be achieved on the social front that continues to persist with traditional interpretations of the differences amongst men and women and continues to justify the inequalities that have persisted all along.

Education, in its content and process, must acknowledge the equality of sexes and shun all discriminations. One recalls having solved sums in the 1950's like: "Three men perform a task in six days while the same is completed by five women in five days. How much time would be needed if they work together?" What more one needed to perpetuate prejudices? All that changed with the advent of the NCERT and the Report of the Kothari Commission in 1966-64. The gender sensitivity aspect has been examined with the curriculum changes in 1978, 1988, 2000 and 2005; each one of which resulted in the preparation of new textbooks. The NCERT trained textbook writers and curriculum developers in states/UTs on how to examine textbooks and other teaching learning materials.[5] Recently, MHRD wrote to the State/UT governments to "modify their existing school curricula and textbooks to include gender positive material". That would require authors who have internalized the significance of the task assigned and further, are free from urban middle class biases. The ministry also suggested changes in the curriculum, system of teacher training and opined that the incorporation of subjects related to self-defence, human body and protection, social health, etc., are on right lines but certain other critical elements are also necessary. What is being done to train government functionaries, including police personnel, to deal with issues that concern women with due sensitivity. Why such a huge sense of insecurity engulfs women from reposing confidence in those who could really make a difference to their self-esteem? The present corrupt, insensitive, unimaginative system of governance requires multi-faceted transformation to make the 'change' happen. Even well-educated women suffer violence in homes, the work places and even while commuting! Experts have identified four significant dimensions that need to be attended to empower women. These dimensions are: cognitive acquisitions, psychological strength, economic security and political support. These are common elements that would determine the curriculum for one and all. Over and above that, it is the political will that could accelerate the change. There too, an attitudinal transformation is necessary. That, everyone knows, is a tough proposition. Every component of society and the system of governance has to realise its responsibility and the need to act — and act at the earliest.

Emergence of Policies and Perspectives

Several Articles of the Constitution of India guarantee gender equality and empower the state to provide special provisions that may be needed for the welfare of women and make the working environment conducive for them. Articles 14, 15, 15(3), 16 and 21(A) are *particularly relevant in the context of equality and education.*

> Article 14. Equality before Law: The State shall not deny any person equality before the law or equal protection of the laws within the territory of India.
>
> Article 15. Prohibition of discrimination on grounds of religion, race, caste, sex or place of Birth:
>
> 1. The state shall not discriminate against any citizen on grounds only of religion, race, caste, sex, place of birth or any of them.
> 2. No citizen shall, on grounds only of religion, race, caste, sex, place of birth or any of them, be subject to any disability, liability, restriction or condition with regard to—
>   (a) access to shop, public restaurants, hotels and places of public entertainment; or
>   (b) the use of wells, tanks, bathing ghats, roads and places of public resort maintained wholly or partly out of state funds or dedicated to the use of general public.
> 3. Nothing in this article shall prevent the State from making any special provision for women and children.

Further Article 16 stipulates equality of opportunity in matters 'relating to employment or appointment to any office under the State'. Article 39 mandates equal pay for equal work; Article 42 pertains to humane conditions in the work place and the provisions of maternity leave. Article 51(A) mentions eleven fundamental duties, one of which enjoins upon every citizen to 'renounce practices derogatory to the dignity of women'. Article 21-A, now after the RTE Act, relates to free and compulsory education to all children in the age group 6-14 years. Proper implementation of the RTE Act, as is well known, remains the key provision. Only adequately educated individuals could be made properly conscious of their rights and duties, the two organically linked elements. The extent and level of internalization of this linkage determines the quality of human life in every society.

The Government of India has, from time to time, appointed several committees and made special provisions for girls and women based upon the recommendations it received from various experts and professional bodies. The National Committee on Women's Education presided over by Smt. Durgabai Deshmukh, in 1959, had recommended general education on par with boys, including professional and vocational skills 'that equip them fully for their duties both in home and outside'. The Kothari Commission made a very significant point: education of girls and women was the key to social transformation! It had recorded its futuristic vision by recommending a common ten-year curriculum 'both for boys and girls'! The National Policy on Education 1986 revised in 1992 summarises the concerns identified over the years and the experiences gained during the implementation of various policies and programmes. The following extracts from the policy would present a comprehensive picture of the approach to education:

4.2 "Education will be used as an agent of basic change in the status of woman. In order to neutralize the accumulated distortions of the past; there will be a well-conceived edge in favour of women. The National Education System will play a positive, interventionist role in the empowerment of women. It will foster the development of new values through redesigned curricula, textbooks, the training and orientation of teachers, decision-makers and administrators, and the active involvement of educational institutions. This will be an act of faith and social engineering. Women's studies will be promoted as a part of various courses and educational institutions encouraged to take up active programmes to further women's development.

4.3 The removal of women's illiteracy and obstacles inhibiting their access to, and retention in, elementary education will receive overriding priority, through provision of special support services, setting of time targets, and effective monitoring. Major emphasis will be laid on Women's participation in vocational, technical and professional education at different levels. The policy of non-discrimination will be pursued vigorously to eliminate sex stereo-typing in vocational and professional courses and to promote women's participation in non-traditional occupations, as well as in the existing and emergent technologies."

After the NPE 86/92, practically every scheme contained in the Programme of Action document, explicitly emphasised the need to take special care of education of girls. The ambitious Operation Blackboard Scheme, which extended support in equipment and teachers to every primary, and later every elementary, school in the country had particularly emphasised on recruitment of lady teachers, insisting that in a two teacher school, one of them must be a lady. That a similar recommendation had to be made by the CABE Committee in 2005 and reiterated in the Eleventh Plan indicates systemic failures over prolonged periods. The Sarva Shiksha Abhiyan (SSA), like the Operation Blackboard, stipulated fifty per cent lady teachers. The reasons remain the same as earlier:[6] "One of the most prominent of the reasons is that many parents will not send their daughters to school if there are no women teachers. The other is that women are found to be more conscientious and caring as teachers." Perusal of the numbers of teachers indicates a significant increase in the number of teachers in schools. Even those who are in the system face several problems and concerns, which require a very sensitive, alert and responsive system of educational management and administration. The implementation strategy requires a very well thought of area specific work plan with inbuilt monitoring mechanisms. In this regard the National Curriculum Framework for School Education,[7] brought out by the NCERT in 2000 observed: "Emphasis in education has moved from 'Equality of Educational Opportunity' (NPE 1968) to Education for Women's Equality and Empowerment (1986). As a result, the curricular and training strategies for the education for girls now demand more attention … removing all gender discrimination and gender bias in school curriculum, textbooks and the process of transaction is absolutely necessary." This Curriculum Framework emphasised "the need to develop and implement gender inclusive and gender sensitive curricular strategies to nurture a generation of girls and boys who are equally competent and are sensitive to one another, and grow up in caring and sharing mode, and not as adversaries."[8] It is indeed encouraging to note that of the 64 lakh school teachers in schools, 29 lakh are women. The percentage of women teachers has been increasing steadily in recent years. From 43.46 per cent in 2008-09, it rose to 44.83 per cent in 2009-10 and 45.51 per cent in 2010-2011.[9] This trend picked up after introduction of the NPE 1986/92 and the scheme of Operation Blackboard could be credited with accelerating it. Removal of certain well known hurdles could further enhance these percentages. However, there are around seven lakh vacant posts of teachers in schools and an equal number consists of para teachers appointed on a pittance as honourarium, are constantly suffering a sense of insecurity. Women are the worst sufferers in uncertain work conditions. As para teachers, they have to depend on the mercy of individuals for extension or regularisation. The systems of governance must pay special attention to such instances which, in a way, amount to harassment and exploitation. In most of the teacher training institutions, females outnumber males amongst student teachers. There are studies that indicate positive impacts of the growing number of women teachers.

To look after the issues of women, with particular emphasis, in higher education, several Departments of Women Studies were set up to conduct researches and surveys that would help in providing better understanding of women issues and lead to more pragmatic and comprehensive policies for women, not only in education, but in other sectors as well. Practically in every Five-Year Plan, women's education was "placed at the forefront of the development programmes in these Plans".[10] A large number of schemes and programmes emerged practically after every Five-Year Plan in the context of women and their education. One of the significant events was the setting up of a Central Advisory Board of Education (CABE) Committee on girl's education and the Common School System in 2005. "It recommended free and compulsory education for girls up to the age of 18 years and emphasised that there should be 'no hidden costs' in the education of girls. The Committee gave a thrust to initiate measures to promote girls education of such nature, force and magnitude that would enable girls to overcome the obstacles posed by factors such as poverty, domestic/sibling responsibilities, girl child labour, low preference to girls education, preference to marriage over education, etc. It also recommended women teachers and women attendants in every institution with provision of suitable working conditions for them so that they can perform their duties effectively, especially in rural areas."[11] If such a recommendation is made, rather reiterated once again, it clearly indicates that most of our well-intentioned formulations in policies and programmes have not yet reached the beneficiaries because of a plethora of impediments that too stand well identified. The Eleventh Five year Plan states the obvious: education is the key instrument for inclusive growth, that opening of easily accessible secondary schools for girls and also coeducational is the critical necessity, particularly as the number of girls willing to move ahead from elementary to secondary stage is increasing appreciably. Perusal of the rise of female literacy rates gives some idea of how far India has moved ahead in educating its women.

The Table below depicts the rise in literacy rates for males, females and the population along with the percentage difference between males and females. This difference though least of all the other periods, still continues to remain at the very high level of 16.68 per cent.

Table 12.1: Rise of Literacy in the post-Independence period

Census Year	*Persons*	*Males*	*Females*	*Male-Female Gap*
1951	18.33	27.16	8.86	18.30
1961	28.30	40.40	15.35	25.05
1971	34.45	45.96	21.97	23.98
1981	43.57	56.38	29.76	26.62
1991	52.21	64.13	39.29	24.84
2001	65.38	75.85	54.16	21.70
2011	74.04	82.14	65.46	16.68

Mere getting basic education or even higher education does not guarantee equality of opportunity to women in a male dominated world. Even good education may not give them power, unless this is augmented by attitudinal transformation within the community and the society on one hand and the males of the species on the other. Even in the educationally advanced countries, good professional education does not guarantee equality of opportunity at the work place. The following illustrates this position:[12]

In her new book 'Lean In', Sheryl Sandberg, Facebook's chief operating officer, recounts a warning she delivered to Harvard Business School students in 2011. "About one-third of the women in this audience will be working full time in 15 years," she told them. "And almost all of you will be working for the guy you are sitting next to."

"Women surpassed men as a percentage of college students in the late 1980s, and by 2009 had become the majority of master's degree students and doctoral candidates. The majority of Americans older than 25 with college degrees are, today, women. Yet just 4.2 per cent of Fortune 500 CEOs are women. So why hasn't women's success in the academy led them to more leadership positions in the world of work?"

Even well educated women may not be getting what is their fundamental right: complete power over their own bodies, minds and the right to un-subjugated motivation and zest for life. Curriculum developers and writers of textual materials at each stage of education require inputs of in-depth surveys and studies in the problems and concerns of girls and women. Violence against women is a serious area of concern for education system.

Violence against Women

Education must help individuals to develop problem solving skills, apart from so much more. Women need these in far greater measure as they do not face a very congenial and respectful environment as they move out of the four walls of their homes. In the year 2012-13, Indian media has reported umpteen cases of terrible violence against girls and women. These could shame any civilized society. These, simultaneously also indicate how inadequate is our understanding of the psychological relationships between the two genders and why violence continues in such a huge measure when the global society is moving ahead to transform itself into a knowledge society! People incessantly talk of creating a peaceful world but keep on manufacturing deadly weapons. The violence perpetuates on the battle field on one hand and it continues to haunt women, right from their homes to places of work, on the other. Why does it happen? Education has to understand it and find solutions and implementable strategies to counter it.

The worst form of this violence is sexual in intent, nature and manifestation. Even after the J.S. Verma Committee Report and subsequent changes in provisions to deal with such crimes, not much deterrent impact is visible in society. There is a great mismatch between what young persons get by way of sex education and the sex-explosion consistently being dished out by media round the clock! Urbanisation, migration for jobs and, loneliness in an alien environment just cannot be ignored in the context of sexual violence. The insensitivity that persists amongst the police and judiciary often makes the victim reluctant to approach them to get their genuine grievances redressed. In matters of sexual violations, it is only now that the victims and their families are gathering courage to come out and complain in spite of the hurdles that all of them anticipate. This trend could be attributed to the spread of education. Even now, women suffer silently in innumerable cases from their well wishers, friends of the family, relatives, and so many others known to them. The alertness in society and the growing family support encouraged by updated legal provisions are bringing the cases of violence to light. One wishes justice also becomes swift and exemplary. Schools and colleges have now special committees to look after cases of harassment to women, which includes violence against them. The Supreme Court, in the well known Vishaka vs. State of Rajasthan Case (1997), had laid down detailed guidelines for all the places of work where women could face harassment. The judgement clearly and emphatically asserted 'Working women have a right to work with dignity and safe from sexual harassment'.

Interpreting Differences

Not much long ago, there was a widespread acceptability of racial differences. This belief in racial superiority and inferiority led to innumerable wars and battles which stand recorded in the history of civilizational growth. The atoneable practices of untouchability, slavery and apartheid were a consequence of such fabricated beliefs. Now, even after the abolition of slavery, apartheid and caste discrimination, these do persist in certain modified forms though to a far lesser extent. Science has exploded the myth of racial superiority, but racial confrontations are no exception. Gender differences, however, are clear and obvious. The role of man and women in reproductive functions is different as they are physiologically different. In the man's world, arguments run like this:[13] "Man is the superior sex, because he is both physically and intellectually superior to women. He is better in leadership, courage, creativity, idealistic and abstract thinking, is more aggressive, more dominant, more adventurous and more ambitious. Woman, on the other hand, is the 'weaker sex', 'Abla', inferior to man in physical strength and intellectual capacities, but more loving, more submissive and more interested in concrete things rather than abstract thinking, in preservation, rather than revolutionary changes, in child bearing and home making, rather than intellectual and artistic creations." All this appear bordering on absurdity to someone who has lived in a cocooned, educated, culturally advanced family and has grown up in an enlightened environment. It would be relevant to recall how girls were being persuaded to opt out of science and mathematics after the fifth grade or so because they were not considered 'intellectually equipped' to cope up with the rigours of learning these two subjects. These were recommended only for boys. It required the vision, and courage, of Dr. D.S. Kothari to emphatically recommend that girls were no deficient in any way to boys and had an equal right to study science and mathematics along with boys. Based upon the Report of the National Commission on Education (1966-64), headed by Dr. Kothari, the 1968 National Policy on Education prescribed ten-year common school curriculum; for both boys and girls; without any discrimination. How forthright this one recommendation was is proved by the millions of girls who have excelled in science, technology, medicine, ICT and every other area. In Board and University examinations, girls invariably do better than boys. Girls themselves have broken umpteen myths, highlighting how different they were, that were imposed upon them for centuries! Girls have proved Swami Vivekananda: educated women shall themselves find solutions to their problems!

The latter half of the 20th century has opened various avenues and vistas for girls and women to prove their worth. There, however, are countries that do not permit women to get a driving license. An innocent 14 year girl Malala Yusufzai is violently attacked, but fortunately survives and becomes a global icon. Yes, most of the men have realised they have to work for the upliftment of women to have harmonious and peaceful families, which in turn shall lead to a harmonious and peaceful world.

There could be innumerable other premises that are still being offered in defence of the man's superiority that invariably points out the necessity of "training women from childhood for their special job and should be encouraged, and even forced whenever necessary to stick to it".[14] Even in educated families, girls are not usually encouraged to become self-dependent while it is a must for boys. Slowly, here again, girls themselves have moved out to the world of work, have courageously confronted problems that arise solely because they were females and have proven their potential. This number must increase as that alone would break the entrenched stereotypes in families and societies.

Over the years, migration to cities and towns is on the rise. Those who move with their families and become part of the urban labour force could be seen in thousands and thousands. They lead a real tough life, suffer illegal wage cuts from the contractors, and are deprived of the benefits of the welfare schemes, because of ignorance or corruption or both. Most of them have no faith in government schools and private schools are beyond their reach. In such families, the worst sufferers are the girl children. If both the parents work as daily wagers, the safety and security of the children, particularly of girls, stands compromised. The social sector support to such children in urban slums and project sites remains inadequate. Hardly any builder or contractor takes the initiative for providing facilities like crèches, health care and transport facilities to schools for the children of hired workers. Access to education is still comparatively far difficult for the girl child than her male counterpart. The factors that impede their participation vary on regional, cultural, social and economic considerations on one hand and the apathy of the system on the other.

Strategies for Empowerment through Education

While evolving specific strategies, one has to comprehensively understand the prevailing conditions and the existing potentialities for eliciting support from sections of the populace. The recent instance of 14-year old Malala Yusufzai, who was shot at for going to school and asking others to study says so much about the strong need for empowering girls through the education route. She is now a role model who has endeared herself globally. Manal al-Sharif is another example of inherent courage; what Indian culture calls *Shakti*. A citizen of Saudi Arabia, she writes about her upbringing:[15] "I was taught that if I left home, I would be fully responsible for any evil that befell me because men cannot be expected to control their instincts. …I was made to stay home…. For Saudi extremists I was *awra*. The word means a sinful thing, an intimate part of the body you should not show. It is against the law to disclose it. By the time I was ten, I was covering myself fully." …We were voiceless. We were faceless. We were nameless. And we were completely invisible." Her rebellion began with daring to drive a car on Riyadh roads with a valid international driving license. It was unimaginable there! She was arrested and jailed. But the fire within was ignited. Here are her Golden words;

> "We believe in full citizenship for women, because a child cannot be free if his mother is not free. A husband cannot be free if his wife is not free. Parents are not free if their daughters are not free. Society is nothing if its women are nothing."

Such example could be located in different situations, conditions and circumstances and could lead to formulation of specific strategies, some of which are mentioned below. Education policies must realise that education helps girls and women to recognise their potential and personality, their social, cultural and economic rights. It enhances their self-images, bestows them with self-assurance, enables them to resist exploitation, oppression and being relegated to a second-class citizen at home or at the work place:

1.1 Even after enactment of the RTE Act, non enrolment of girls in schools remains visible in certain situations like migrant workers, inaccessible areas, absence of crèches and Balwadis, etc. A pragmatic view has to be taken, the system must continuously monitor cases of non-enrolment of girl students, delineate specific impeders and try to find solutions, by taking the parents into confidence. Mere provision of punitive action against parents is not sufficient.

1.2 There is a tendency on the part of the bureaucracy, functionaries of the education departments and the management systems to take the issue of provisions of toilets lightly. Millions of girls drop out of schools at the age of 11-12 years solely because of non-availability of separate functional toilets.

1.3 Absence of lady teachers, particularly in distant, far flung and rural areas is another main cause of girls opting out early and are, thus, deprived of moving to higher education. Repeated assurances contained in the policies and programmes need speedy and sincere implementation. A well educated girl impacts the village or the community far more effectively than a boy. She could be an asset in achieving attitudinal transformation on various aspects including the education of girls and need to give them equality in homes as well.

1.4 Every educational plan and its implementation must internalise and specifically articulate that the goals of universal education, egalitarian society, equality and development just cannot be attained without every girl being brought to the fold of elementary education and further, every impediment towards her moving to higher education is removed by the state and the society. The presence of women in sectors that require higher level skills invigorates the work culture.

1.5 Prevention of crimes against women must get explicit priority in the curriculum in schools and the teacher training institutions. Specific mention of the constitutional guarantees that pertain to women rights must also become the part of legal and constitutional literacy that must be imparted before the boy or the girl leaves school. Studies in these areas should also be encouraged at the university level through special courses and elective papers. Researches deserve sponsorship and the outcomes may lead to better understanding and refinements in policy renewals.

1.6 Education must prepare women for entrepreneurship, self employment and for taking up skilled and professional assignments. Women's access to employment could be substantially increased if specific arrangements are put in place to provide skill orientation to any girl or women who may be interested in acquiring or augmenting professional skills.

1.7 Good education and its appropriate utilisation by one woman impacts scores of others. Names like Vandana Siva, Kiran Bedi, Ila Bhatt, Kalpana Chawala, Sania Mirza or Saina Nehwal cast an impact on innumerable girls and their families. So do women in colleges, universities, in ICT, in the corporate sector and other upcoming avenues.

1.8 The deficiency of trained teachers in rural and tribal areas requires some fresh thinking. It should be possible to pick up girls from a tribal district after class Eight, recruit them as probationary teachers, train them for four/ five years in residential training schools with free boarding lodging and a stipend. One could be rest assured that at least ninety per cent of them shall be in schools even after marriage which does not take them to too distant a place. This strategy could be implemented even in the existing DIETS most of which, in rural and tribal areas, have large campuses and even huge accommodation to function as residential institutions.

1.9 Provision of government teacher training institutions for girls in rural and tribal areas could make a big impact as it would substantially reduce dropouts and enhance retention. It would greatly generate people's confidence in girl's education if girls, brought to these institutions after eight years of schooling, are treated as probationary teachers, looked after fully by the State and given a small stipend. This would greatly reduce non-availability of trained teachers in these areas and also the perpetual teacher absenteeism.

1.10 Married women often suffer abuse and violence in their matrimonial homes, without being able to share their woes with the parental homes. The school curriculum should stress on the importance of family ties. Girls must be acquainted with the lasting value of family ties and necessity of interacting and 'sharing' with their mother and also with other near and dear ones.

1.11 There is a need to create a national level Women's body to monitor media portrayal of women and children in the print media, Television and Films on a regular basis. Unscrupulous exploitation of women and children in films, intended solely at commercial gains, frequently ignore the distracting influences that manifest themselves in severe aberrations in society. It could set up monitoring cells in educational institutions and keep in touch with teachers and parents to ascertain their response.

1.12 It is rather unfortunate that a large number of families continue to give first preference to the boy child. Girls lose out even on health care and food. Schools, teachers and voluntary organisations could combine together to combat these unhealthy traditional practices.

1.13 Education must take note of the fact that urban sex ratios are more skewed than those in rural areas. The point of concern is: have all the provisions for preventing sex discrimination tests have made little impact on educated urban population? Has education not impacted this aspect?

1.14 Educational endeavours need augmentation from the media, opinion makers, professionals particularly the medical practitioners, who need to come together and assist schools and institutions.

Media, opinion leaders and the icons of the people and young persons could also supplement and augment the educational efforts. An intensive networking could result in tangible outcomes. Let it be reiterated that good quality education remains the most strengthful strategy to empower women and give them their due place in each and every aspect of human endeavour.

(September 15, 2013)

Notes

1. World Declaration on Education for All, Jomtien, Thailand, Published by UNESCO, 1990.
2. *My India: The India Eternal*, Swami Vivekananda, Ramakrishna Mission Institute of Culture, Calcutta, July 2000.
3. Akshya Mukul, Upper primary school Enrolment rises by 4.8 per cent, *The Times of India*, September 14, 2013, New Delhi.
4. Subodh Verma, Sex ratio skew worsens with age: Girls lose out on food, healthcare, *The Sunday Times*, September 8; 2013, New Delhi.
5. Rajput, J.S., Curriculum needs external support for gender equality, *The Sunday Standard*, September 15, 2013, p. 8 (magazine), New Delhi.
6. Sharma, Kavita A., Empowering Women through Education: Women as Agents of Change, in Women and Development: Self, Society and Empowerment, 2012, Primus Books New Delhi, p. 75.
7. National Curriculum Framework for School Education, NCERT, 2000, New Delhi, p. 9.
8. National Curriculum Framework for School Education, 2000, NCERT, New Delhi.

9. Hemali Chhapia, Times News Service, *Times of India*, September 5, 2012.
10. Anita Nuna and Poonam Agrawal, Post Independence Perspective on Girls Education, Dialogue, *A journal of Astha Bharati* New Delhi, p. 162, Vol 12, No. 4 April-June 2011.
11. *Ibid.*, pp. 161-162.
12. Garance Franke-Ruta, Why Isn't Better Education Giving Women More Power? http://the atlantic.com/magazine/print/2013/04/miss-education/309276/
13. *The Concept of Equality*, Susmita Bhattacharya, 2002, p. 64, Writers Workshop, 162/92 Lake Gardens Calcutta 700 045.
14. *Ibid.*, p. 65.
15. Manal addressed the Oslo Freedom Forum, 8 May 2012, and delivered the speech which the *Reader's Digest*, India published in its August 2013 issue, pp. 118 to 123.

13

Human Rights, Education and the Marginalised Groups

Indian Context

The civilization and culture of India was initially moulded by great thinkers, scholars and committed individuals and institutions. The Rig-Veda, the oldest amongst these pronounces that all human beings are equal and are brothers. Every human being is expected to repay the debt he owes to the super powers and nature, to the parents and the society and to the learned and knowledgeable. In fact, these three outline the path to lead a fruitful and satisfying life. Indian society grew as a duty-based society in which every duty performed is essentially giving someone else his rights. Implications of performance of one's duty are in fact a statement of how to give others their rights. "Your Right is to perform your Duty" is the *Mantra* that, in its intent, content and import, continues to baffle people even in the present times. The global history, however, became a narration of injuries, humiliation, violence and deprivations inflicted by some on many. A situation developed in which the issue of human rights appeared extremely significant. The intention globally remains same and is best expressed in the following that forms part of the judgement of the Supreme Court of India[1]. Referring to the Fundamental Rights incorporated in the Part III of the Constitution of India, the Court said:

> "These Fundamental rights represent the basic values cherished by the people of this country since the Vedic times and they are calculated to protect the dignity of the individual and create conditions in which every human being can develop his personality to the fullest extent."

One could also say that the entire canvas of rights and duties is organically linked and is essentially an exercise in ensuring how human beings internalize the highest ideal of human life: Let all people be happy. It has not been easy to let 'all' enjoy their rights, though the concept is meant for one and all. Hence the need to pay greater attention to those often termed as marginalized groups. People living in peace suddenly become marginalized because some social or religious disturbance takes place or some natural calamity suddenly impacts them.

There could be several technical, sociological and anthropological definitions and classifications on this count. These do help in visualizing general perceptions about the people, groups and communities considered marginalized. It also helps understand why societies throw out certain section from amongst their own to the periphery! An analysis on these lines could precisely reveal the circumstances, perceptions and the factors that may have resulted in the discrimination being inflicted on a certain set of people who stand deprived of what others have confiscated, confined and declared it as applicable to 'them' only! As different civilizations evolved, flourished and several even banished, serious studies and discourses have been conducted globally on what led to the emergence and institutionalization of the practices like slavery, colonialism, apartheid, racial discrimination, gender discrimination, caste categorization and the like. Slavery was the worst of such practices and was the first of the abhorrent practices that was abolished formally. By the end of the 20th century, human beings had well understood the devastating influences of marginalizing groups and communities on one pretext or the other and resolved to eliminate these completely.

When a set of people is pushed outside a cohesive group, tribe, community or society, they stand marginalized and that essentially means depriving them of their due on par with the decision makers. The way natives and the original groups were edged out in their own countries come in this category. Similarly, the poor, deprived, deficient and disabled, elderly obviously come in this category. Excluded subgroups and minorities could also find themselves in such a position that deprives them of human dignity and discriminates on one pretext or the other. It could also be said that those reduced to powerless position, though part of the society, stand marginalized. They become less important and their importance is deliberately reduced in a planned manner. It is not easy to get an overarching definition of marginalization. The EFA Global Monitoring Report 2010: Reaching the Marginalized, however, defines marginalization as "a form of acute and persistent disadvantage rooted in underlying social inequalities". Some examples of the most disadvantaged sections of society are girls and women, hard-to-reach groups such as indigenous people and ethnic minorities, poor households, people living in informal settlements, individuals with disabilities, rural populations, nomadic tribes, those affected by armed conflict, refugees, patients of HIV and AIDS and street and working children. It is indeed ironical that women and girls are the worst sufferers on several counts though they are the backbone of every society. Apparently, in spite of several corrective measures, girls and women from practically every strata of the society still remain a marginalized group and, hence, need to be dealt with extra caution and empowering provisions.

The Current Scenario

The issue of human rights was always in the conscience of right thinking and enlightened individuals even in ancient times. In the Indian context even the folklore speaks about *Rajdharma* that must treat everyone on equal footing. Several historical instances could be cited of saints, Rishis and Kings who acknowledged human rights and the 'equality of human beings'. However, simultaneously and because of vested interests, certain practices developed that led to deprivation of human rights of the people, again, on one pretext or the other. The well known novel *Roots* by Alex Haley narrates the outcome of his research conducted studiously to trace out his parental lineage. He successfully did so and narrates the journey of his past twelve generations. It was legal to raid villages in Africa, put the captured 'slave' into dehumanizing conditions in ships, transport them to America and auction them! The rights of the Masters would make a revolting reading to the present generations. The measure and magnitude of human understanding on the equality of human beings has developed over the centuries and taken a concrete and sustainable shape only after the sufferings that the two World Wars have inflicted on humanity in the 20th century. That certain sections of the society have been deprived of their human rights for ages together caught the attention of the world community and the United Nations. The Universal Declaration of Human Rights (UDHR) of 1948 is an outcome of the same. Its Preamble says it all "whereas recognition of the inherent dignity and of equal and inalienable rights of all members of human family is the foundation of freedom, justice and peace in the world." Any act, provision, practice that disturbs the notion of equality in any manner needs to be examined and discarded. The

Constitution of India very specifically takes note of this requirement of giving everyone his/her rights and its Part III containing Articles from 12 to 35 deal with Fundamental Rights. These basically cover all that is contained in the UDHR and have extra emphasis on aspects that are particularly relevant to the Indian context.

Those legal provisions or the Constitutional mandates alone are not sufficient to root out discriminatory practices unless the society and the community internalize their adverse consequences and resolve to banish any discriminatory practices that impinge upon the universally accepted basic rights of all human beings. The framers of the Constitution of India were the veterans of the freedom struggle, men and women of courage and sacrifice. Filled with the spirit of patriotism and dedicated to social transformation of the people, they had studiously acquired a thorough understanding of the people, and India and the strength of its multifarious diversities. They also knew what had impeded the growth and advancement of the country and which of the practices had to be shunned completely. They knew the emerging aspirations of the people and what was necessary to achieve social, religious and cultural cohesion in the Indian society that could boost every conceivable diversity that could present anywhere on the planet earth! Mahatma Gandhi was deeply concerned on the shape of India and the lives of the people of India after independence, as is evident in a letter he wrote in 1922:

> "We should remember that immediately on the attainment of freedom our people are not going to secure happiness. As we become independent, all the defects of the system of elections, injustice, the tyranny of the richer classes as also the burden of running administration are bound to come upon us. People would begin to feel that during those days, there was more justice, there was better administration, there was peace, and there was honesty to a great extent among the administrators compared to the days after independence. The only benefit of independence, however, would be that we would get rid of slavery and the blot of insult resulting therefrom.
>
> "But there is hope, if education spreads throughout the country. From that people would develop from their childhood qualities of pure conduct, God fearing, love. Swaraj would give us happiness only when we attain success in the task. Otherwise India would become the abode for grave injustice and tyranny of the rulers."

This letter identifies the problem and also offers the solution; extend good quality education to one and all. Earlier Swami Vivekananda had said in the context of women that give them education and then they would solve their own problems. The breadth of vision was also evident when Mahatma gave his own Talisman to every Indian how to move towards equality of all human beings in its various aspects, and how everyone could contribute to it and thus enlarge his/her own sense of fulfilling societal obligations and derive tremendous satisfaction out of it:

> "I will give you a Talisman. Whenever you are in doubt or when the self becomes too much with you, apply the following test: 'Recall the face of the poorest and the weakest man whom you may have seen and ask yourself if the step you contemplate is going to be of any use to him. Will he gain anything by it? Will it restore him to a control over his own life and destiny? In other words, will it lead to Swaraj for the hungry and spiritually starving millions?' Then you will find your doubts and yourself melting away."

This oft-quoted statement of Gandhi Ji particularly reveals comprehensively the tasks before the resourceful and those in positions of power. They only have to translate it into actual action points in the area of their assignment. Great assistance and understanding emerges from another statement of Gandhi Ji that has eternal relevance for every human being: World has a sufficient resource to meet the needs of everyone but not the greed of anyone. Any analysis of human rights violation in India has to take note of the damage caused due to the unbridled human urge to decimate natural resources for materialistic gains without appreciating how critical it is to maintain the delicate balance between the nature and human beings. This unchecked exploitation has inflicted unaccountable miseries on the tribal population in every part of India. Though laws have been enacted, provisions made but the practices do continue, sometimes even under official patronage that comes out of inappropriate perceptions of the ideology of development. Urbanization, industrialization and modernization may have generated wealth and contributed to 'development and progress' but have simultaneously displaced, disoriented and deprived millions of rural folks and tribal people in practically every part of India of their livelihood, tradition, history and culture. It has created wider gaps and bitter discriminations.

Equality of Opportunity

Democracy, the best available model of government (and governance), comprehensive growth and inclusive progress is meaningful only when it bestows on every individual the right to equality of opportunity of access and success in moving ahead to improve the overall quality of life. Factors like caste, creed, gender, skin colour, regional location, religion, faith and any other such diversity should not be allowed to come in the way as impediments. Article 15 of the Constitution of India prohibits discrimination on 'grounds of religion, race, caste, sex or place of birth' in very clear terms: "15(1) The State shall not discriminate against any citizen on grounds only of religion, race, caste, sex, place of birth or any of them." Even those who may not have seen or read the Constitution of India are, by now, well familiar with the essence of Article 14 that deals with Equality before Law: "The State shall not deny to any person equality before the law or equal protection of laws within the territory of India." Speak to anyone from any strata of the society; the general response would be the same: that is just not happening! To avail the protection of law is just not within the reach of the poor and marginalized sections of the society. These and other similar provisions have not yet been institutionalized in the diverse social context and hence, numerous instances of frequent violations of such provisions are being reported on regular basis. The stratified stages of the system remain vulnerable to the pressures and influences of the resourceful and the powerful. There are umpteen instances of social and racial discrimination inflicted on the people from Northeast. Aware of several prevalent discriminatory practices that were unacceptable, the framers of the constitution were very specific in making clear and explicit provisions on equality and non-discrimination, as is also evident in the Article 15(2) (a): "No citizen shall, on grounds only of religion, race, caste, sex, place of birth or any of them, be subject to any disability, liability, restriction or condition with regard to (a) access to shops, public restaurants, hotels and places of public entertainment;" A large number of young boys and girls come to Delhi and other parts of India that have educational institutions of repute. They come with high hopes to fulfill their dreams and to make it good and desirable in life. For decades together, they have suffered social, emotional and physical discrimination that speaks very poorly of any civilized society. Educational institutions in Delhi, the local community and the system of governance could have responded to ameliorate unacceptable discrimination inflicted on these young persons. The failure on this front must be acknowledged sincerely. It has to be coupled with a serious resolve to give the Northeast children their due as proud Indians.

Girl Child and Women

On February 17, 2014, a Report on Women Empowerment was presented in the Parliament of India. Crimes against women are on the rise and apparently all steps put in place in this context are not showing much impact in checking these crimes. 2,28,650 was the number of crimes against women in the country in 2011 while the number was 2,13,585 in 2010. It is an increase of 7.1 per cent. The numbers in 2009 and 2008 were 2,03,804 and 1,95,856 respectively. One could cite several cases of the recent past which have shaken the conscience of the entire country. That the crime against women begins right from the stage of conception is well known. In the year 2011 the ratio of male female stood at 1000: 940. In certain states, it is lower than 900. The position of the Child sex ratio is still worse. In the age group 0-6, there are only 914 girls against 1000 boys. The issue of female foeticide and infanticide presents a very sordid social practice that unfortunately has entered the homes of highly educated and professionally trained persons. While there is visible improvements amongst the educated in respect of the age of marriage, the same could not be said of practices like dowry.

In the context of women and girls, the very concept marginalization takes a different shape. They constitute 49 per cent of the population but are still marginalized! Their sufferings are multifarious and have persisted for ages in practically every society. Lack of education and economic and social deprivation, resulting out of practices like that of untouchability, have added to their woes. Their sufferings at the hands of relatives persist, as they get educated and join work force, they suffer at the hands of their colleagues and bosses and are frequently the victims of sexual advances and exploitation. One third of the crimes of rape are committed by persons known to the victims. A very high percentage of these consist of family members and relatives. Women suffer in cases of property rights which in actual practice are heavily tilted towards the male in most parts of the country. Probably every educated women needs to think and analyze her responsibility on the continuance of dowry and female infanticide even in educated families! They could be the best guides to women and girls on their rights. Initiatives like SEWA and several efforts of NGO's and VAs have resulted in women asserting their rights. Legal provisions have also played a positive role. But in cases of women and girls, the tolerance of atrocities can just not be partial; it has to be hundred and one per cent elimination. Economic sustainability helps a great deal in women and girls getting their rights. In many cases comprehensive plans and programmes, duly coordinated, to empower women have succeeded in extricating women out of marginalization and deprivation. It has been established very firmly that the conditions women could improve only when they become the part of power structure.

Schedule Castes/Schedule Tribes and Dalits

The proceedings of the Constituent Assembly that drafted the Constitution of India would reveal highly informed, knowledgeable and in-depth discussion on reservations. The Constitution of India had taken due note of the fact how these groups remained relegated to humiliating conditions both socially and economically. Even in this case, suggestions to make reservations for longer period than ten years were not accepted in the hope that the things could change within the next decade. There have been several subsequent extensions. Gradually, the provisions of reservations have been extended to OBCs and certain other groups as well. Several of these provisions have given positive results but the dissemination of the intended upliftment and upgradation has, once again, not reached uniformly the different layers even within the specified groups. The fact of creamy layers developing and cornering the benefits had to be accepted. On the other hand, certain states have classified those who have suffered most as *Mahadalits*, the utility of which remains questionable in a system that reels under corruption and political maneuverings. Even now, the cases of prevailing untouchability are sporadically reported. The caste-based political parties have not only grown but have even assumed power in states. These trends are the obvious consequences of lack of political will. When party politics overtakes national interests, the challenge before the nation becomes much tougher. This realty must be acknowledged as it creates a great stumbling block in people getting their rights.

People are generally familiar with the miseries inflicted on the Scheduled Castes in India as the two come in contact with each other practically in every village, town and city in India. The same awareness is not that prevalent about the scheduled tribes which mostly inhabit the forest lands and areas that are rich in mineral resources. It could be the envy of any nation that over twenty thousand varieties of minerals are available in India. People generally know of the iron ores, coal, bauxite, chromites, oil reserves and others. As the explorations and the mining activities grew, innumerable sufferings were inflicted upon the traditional habitants of these places who had lived a simple life in total harmony with nature. They were displaced, despised and often treated as burdensome impediments. They were, and are, exploited by traders, government officers and the greedy corporates. While riches have been accumulated on the extraction from tribal areas by select few, the lot of the tribal people has remained rather miserable in most of the places. Often one reads about the assurances issued by government and its other bodies promising to ameliorate the lot of the tribal people. In the year 2008, a National Policy on Mining was also announced by the Government of India. Formally, one could find a list of several steps that have been taken to benefit them but the story still remains rather shoddy.

Minorities

This is probably the most sensitive of the areas that needs constant monitoring as it constitutes the backbone of social cohesion and religious amity. The Constitution takes specific note of the needs of the minorities and has made provisions accordingly, particularly under Articles 29 and 30. All those 'having a distinct language, script or culture' of their own 'shall have the right to conserve the same'. Further no educational institution could deny admission on grounds only of religion, race, caste, language or any of them. Minorities, linguistic or religious, have a right 'to establish and administer educational institutions of their choice' and further, that state shall not discriminate 'against any institution on the ground that it is under the management of a minority, whether based on religion or language.'

The issue that often comes up for deliberations and discussions pertains to socio-economic and educational backwardness of the Muslim community in India. It has been formally confirmed by the Ranganath Mishra Committee and the Sachar Committee, both of which have made several recommendations to improve the conditions. The Muslim community has now realized the importance of educating their children, both boys and girls, in modern education as well, along with the traditional religious education. Certain conservative elements within the community have not been very supportive of the 'change'. If it were not so, the Muslim community would certainly have moved ahead at a faster pace. It is the right of Muslim children to get the facilities for education in the formal system in their mother tongue. They have often been denied this right in even Muslim concentration areas. Further they are denied this right to education when the government schools are practically non-functional without adequate infrastructure facilities and teachers in sufficient numbers.

Towards Universality of Human Rights

Human rights are universal in their intent and purpose but these are violated unabashedly by those in power, and the resourceful, for their vested interests. When the colonial era was in its sunset, the UDHR was found necessary. Independence was in fact also the retortion of the nation's human rights, if considered in a boarder sense. What could be the meaning of human rights for a nation and its populace under a colonial yoke? Within the nation, independence would have been a futile exercise for the so-called 'untouchables' if the obnoxious practice was not abolished with firmness and a determined resolve. No nation could claim equality of opportunity and human dignity if the following groups are left to suffer the discrimination that has perpetuated for centuries together:

1. Women harassed at the work place, in trains, in buses, parks, educational institutions,
2. Continuance of the practice of manual scavenging,
3. Sporadic cases of the practice of discrimination based on caste system,
4. Discrimination in jobs with disabled, Dalits or minorities,
5. Practice of child labour in brick kilns, stone quarries, bangle making, hotels and *dhabas*, in homes, construction works, glass industry, diamond cutting, lock industry, hazardous professions like making of crackers, ship wrecking, carpet weaving, and several others,
6. Victims of group violence, ethnic violence or religious fundamentalism,
7. Children of nomadic tribes and their health and education
8. Widows, discarded and destitute women
9. Several other groups that may be termed marginalized but deserve immediate, prompt and effective attention.

Every day one comes across children, girls and persons who are being denied their rights and are destined to live a miserable life. Who is not familiar with the street children, beggars on the street, rag pickers and children working in hotels and restaurants on the roadside? Laws are there, Right to Education Act is there, but social consciousness has not yet risen to that level in a uniform fashion. When a newly born child is left abandoned, it raises serious doubts about the levels of civilization of the society. As urbanization grows and education expands, one comes across several contradictions in human behaviour which were not anticipated. See the fate of the children of millions of construction workers who eke out a living in extremely tough conditions. While on paper, there are provisions for crèches and schooling of their children, everyone knows that implementation beyond the legal provisions depends on the 'will' of the implementers and those supposed to monitor the provisions. Every child deserves a family which is not available to many and alternatives need to be strengthened. Then follow the rights pertaining to education, juvenile justice, sexual abuse, issues of adoption, child labour, juvenile homes, correctional institutions, and finally supportive conditions to acquire skills in getting ready to earn a livelihood. Several issues linked to juvenile justice have emerged in recent years. Like the query 'who is marginalized', questions have risen on the very definition of juveniles. Errant behaviours and criminal tendencies could trace their origin to the deficiencies in the inadequacy of congenial conditions necessary for proper upbringing and growing up. Deprivation of parental care, non-availability of water, food, shelter, clothing, medical care, play materials could contribute to juvenile delinquency which gets aggravated consequent on the societal neglect.

In Indian context, a major issue of the Human Rights is in the conflict zones. Northeast has suffered most, so has also been the case of Jammu and Kashmir. The Armed Force Special Powers Act (AFSPA) traces its origin to the Armed Force (Special Powers) Ordinance of 1942 which was the need of the British to suppress the Quit India movement. Obviously, it does not speak high of the system of governance when Northeast suffers AFSPA for over half a century. No nation can afford to let such conditions prolong for decades together. Should armed defense forces be employed in interior areas for such long durations? It does impinge upon the human rights of one and all in these areas as every individual, even if not personally harassed, does find his human dignity being compromised and his liberties curtailed!

To give human dignity to every citizen is the corner stone of the Constitution of India. That requires an assurance of security, both internal and external, from the state to individual. It translates to maintenance of peace and order. Towards this, Police is granted special and specific powers to fulfill these responsibilities. They should principally be responsible to people. Their job is to serve people and even educate them on certain counts. It is widely agreed upon that

Police personnel lack right kind of training and remain particularly deficient in handling the matters concerning human rights and human dignity.

One could attempt to recount and recall the provisions and projects to ameliorate the lot of those in the grip of poverty for decades together. These exist in abundance. Corruption eats away not only the monetary part of it but in fact the rights of the deprived. The scams and scandals are the cases of deprivation of human rights of the weakest. These impact the economy of the country, and sufferings consequent to the inadequacy of resources for welfare measures like health and education suffer considerably. And the last in the line suffer most. If there is no money for refugee camps, children suffer, their health and education suffer! The system of governance needs to gird up its loins to redress the situation. After all, black money and corruption-riches are revealing instance of depriving many of their rights and what is genuinely their due.

What can be Done?

1. Most parts of this country provide education in multi-religious classrooms. Basic human values are inculcated here, based upon the background of the family education initially received by every child. In the second decade of the 21st century, it is so easy to let the child realize that the "World is but one Family"! How each one of us is enjoying the benefits of the inventions, discoveries, innovations contributed by the thinkers, scientists, technologists and others! They were from different countries, different religions, nationalities, languages, culture but they all worked for the human beings without any distinction. Even those who suffered severe handicapped like the poet Milton, physicist Stefan Hawking have all enriched this planet and made it better place to live. Knowledge knows no boundaries and it cuts across diversity of any kind. Then how any group of human beings could deprive others and snatch away their right to equality? This spirit must reverberate in every individual and group activity, in places of action and activity, in gatherings of learners and the learned, in legislations and public interactions of those who could make a difference. It has to be approved in families and family functions.

2. Rights would flow to every marginalized group once a universal acceptance of moral, ethical and humanistic values is not only sincerely accepted in covenants and legislative Acts, but also internalized by individuals and families. Constitution of India strictly abolished untouchabilty. But law alone is not sufficient; it requires social action

and acceptance. Generational change is bringing about a positive change. Same is the case in respect of child marriages. It is education, advocacy and awareness resulting there form that shall make the difference.

3. The system of governance is more focused on authority, perks and privileges instead of treating the opportunity to serve the 'last man in the line' with zeal and enthusiasm. Why could a Police Inspector not become the most popular person amongst honest and right thinking citizens? This would apply to policy makers as well. You just cannot displace a whole set of people; hundreds of thousands of them in tribal areas to establish an industry just by offering the pittance of a cash compensation and leave them to their fate!

4. Defects of elections reduce human angle and the commerce and business or the market takes over the objectives of the resourceful, resulting in the unfathomable sufferings on the already ostracized and deprived.

5. Every nation faces economic crisis. It is more serious in countries that have not yet delineated the right mix of the 'ideology of progress'. Many nations which got rid of the colonial yoke suffered as they could not create a model of growth and development that was 'rooted to their culture and committed to progress'. It may benefit some and increase the number of billionaires in that country. In times of unbridled materialistic pursuits, it has deprived millions across the globe of their rights. Transplanted models often ruin the acceptor countries and the marginalized are the worst sufferers.

6. The access of Media is now universal. In small towns, people get supplements in newspapers early morning that deal with the district and even block and village level happenings. The watchdog role of media has helped in several ways. Certain unacceptable practices have also crept in to the system. Media can play a very useful role in generating awareness of people's rights, responsibilities and also highlight issues that the administration may like to suppress. Media, both print and electronic, has done this successfully in several cases and received public appreciation for the same.

7. Criminalization of politics is not a small factor in suppression of human rights. Once criminal elements, assisted by their muscle power, rise in the hierarchy of power, people's confidence in the democratic values erodes gradually. Several steps in this direction have been initiated by the Election Commission and the Parliament. These need to be pursued vigorously and taken to a stage when those with criminal cases against them shall not become law makers.

8. Voluntary action; VAs and NGOs; are supposed to play a vital

role in ensuring human rights to persons at the periphery, not in a position to assert, or seek justice on their own. The numbers of VAs have grown and it is indeed surprising that India now has a VA for every six hundred people! Many of these flushed with money, from internal and external inputs are suspected of deviating from their stated objectives. These need to assist in regaining their credibility.

9. Invest in elementary education universally, provide special provisions to ensure that girls; belonging to SC/ST, from tribal areas and from every section of society that is culturally and economically deprived; are given special consideration on their needs and requirements. They must get good quality education and skill orientation up to class eight if not ten.

Conclusions

Every civilization has invariably pleaded for internalization of human values, for universal brotherhood, for peace and dignity to others. It is also a fact that in numerous instances, these basic human aspects have been totally ignored and human beings have suffered unimaginable levels of subjugation, humiliation and sub-human treatment. Vast chunks of people have suffered violence for no fault of theirs. The very recognition of the need for an UDHR is an acknowledgement of the failure of human ingenuity to comprehend the essence of being a 'human being'! Further absence of comprehension to realize that good quality human life depends on two major factors: cordiality of the relationships between human beings, and realization of the human responsibility to maintain the sensitive relationship between man and the nature. In the Indian context, Mahatma Gandhi strived throughout his life that people get their rights like freedom from foreign rule, equality in social, equality of opportunity of access and success, freedom from social and cultural subjugation and practices of discrimination, and many more. Rights depend on human needs. One's needs require someone else to perform his duties. In the bracer perspective, it would mean performance of duties by one and all and only then rights would ensue. It would also require certain attitudinal changes. Many of those practising untouchability, under unacceptable notions, thought, they were performing what was divinely ordained upon them! Those suffering the custom had also accepted it as their fate! Both were wrong. They needed education and that became the duty of the enlightened ones in the society. Slavery and apartheid are other examples. Each could be examined in the context of vested interests, in the social, cultural and economic imperatives.

A civilized society is one that cares for each of its child, gives due rights to the girl child on the basis of gender equality. It prepares them, without any discrimination on any count in education and skill development. It imparts and nurtures humanistic, moral and ethical values along with the democratic values. The citizens thus internalize the concept of eternal unity of human beings irrespective of any diversity that may be cited otherwise. Nations are served well by strong and alert citizens who are equipped with education and skills needed to be partners in the process of national development and human evolution. Indian society is a duty based society and this is best expressed in the following words of Mahatma Gandhi:

> "I learned from my illiterate but wise mother that all rights to be deserved and preserved come from duty well done. Thus the very right to live accrues to us when we do the duty of the citizenship of the world. From this one Fundamental statement, perhaps it is easy enough to define duties of man and woman and correlate every right to some corresponding duty to be first performed..."

This is the most comprehensive and effective statements that could guide all those who strive to let people, particularly the marginalized groups, get their rights. That they are not getting their rights is a direct consequence of someone else usurping what genuinely belongs to the deprived. Some day, exploitation, extractions and miseries shall also vanish like the practices of slavery and apartheid. The onus to achieve it lies with the young of India.

(February 25, 2014)

Note

1 In the case of Maneka Gandhi vs. Union of India [1978(1) S.C.C. 248].

14

Policy Perceptions on Value Education

Continuity of Imperatives and Implications

The import of the fast pace of change in every sector of human endeavour is being experienced, and analysed. The implications are bring deliberated upon seriously throughout the globe. It is unavoidable and hence a necessary survival task before every one. There is no nation, which does not face problems and crises of its own. Some of these are universal. Each nation is continuously facing an economic crisis that was highlighted by the meltdown of 2008. Then there is the crisis of the ideology of progress. The magnitude may differ, but its presence is undeniable. Equally, if not more, significant is the presence of 'some sort of a moral crisis'. None of these three is new. These have persisted all along, but their nature and import have dimensions today that were never experienced before in such a measure. These are also the times of erosion of human values, declining mutual trust, decreasing religious amity and declining social harmony. Strangely enough, these are also the times when all human beings have become 'neighbours' in a global village, thanks to the advances in information and communication technology. Intensive social, cultural and religious interactions have become more convenient. There are far greater opportunities to initiate dialogues and debates and arrive at solutions that may help the cause of the poor and downtrodden, the deprived and the deficient. The world, however, is busy discussing nuclear warfare, violence, terrorism and fundamentalism. The spread of hatred, violence, destruction and devastation continues unabated in times when human beings have the wherewithal, knowledge and technology to make life better for everyone. Is it not really strange that with adequate natural resources around and sufficient human knowledge and know-how being possessed by human beings, millions and millions are hungry, undernourished and living in subhuman conditions! Gandhiji had summarised the situation rather prophetically: Nature has enough to meet every body's needs, but not anybody's greed. There could be no statement that is so powerful and comprehensive to present the significance of the need to preserve the man-nature relationship. That can happen only when very strong human bonding, and man to man relationship of love, care and trust are genuinely established. It can be preserved only when society adheres to eternal human values and ponders seriously on the spiritual objectives and goals of life.

The rich Indian tradition in spiritual quest is respectfully acknowledged the world over. Everyone looks towards India to lead the world on the path that could bring in bliss and '*Ananda*'. Millions in the affluent families and in the developed countries have experienced that materialistic accumulations do not necessarily lead to a happy and blissful life (Rama Jois 1997).

> *Vidya dadati Vinayan. Vinyadyati Patratm*
> *Patratwad Dhanamapnoti Dhanaddharmamtatahsukham.*
> (Education imparts intellectual culture;
> Intellectual culture secures capacity and stability;
> Capacity and stability enables one to secure wealth;
> Wealth so secured enables to conform to Dharma
> Which, in turn, secures happiness.)

Reverting back to the present day education system, we are all aware that India has a federal system which has inbuilt procedures to evolve and accept national policies on education. These were formulated in 1968, 1986 and 1992. The recommendations of different committees and commissions are supposed to augment policy formulation and also in some cases, help in evolving plans and programmes in implementing these policies. The Constitution of India is the supreme document, which assures "to secure to all its citizens:

> Justce, social, economic and political;
> Liberty of thought, expression, belief, faith and worship;
> Equalty of status and opportunity;
> And to promote among them all
> Fraternty assuring the dignity of the individual and the unity and integrity of the nation:"

It is one of the most profound statements on democratic and human values. These assurances, the attainment of which could lead to an ideal democracy, can be fulfilled only in a society in which "every one performs his/her ordained duty and consequently, everyone else gets his/her rights". In such a society, there ought to be no conflict of rights and duties if the people follow the real spirit and intent of the thought. How to move ahead needs to be determined and put in policy formulations and action plans regularly and continuously. Just to illustrate the point, some of the recommendations could be recalled.

The Report of the Religious education committee appointed by the Central Advisory Board of education (CABE) in 1946 had this to say:

> "The fundamental importance of the spiritual and moral values of life must be recognised in any scheme of education.
>
> Spiritual and moral teaching common to all religions should be an integral part of the curriculum and provision of facilities for instruction therein should be a responsibility of the state.
>
> An 'agreed' syllabus incorporating the spiritual and moral teachings common to all religions should be formulated.
>
> In every school there will be every day a short period for meditation before the work of the day begins. The school should be assembled for this period."

This report was available at the time of independence. The priorities and engagements were different at that stage. The spiritual and mind component was lost in the wake of expansion of education which too was an urgent need. The emphasis was reiterated in the report of the University Education Commission headed by the legendary teacher, philosopher and statesman Dr. Radhakrishnan, a great scholar of ancient Indian and western scriptures, who desired that

> "We must habituate students to right emotions; induce to them the formation of good moral, mental and physical habits. Only what one accepts willingly becomes a part of oneself. All else is a mask."
>
> "We must civilize the human heart. Education of the emotions and discipline of the will are essential parts of a sound system of education. Religion is a permeative influence, a quality of life, an elevation of purpose. Our institutions, if they are to impart religious vitality, should have simplicity and an atmosphere of consecration that permanently influences lives."

The greatness of the outstanding philosopher that Radhakrishnan was is evident in his writings on education and remains fresh and relevant as in his own times (Radhakrishnan, 1990):

> "We must develop the freshness of feeling for nature, the sensitiveness of soul to human needs. We must foster the freedom of the mind, the humanity of the heart, the integrity of the individual. Even from the nurseries, we must train human beings by unconscious influence and conscious effort to love truth, beauty and goodness. A famous Church Father in the Middle Ages, Bernard of Chairvaux, in a Latin hymn, asks. "Who will achieve universal peace?" and answers, "The disciplined, the dedicated, the pure in heart and the gentle in spirit." No machinery which the art of man can devise will work unless there is behind it the proper temper of mind. To create and maintained that temper should be the aim of education in a civilized society." (Radhakrishnan, S.)

This Education Commission, headed by Dr. Radhakrishnan, had made a very vital point, which, today unfortunately, is visible more in breach than adherence. It had stated that: "The best method of suggestion is by personal example, daily life and work and books read from day to day." It immediately reminds one of what Gandhiji had said: 'my life is my message'. What the young persons of today see around them is a far cry from what should be presented before them by the society. The Mudaliar Commission (1952-53), once again, puts these concepts in the following words:

> "If a democracy like ours is to survive-a democracy which harbours so many faiths, races and communities—education must cultivate in our youth and openness of mind and largeness of heart which would make them capable of entertaining and blending in to a harmonious pattern differences in ideas and behvaiour. It is possible for every school to do so, not only through the proper presentation of various school subjects, particularly the humanities and social sciences, but also by utilising the resources and opportunities provided by the fact that its students are drawn from different castes, creeds and classes. If they can first learn to live pleasantly and peacefully in the small community of the school; this training will enable them to do so later in the larger community outside."

India had several leaders after independence who enjoyed public adulation and admiration that probably can hardly be visualised by the young generation of today, which is observing the decline of regard for political leadership on a daily basis. Even during the first decade after independence, value decline was visible in public life. It had set in immediately after the elected representatives had begun to enjoy the luxury of being in 'office' and unimaginable perks and 'hidden possible benefits' that could be theirs just for asking! Such a presence at that stage was miniscule only but the need to nip it in the initial stages was certainly obvious. Education and its potential in creating a value-based society were perceived as the best way to achieve the objective. The Committee on Religious and Moral Instruction under the Chairmanship of Sri Prakasa submitted a report in 1960. It dealt with the issue in great detail. It emphasised on 'deliberate inculcation of moral and spiritual values from the earliest years of our lives' to preserve the 'old bonds' that kept men together in an increasingly worsening situation and recommended:

> "We have to lay special stress on the teaching of moral and spiritual values. Moral values particularly refer to conduct of man towards man in the various situations in which human beings come together—in home, in social and economic fields, and in the life of outside world generally. It is essential that from the earliest childhood, moral values should be inculcated in us. We have to influence the home first. We fear that our homes are not what they ought to be. Habits, both of mind and body, formed in the earlier years at home persist, and influence our lives afterwards."
>
> "Just as moral values affect the relations between man and man, so do spiritual values in his relation with himself. The individual is not only a body; he is also a soul. He does not live by bread alone; he wants inner peace and happiness. If he loses all spiritual values, he loses the possibility of being at peace with himself. It is necessary to have some faith in things beyond flesh, some identification with a purpose greater than oneself, in order to achieve this mental equilibrium."

This report specifically refers to the 'realisation of social obligations' and wants the virtues to 'devote ourselves to the welfare of others' to be inculcated in the early years. Such virtues can be a consequence of an appreciation of moral and spiritual values, which must be taken up in schools and colleges. It says emphatically: 'A nation that deprives itself of these, and only concentrates on material concerns—however important they may be—would be like a body without a soul.' These days thousands of farmers are committing suicides, millions are being uprooted and displaced to give their land to the corporate houses for development purposes, over 40 per cent children are malnourished and thirty crores of Indians admittedly live below the poverty line and source of survival. One wonders how long India shall continue to neglect the stipulations on values and ethics, repeatedly emphasised by those who had predicted the shape of things based on their experience, knowledge and sacrifice. In short, these are the times when 'me, my family' has overtaken the traditional concern for others, the importance of '*Sewa*', and concern for all, including Nature. The Sri Prakasa report covers every aspect that would help young persons learn their duties to self, society, neighbours and other human beings and animals. It also refers to the importance of good manners and promoting the virtues of reverence and courtesy, which are 'badly needed in the society'. In its stage-wise recommendations it wants simple and interesting stories about the lives and teachings of prophets, saints and religious leaders to be included in the syllabus for language teaching. It however, clearly states that "Dogmas and rituals of religion should be excluded from moral instruction for which two periods per week should be set aside. Then it makes probably its most important recommendation for the secondary stage, the relevance of which deserves to be examined not only in the Indian context, but also globally:

> "Secondary stage...The essential teachings of the great world religions should be studied as part of the curriculum pertaining to social studies and history. Simple texts and stories concerning different religions may be included in the teaching of languages and general reading."

India suffered partition and had experienced the brutal pain of communalism at the time of independence. Its leaders were, naturally, concerned to revitalise the forces of communal harmony and social cohesion. A committee on Emotional Integration submitted its Report in 1961 the following recommendation of which deserves to be noted:

> "Although it is not possible to provide religious education as a part of curriculum for schools in a secular state, education will be incomplete if students are not helped to appreciate the spiritual values which the various religions represent to the people. Talks, open to all, on the teaching of various religions by able and competent persons may be arranged in schools."

Whatever has been described above clearly indicates the unease in the relationship between secularism and religions in the context of teaching and learning in schools. It clearly emerges that no commission or committee has recommended religious education being imparted in schools. However, it also emerges equally prominently that practically each one has supported the inculcation of values and awareness about the basics of all religions being imparted in schools to the children as means to help them imbibe values moral and ethical and also to inculcate the value to serve others. The issue was taken up for a profound analysis and in-depth deliberation by the Education Commission (1964-66), which submitted its monumental Report, entitled "*Education and National Development*", which resulted in the formulation of the National Policy on Education of 1968. The Commission, (Ministry of Education; 1966) also known as Kothari Commission, had this to say:

> "One has to make a distinction between 'religious education' and 'education about religions'. The former is largely concerned with the teaching of the tenets and practices of a particular religion, generally in the form in which the religious group envisages them, whereas the latter is a study of religions and religious thought from a broad point of view—the eternal quest for the spirit. It would not be practicable for a secular state with many religions to provide education in any one religion. It is, however, necessary for a multi religious democratic state to promote a tolerant study of all religions so that its citizens can understand each other better and live amicably together. We suggest that a syllabus giving well-chosen information about each of the major religions should be included as a part of the course in citizenship or as a part of general education to be introduced in schools and colleges up to first degree. It should highlight the fundamental similarities in the great religions of the world and emphasis they place on cultivation of certain broadly comparable moral and spiritual values. It would be a great advantage to have a common course on this subject in all parts of the country and common textbooks should be prepared at the national level by competent and suitable experts on each religion. When these courses have been prepared, it would be worthwhile to have these scrutinised by a small committee of eminent persons belonging to different religions to ensure that nothing is included in them to which any religious group could take legitimate objection."

The above contentions reverberate in the Ramamurti Committee Report of 1990 in the following words:

> "Back in 1937, the Zakir Husain Committee, appointed by the All India National Education Conference, and presided over by Mahatma Gandhi, held up the ideal of development of a citizenship in an organised, civilised, democratic and cooperative community and recommended that a course in history in civics and in current events, combined with a reverential study of the different religions of the world, showing how in essence they meet in perfect harmony, should be introduced."

The Committee was also clear about the place of values in education:

> "The social dimension of education necessitates that education be essentially value-based...Imparting of value education should be an integral part of the entire educational process and school climate, as distinct from dissemination of values through special classes or lectures in morality or through mechanical textbook based learning methods."

The essence of the approach and thinking on value education comes out clearly in some of the selected extracts given above. This list could be expanded but the essence of the recommendation would largely remain the same. A core group on Value Orientation of Education was set up in 1992 and it gave its views on the main problem that has come in the way of implementation of value education in the country. This Report make this abundantly clear:

> "The term 'secularism' in the Indian constitution is intended only to secure that no discrimination is practised by the State against any sect on grounds of religion or faith and that people, belonging to all religious persuasions, are enabled to enjoy equal freedom in the matter of practising and propagating their religion. In the name of 'secularism', in spite of the richest cultural and spiritual heritage, the youth of this country have been denied even the barest minimum opportunity to imbibe simple basic values by imposing a taboo on all moral and spiritual teachings in educational institutions. Secularism means equal respect for all religions. Secularism within the Indian context means comprehensiveness in which all religions receive equal protection, treatment and respect. It also encourages us to approach everything, whether

> material or spiritual, with a sense of sacredness. Indian secularism encourages unity of all religions and faiths and promotion of human values, which are universal."

Education in the New Millennium

The 1986 National Policy on Education, revised in 1992 (NPE 1986/92) very clearly noted 'the growing concern over the erosion of essential values and an increasing cynicism in society'. As expected, it emphasised the need for the curricular changes to make education 'a forceful tool for the cultivation of social and moral values'. It went ahead to plead further: "In our culturally plural society, education should foster universal and eternal values, oriented towards the unity and integration of our people. Such value education should help eliminate obscurantism, religious fanaticism, violence, superstition and fatalism." This was the need of the times and also a chance to link education to the ethos, heritage and culture, the essential ingredients to perceive a model of national education. The essential spirit of the policy recommendation found a forceful endorsement in the 86th Report of the Department-Related parliamentary Standing Committee for the Ministry of Human Resources Development. This was a report on Value education and was submitted to both the Houses of Parliament of India on February 26, 1999. As per the standard practice, it was passed on to the concerned ministry for implementation with the authority of the Parliament of India behind it.

Two of the recommendations pertained to values and religions in very clear terms. It identified Truth (*Sathya*), Righteous Conduct (*Dharma*), Peace (*Shanti*), Love (*Prema*) and Non-violence (*Ahimsa*) as the universal values which could become the foundations of education programmes. The Committee also emphasised that, in view of the diversities of all perceptible types in the country, young persons must imbibe national values. They should be familiar with the history of India's freedom struggle, cultural heritage, constitutional obligations and the features comprising our national identity. The most prominent and 'bold' recommendation was concerning religions. The Committee went ahead with the following:

> "Another aspect that must be given some thought is religion, which is the most misused and misunderstood concept. The process of making the students acquainted with the basics of all religions, the values inherent therein and also a comparative study of philosophy of all religions should begin

> at the middle stage in schools and continue up to the university level. Students have to be made aware that that the basic concept behind every religion is common, only the practice differ. Even if there are differences of opinion in certain areas, people have to learn to coexist and carry no hatred against any religion."

The process of the renewal of the school curriculum completed in the year 2000 (NCFSE, 2000) seriously considered the above-mentioned recommendations as an expression of the continuity of India's heritage of acceptance of diversity, which emanated out of the ancient Indian storehouse of scholarship knowledge and wisdom. In a world torn asunder practically every day due to religious fanaticism and terrorism, the value of non-aggression has to become the key concept spread over the entire process of teaching and learning. Whatever be the other reasons and causes, the two nation theory that led to the bleeding partition of India was certainly an outcome of lack of mutual trust and absence of true understanding amongst the two major communities of India divided on religious lines. If only the human values common to both the religions had been internalised across the board, the politicians would not have been allowed to play that disastrous game. No further justification would be needed in the current times to strive hard to let all the young persons know the basics of all the religions and develop mutual respect. This alone can lead to re-establishing the much needed social cordiality and religious harmony in India. This could be achieved only when the citizens are prepared with an attitude to not only strive to do 'good,' but also remain ever alert to work and suffer for 'good'. Their endeavour must always aim to achieve the most sought after: *Sathyam, Shivam and Sundaram;* Truth, Goodness and Beauty. Help comes in achieving this attitudinal transformation from the inheritance of history, culture and customs. Help comes from the inherited traditions, scriptures, epics and literature the value of which, despite planned efforts to demolish it, is universally recognised and realised. Such an education cannot 'be organised except on a 'religious basis'. While pleading for such an education, C. Rajagoplachari (1978) wrote: "To misunderstand the 'secularity' to which people think we are pledged, and to treat religion as untouchable is one of the many unfortunate follies our government has fallen into. It is not impossible, or even very difficult, to deal with and include in a nation-wide effort to make men truly religious, each in the way shown by his or her own religion, and add to it a spirit of understanding and respect for other people's religion and way of life." In continuation, this outstanding statesman-cum-scholar gives an advice in terms a basic principle: "The conclusion of the matter as I see it is that parliamentary democracy will be a waste of expense and produce no good unless this true education of the people is undertaken by a general consensus among all statesmen and politicians." (Rajagoplachari, C., *Rescue Democracy from Money Power*, Bhartiya Vidya Bhavan, Bombay, 1978). The significance of such futuristic perceptions is being realised by men and women of eminence and achievement more and more as the time passersby; one witnesses greater deterioration in adherence to human values. N.R. Narayana Murthy; the father of Infosys and icon of the young of India at this juncture is very clear on values, secularism and religion (Narayana Murthy, 2009):

> "It is important to accept and appreciate that India is a pluralistic society. Historically, India has suffered due to poor teamwork. Good teamwork requires leveraging the strength of diversity in our thoughts and beliefs. To realise this strength, we have to demonstrate respect and tolerance towards the opinion and beliefs of others, while holding onto the good things in us..... For me secularism is about respecting every religion and appreciating the positive aspects of each faith. ... Every religion teaches man to be good and have its positive aspects; be it the quest for knowledge of the Hinduism, the tolerance of Sikhism, the sacrifice embodied by Christianity, the brotherhood of Islam or the compassion of Buddhism."

The world of today is sick as it suffers from violence, bloodshed, terrorism, distrust and bigotry practically everywhere and at every moment. The world of tomorrow needs a healing touch and a curative balm to put it back on the health track. The quintessence of ancient Indian culture has faced all possible onslaughts over the ages but has survived as it accepts unbreakable unity and the universality of all human beings. In terms of values, it can be put in five inter-related ideals that find consistent mention in practically all the epics and scriptures that Ancient Indian seekers of the ultimate truth have presented to the humanity. Conflicts, strife, wars, battles and violence occur at various intervals, mostly due to ignorance, ego and misinterpretations. The five ideals that survive eternally are: Truth (*Sathya*), *Dharma* (Righteous conduct), Peace (*Shanti*), Love (*Prema*) and Nonviolence (*Ahimsa*). Those who internalise these will find equal substance in every religion and faith, an essential requirement for the very survival of the planet earth and the existence of humanity on it.

It is a great irony of the present times that religions, which actually should be leading towards social cohesion and religious harmony, are being used to achieve just the opposite. India's age-old wisdom very clearly predicts the way out: "*Samavaya eva Sadhuh*—Concord alone is correct and proper". This wisdom was not confined only for discourses and discussions amongst the learned scholars but was put to practice as a way of life at each stage. Dr. Radhakrishnan and Swami Ranganathananda have referred in their academic contributions to a quotation from the book: "Murray's Discoveries and Travels in Asia; (Vol. 2, p. 20). It describes one of the many historical events that highlight the essence of Indian culture and conduct as testified by foreign visitors and emissaries. This one refers to Abdul Razak who came to India as the Envoy from the Court of Persia to Indian states:

> "The people (of Calicut) are infidels; consequently, I consider myself in an enemy's country, as the Mohammedans consider everyone who has not received the Koran. Yet, I admit that I meet with perfect toleration, and even favour; we have two mosques and are allowed to pray in public".

Once it is accepted that there is a divine spark and limitless potential in every individual irrespective of caste, colour, creed or religion, there shall be no place for aggression, fundamentalism and, hence, violence and terrorism. The human ingenuity would be in a position to devote itself with greater commitment and devotion to further its quest for the search of truth in order to make life better for the fellow human beings. A.P.J. Abdul Kalam (Abdul Kalam; 2006) recalls this aspect of the Indian culture in a universally comprehensible manner. He quoted the advice Gandhiji received early in his life from his from his mother: "Son, in your entire life if you can save or better someone's life, your birth as a human being and your life is a success. You have the blessings of the Almighty." It enlightens the path in search of solutions to the problems of humanity.

The weakening of morals and ethics, the growing impact of erosion of values all around, materialistic pursuits of the powerful and the icons, ever-expanding consumerism, growing violence and bigotry, all taken together, clearly point out that education should aim at character building. Value internalisation and establishing a symphony of 'self, society and nature' is the only possible alternative available for human survival on the planet earth.

References

Government of India, 1962, The Report of the University Education Commission (December 1948–August 1949), Volume I, New Delhi, Ministry of Education.

Abdul Kalam, A.P.J., *What can I give You*, 2006, Foundation for Unity of Religions and Enlightened Citizenship, New Delhi.

Government of India, National Policy on Education, 1986/92, Ministry of Human Resources Development, 1992, New Delhi.

Government of India, 1992, Report of Core Group on Value Orientation of Education, New Delhi.

Government of India, Value Education, 1999, Report of the Standing Committee of Parliament for the Ministry of Human Resources Development, Rajya Sabha Secretariat, New Delhi.

Ministry of Education, 1966, Education and National Development—Report of the Education Commission (Kothari Commission), 1966, Ministry of Education, Government of India, New Delhi.

National Curriculum Framework for School Education (NCFSE), 2000, National Council for Educational Research and Training (NCERT), New Delhi.

Radhakrishnan, S., *Radhakrishnan Reader: An Anthology*, 1990 (Third edition); p. 510, Bhartiya Vidya Bhavan; Bombay.

Rajagoplachari, C., *Rescue Democracy from Money Power*, Bhartiya Vidya Bhavan, Bombay, 1978).

Rama Jois, M., Human Rights and Indian Values, 1997, National Council for Teacher Education, New Delhi, p. 25.

Ramamurthy *et al.*, Report of the Committee for Review of National Policy of Education, 1986.

UNESCO, Learning: The Treasure Within, 1996, Report to the UNESCO of the International Commission on Education for the Twenty-First Century, UNESCO Publishing, Paris.

Narayana Murthy, N.R., *A Better India a Better World*, 2009, Penguin Books India; p. 43.

English Book 1 Additional chapters Nov. 2014.

15

Role of Education in Peace Process

Combating Terrorism through Creation of Awareness and Educating People

"I learned from my illiterate, but wise, mother that all rights to be deserved and preserved come from duty well done. Thus the very right to live accrues to us when we do the duty of citizenship of the world. From this one fundamental statement, perhaps it is easy enough to define duties of man and women and correlate every right to some corresponding duty to be first performed."

—*Mahatma Gandhi*

The progress and development of the human race on earth has been a continuous and evolving process that always moves ahead. During the last couple of centuries, there has been so much to be happy about: end of slavery, rejection of apartheid, death of colonialism, great scientific discoveries including man's landing on the moon, deep human access into the secrets of nature. This list can indeed be very long. Systems of governance also changed with times. Democracy was visualised as the best alternative that would bring in dignity, self-respect and equality of opportunity even to the most deprived, exploited and marginalised in society. Though a global phenomenon, these aspirations are comprehensively included in the Preamble to the Constitution of India which promises to secure to all its citizens "Justice; social, economic and political; Liberty of thought, expression, belief, faith and worship; Equalty of status and of opportunity; and to promote amongst them all Fraternity assuring the dignity of the individual and the unity and integrity of the nation". There could hardly be any statement that best summarised the hopes and expectations of the thinkers and intellectuals, on one hand, and of the suffering masses, on the other. The Constitution of India has explicit provisions on fundamental rights but had nothing initially on the fundamental duties. It was drafted and finalised by persons of exceptional calibre. They had followed noble ideals to liberate the country, promote national integration and communal harmony, secularism and the preservation of the rich culture and heritage of India. They presumed these as basic values initially nurtured by the family, tradition and the community. These were to be internalised by every citizen. In fact, they found the fundamental duties as an integral part of life. It was presumed that these were being covered under the very Preamble of the Constitution. However, the trends and practices that followed in the subsequent two-three decades clearly established the need for an explicit amendment in the Constitution of India in 1976 to include fundamental duties. It has to be viewed as a serious initiative to augment the struggle for giving human rights to each and every individual, irrespective of his/her position in the socio-economic and cultural hierarchy. It is clear from the contents of Article 51 (A):

It shall be the duty of every citizen of India:

(a) to abide by the Constitution and respect its ideals and institutions, the National Flag and the National Anthem;
(b) to cherish and follow the noble ideals which inspired our national struggle for freedom;
(c) to uphold and protect the sovereignty, unity and integrity of India;
(d) to defend the country and render national service when called upon to do so;
(e) to promote harmony and the spirit of common brotherhood amongst all the people of India transcending religious, linguistic and regional or sectional diversities; to renounce practices derogatory to the dignity of women;
(f) to value and preserve the rich heritage of our composite culture;
(g) to protect and improve the natural environment including forests, lakes, rivers and wild life, and to have compassion for living creatures;
(h) to develop the scientific temper, humanism and the spirit of inquiry and reform;
(i) to safeguard public property and to abjure violence;
(j) to strive towards excellence in all spheres of individual and

collective activity so that the nation constantly rises to higher levels of endeavour and achievement.

On 12th December 2002 the following was added after (j) under 86th constitution amendment

(k) who is a parent or guardian to provide opportunities for education to his child or, as the case may be, ward between the age of six and fourteen years.

A perusal of these would, once again, establish the organic relationship between fundamental rights and fundamental duties. It is well established that the traditional Indian society is duty and sacrifice oriented. The joint family system, the village level cohesion and community fellowship are some of the traditional examples of the duty-orientation of Indian society that could be seen in every nook and corner of the country. It is also a fact that Indian society, because of various factors and reasons, got embroiled in practices that created segregations of various types. What followed as a consequence were exploitation, neglect and humiliation of a very large section of the society. The caste system deprived generations after generations of their basic human rights for ages. The Constitution took note of the rights of such groups and made provisions for abolition of abhorrent practices and for prevention of exploitative practices and traditions. It also made clear and effective provisions for positive discriminations to empower groups of people to assert their rights and avail of the same.

In the beginning of 21st century, the global village is a universally insecure habitation. Think of 9/11, and one could enlist umpteen instances of insane human killings. While the world was worrying about the ever-increasing nuclear weaponry that could destroy the planet several times, fundamentalism and terrorism have opened another threat of a disastrous magnitude. Can anyone ignore the gross violations of human rights that are taking place in countries like Iraq, Afghanistan, Pakistan, Nepal, Bosnia, Palestine and several other countries? It is violence, and its retaliation by state and external agencies has deprived millions of their basic human rights. The violence by Naxalites that has already spread to over one-third of all the districts of India is no small threat in the realm of terrorism.

The world needs a culture of peace. Its multi-dimensionality was illustrated by Dr. Martin Luther King Jr, when he said "Peace is not only the absence of war but the presence of justice and brotherhood". The present position is that no family, no nation can live in peace unless the neighbouring families and other nations of the worlds are also living in peace. This is an era of connectivity and, hence, mutual dependence. Indian thought is very clear on how it can be achieved—no happiness, joy of life or peaceful existence can be enjoyed unless one achieves 'peace within'! The need to internalise the concepts of Ahimsa, universal brotherhood, compassion, service to others are generally lost in an environment of visible world-wide erosion of social and moral values in the present context. The transgression of the eternal human values can happen only at the cost of the rights of others or at the cost of damaging the man-nature relationship. Violence is bound to be the outcome in some form or the other. A climate of peace can be created only when it is accepted as a shared agenda and all concerned strive to achieve it.

The seeds of moral orientations are sown initially at home by the parents, family and the immediate community. Gradually the children begin to observe 'how far others are practising what they preach to them'! The schools come next. Here again, the practices and the models that teachers put before them have a greater impact than what is 'taught' to them on a routine basis on 'how to become good individuals and citizens'! As they grow up, they become keen observers of the 'degeneration of social and moral values in society' all around and particularly amongst those who were supposed to be role models or even icons for them (O.S. Dewal, 2008). Such a background becomes conducive to get attracted towards a value-less conduct and young persons could easily fall prey to vested interests that thrive on exploitation of the innocent and gullible and indulge in violence and terrorism of a varied nature. These are also the main causes of violence that one faces and witnesses in everyday life. A peace-loving society, that is living a value based community life and is ever alert to the changes that take place all around as a rule of nature, shall never produce violence and hence could be free from fear. Even that has limitations. No society can remain in peace in isolation to others! It is a global village in which all are neighbours; whether they like it or not. Consequently, everyone has to learn to be 'neighbourly' to everyone else. If that be so, no transgression of human rights would be possible.

What are the major factors that a common person comprehends about the expanding dread of terrorism? What makes young boys be attracted by the disruptive agenda of the terrorists? How are they able to recruit them and prepare them to become suicide bombers? How do they generate and spread communal frenzy and create violence of the most obnoxious variety? While the scholarly and the researcher are obviously busy analysing the socio-economic, ethnic and cultural contributing factors, for the common person it is merely "exploitation of ignorance by the crafty, wily and the value-deprived". Terrorism is unscrupulous exploitation of religion, poverty and ignorance. It shall continue to flourish as long as ignorance and illiteracy cloud reason, logic and human values. Terrorism is being related to religions which is the harrowing trend and has already caused irreparable damage to the thread of social harmony and religious amity in multi-religious countries. India has suffered terrorism of various varieties for decades together. It comes both from religious fundamentalists and also from the blind followers of certain discredited ideological moorings; the Naxalites. They mostly net the ignorant, deprived and socially neglected. Of course, their leadership has the support of conservative clergy and certain set of intellectuals still adhering to failed ideological loyalties. Misinterpretations of religious practices and principles by the insecure clergy influence the gullible easily. They do not hesitate to convert young boys in their early teens as human bombs. The systemic exploitation of natural resources by vested interests supported by the corrupt in the state systems has consistently contributed to generating conducive climate for Naxalites and Maoists.

Education, Tensions and Sins

What facilitates the access of the terrorists to young persons and the masses? It is their poverty, unemployment, the vice-like grip of the clergy and, above all, their ignorance and inability to see through the design of the vested interests. When it comes to ignorance, education must come in full force in the 21st century. It should have the boldness to include in its curriculum the essence of secularism which is the prime requisite for "learning to live together and work together"! In a secular society, interpretations of secularism need to present all the sensitivity it deserves in pluralistic society. Religions are a reality. Indian society is religious and, in no way, it comes in conflict with the secular fabric of the Indian state being secular. Those who understand Indian tradition and culture would accept it unhesitatingly that a truly religious person would necessarily be secular. Only such a person would evolve to see goodness in all religions. He would be most suited to highlight the eternal commonalities of all religions and the singularity of the highest objective of all religions. Such a person would be in peace with others as he would be in peace with himself. This comes out very interestingly in one of the conversations that Gandhiji had with Sir E. Stanley Jones. (Gangrade, 2001)

> **Stanley Jones**: You are the leading Hindu of India. What would you say to me as a Christian, as to what Christians should do to make Christianity is more naturalised in India—not a foreign thing, identified with a foreign government and a foreign civilization, but a part of the national life of India and contribute its power to India's uplift and moral change.
> **M.K. Gandhi**: First, I would suggest that all of you Christians, missionaries must begin to live like Jesus Christ,
> Second, that you practice your religion without adulterating it or toning it down,
> Third, that you emphasise love and make it your working force, for love is central in Christianity,
> Fourth, that you study the non-Christian religions more sympathetically to find out the good that is in them to have a more sympathetic approach towards people.

Obviously, this analysis is universally applicable to all the adherents of their respective religions. It would benefit everyone who, following these four, gets converted to his/her own religion! When that happens, there is no scope left for any ill-will against neither any religion nor any individual. In the absence of ill-will, biases and prejudices, the vacant space has to be, naturally, occupied with love, brotherhood and understanding.

The present position is that terrorism and fundamentalism are often being related to one or the other religions. Basically, it is also being understood that a person becomes a religious fanatic or a fundamentalist only because his upbringing deprives him of the right education and the true realities of his/her own religion. This could be because of ignorance of the same in the immediate environment, a planned strategy by the set of clerics to sustain their hegemony that survives on ignorance, a well thought of strategy to indoctrinate young boys and girls in the initial tender and sensitive years. Examples of all these categories are before the nations of the world. Violence in Sri Lanka, Iraq, Bosnia, and Naxal-infested districts of India has certainly different motivational factors behind it. It can, however, be safely stated that essentially it all arises due to the lack of education in eternal human values, proper understanding of ones own traditions, practices and cultures and, of course, falling prey to vested interests.

Why has there been such an erosion of human values. The world has become an insecure place for practically everyone, even the mightiest as was evidenced by 9/11. When developing nations should be taking care of their hungry and malnourished, they are spending huge amounts on security and defence preparedness! In certain cases, internal security requires more attention than the external threat. Where has the world faltered? While annihilating colonialism, apartheid and making sincere efforts to do away with caste and racial discriminations, did the global leadership ignore certain basic essentials in the process of development and growth? Has the content and process of education been deficient on crucial counts to bring the world to the tensions that it is suffering at this stage? These tensions have been identified in the Report to UNESCO of the International Commission on Education for the Twenty-First Century entitled "Learning: The Treasure Within" (UNESCO, 1996).

- The tension between the global and the local
- The tension between the universal and the individual
- The tension between tradition and modernity
- The tension between long-term and short term considerations
- The Tension between the need for competition and concern for equality
- The tension between extraordinary expansion of knowledge and human being's capacity to assimilate
- The tension between the spiritual and the material

The above were identified in 1996 and have definitely a much higher measure of magnitude at the present juncture than any evidence of diminishing of the tensions even in a single category. Examine these in the light of what Gandhi had written in 1925, on what he called the seven sins:

- Politics without principles
- Pleasure without conscience
- Commerce without ethics
- Knowledge without character
- Science without humanity
- Wealth without work
- Worship without sacrifice

If the education process was geared to take note of the seven sins that Gandhiji had identified much earlier, the world today would not have been pitted to face with the seven tensions. These are timeless issues and concerns. These persist because of certain well known and well understood inherent weaknesses of human kind that are, once again, universal and independent of region, caste, creed or religion. If one sits to examine the curriculum of universal elementary education, is it possible to ignore the fact that the tensions and sins mentioned above must constitute the core of essential human concerns in the globalised world. As long the seven sins continued to be committed, the seven tensions shall continue to rise in the same proportion. The first major step is to scrutinise the pace of universal and eternal human values in the comprehensive curriculum of teaching and learning in schools and institutions. Now, when the source of learning is no more mainly confined to the family and the schools, several other sources would also come into the picture. Media, both electronic and print, has totally absolved itself of social obligations and is insensitive even to the requirements of children. In an examination-oriented system, the situation becomes more acute as little time is made available in schools and other institutions to inculcate and nurture values, ethics and morals. This deserves a detailed analysis and consideration.

Delivering the Convocation Address at the Mysore University on December 16, 1962 Professor D.S. Kothari remarked: "The mention of atomic age immediately calls to our minds the unprecedented peril, both in depth and extent, which faces mankind in the shape of a possible misuse, deliberate or accidental, of nuclear knowledge. Indeed, nothing less than civilisation and human survival are at stake. If this simple fact is not widely apparent and forcefully realised as it ought to be, it is largely because there has not been enough serious and sustained effort to inform us about it." (Kothari, 2000). At that stage, eminent scientists were concerned about the dreaded possibility of the extinction of human species as a consequence of struggles for political authority and the unquenchable urge for economic hegemony. The Cuban crisis was fresh in the minds of people when professor Kothari delivered the Convocation Address in Gujarat in which he went on to elaborate: "The balance of terror has to be replaced by common-links of cooperation and common endeavour in the pursuit of high ideals and goals. The present unfortunate and tragic situation is essentially a reflection of the widening gap between rapidly expanding scientific and technological knowledge, on one hand, and political wisdom, statesmanship and ethical values, on the other. Science and spirituality or 'atom' and non-violence are not in balance. It is the imbalance that mankind must seek to redress."

And this imbalance, perceived over half a century ago, is now a dreadful reality. Fundamentalism and terrorism were not so frequently seen in usage at that stage but the decline in value systems had already begun to show its ugly face. Never before mankind had so much of knowledge and wisdom to understand, explore and utilise for its own benefit the secrets of nature. Never before were conditions so conducive for making contacts, continuing dialogues and rendering humanitarian help at any point of the globe as is available to mankind today. All this has been possible through the sustained endeavour that humankind had put in exploring the forces of natures for several millennia. It is another fact that never before there was so much hunger, poverty, violence and bigotry as of today. Never before, fundamentalism was such a serious threat as of today! And it is so in spite of the fact that now it is possible that every child could be given the level of nourishment needed, the global distribution system can be put to practice. But this is not happening. The basic fundamental right of every human being born on planet earth to get food, clothing and shelter is being denied by those who are supposed to be the trustees of the future generations. In one of the *hadith*, the Prophet said, "The son of Adam has basic rights on three things, a house to live in, a piece of cloth to cover his body, a loaf of bread and water." (Akbar, 2009). One could quote such prescriptions from every civilization and every religion. That this knowledge and awareness has remained a sealed book for all these years is one contributing factor for the suffering of the millions even in 21st century. One must reflect back on the last century and visualise the glorious efforts to expand education to everyone; to enable them to know what is their due and how they are not only being deprived of their share but in the process are also being exploited, humiliated and denied the right of education, knowledge and learning. Masses were never allowed to have access to education and leaning. In some places, it was caste system, elsewhere the colour of the skin or even royal claims to divinity and the dictates that flowed from the exalted ones! The contemporary times were well articulated by Dr. Radhakrishnan: "If there is any phenomenon which is characteristic of our times, it is mingling of people, races, culture and religions. Never before has such a meeting taken place in the history of our world" (Radhakrishnan, 1968). In such an intermingling, there can be no place for prejudices based on ethnicity, religion, race or any other count. The situation once again highlights the role of education, educational institutions and the process of teaching and learning.

In Schools and Colleges

It is the schools and colleges in countries like India where practically every classroom is a multi-religious congregation and the same applies to the set of teachers in any particular establishment. Essentially the teacher, and more particularly the teacher trainer, could play a critical role in imparting education that would prepare, "soldiers of communal harmony and human values".

The 1986 National Policy on Education, revised in 1992 (NPE 1986/92) very clearly noted 'the growing concern over the erosion of essential values and an increasing cynicism in the society'. As expected it emphasised the need for the curricular changes to make education 'a forceful tool for the cultivation of social and moral values'. It went ahead to plead further: "In our culturally plural society, education should foster universal and eternal values, oriented towards the unity and integration of our people. Such value education should help eliminate obscurantism, religious fanaticism, violence, superstition and fatalism." The National Council for Teacher Education (NCTE) developed a curriculum framework for teacher education in 1998 (NCTE, 1998) and summarised the essence of the tasks before the teacher education institutions in the following words:

> "Increasing delinquency, violence, terrorism and fissiparous tendencies and use of inappropriate means to get one's ends served are threats to national integration and social cohesion. Democracy, violence and terrorism cannot coexist. Education has to develop a peace loving personality and the programme of teacher education has to contribute in this regard."

This was the need of the times and also a chance to link education to Indian ethos, values, heritage and culture, the essential ingredient to perceive a model of national education. The essential spirit of the policy recommendation found a forceful endorsement in the 86th Report of the Department-Related parliamentary Standing Committee for the Ministry of Human Resources Development (Value Education, 1999). This was a report on Value education and was submitted to both the Houses of Parliament of India on February 26, 1999. As per the standard practice it was passed on to the concerned ministry for implementation with the authority of the Parliament of India behind it.

Two of the recommendations pertained to values and religions in very clear terms. It identified Truth (*Sathya*), Righteous Conduct (*Dharma*), Peace (*Shanti*), Love (*Prema)* and Non-violence (*Ahimsa)* as universal values which could become the foundations of education programmes. The Committee also emphasised that in view of the diversities of all perceptible types in the country, young persons must imbibe national values. They should be familiar with the history of India's freedom struggle, cultural heritage, constitutional obligations and the features comprising our national identity. The most prominent and 'bold' recommendation was concerning religions. The Committee went ahead with the following:

> "Another aspect that must be given some thought is religion, which is the most misused and misunderstood concept. The process of making the students acquainted with the basics of all religions, the values inherent therein and also a comparative study of philosophy of all religions should begin at the middle stage in schools and continue up to the university level. Students have to be made aware that that the basic concept behind every religion is common, only the practices differ. Even if there are differences of opinion in certain areas, people have to learn to coexist and carry no hatred against any religion."

The process of the renewal of the school curriculum completed in the year 2000 (NCFSE, 2000) seriously considered the above-mentioned recommendations as an expression of the continuity of India's heritage of acceptance of diversity, which emanated out of the ancient Indian storehouse of scholarship knowledge and wisdom. In a world torn asunder practically every day due to religious fanaticism and terrorism, the value of non-aggression has to become the key concept spread over the entire process of teaching and learning. Whatever be the other reasons and causes, the two nation theory that led to the bleeding partition of India was certainly an outcome of lack of mutual trust and absence of true understanding amongst the two major communities of India divided on religious lines. If only the human values common to both the religions had been internalized across the board, the politicians would not have been allowed to play that disastrous game. No further justification would be needed in the current times to strive hard to let all the young persons know the basics of all the religions and develop mutual respect. This alone can lead to re-establishing the much needed social cordiality and religious harmony in India. This could be achieved only when the citizens are prepared with an attitude to not only strive, but to do 'good' but also remain ever alert to work and suffer for 'good'. Their endeavour must always aim to achieve the most sought after: *Satyam, Shivam and Sundaram;* Truth, Goodness and Beauty. Help comes in achieving this attitudinal transformation from the inheritance of history, culture and customs. Help comes from the inherited traditions, scriptures, epics and literature, the value of which, despite planned efforts to demolish it, is universally recognised and realised. Such an education cannot be organised except on a 'religious basis'. While pleading for such an education, C. Rajagoplachari wrote: "To misunderstand the 'secularity' to which people think we are pledged, and to treat religion as untouchable is one of the many unfortunate follies our government has fallen into. It is not impossible, or even very difficult, to deal with and include in a nation-wide effort to make men truly religious, each in the way shown by his or her own religion, and add to it a spirit of understanding and respect for other people's religion and way of life." In continuation, this outstanding statesman-cum-scholar gives an advice in terms of a basic principle: "The conclusion of the matter as I see it is that parliamentary democracy will be a waste of expense and produce no good unless this true education of the people is undertaken by a general consensus among all statesmen and politicians." (Rajagoplachari, 1978).

The world of today is sick as it suffers from violence, bloodshed, terrorism, distrust and bigotry practically everywhere and at every moment. The world of tomorrow needs a healing touch and a curative balm to put it back on the health track. The quintessence of ancient Indian culture has faced all possible onslaughts over the ages, but has overcome these, as it accepts unbreakable unity and the universality of all human beings. In terms of values it can be put in five inter-related ideals that find consistent mention in practically all the epics and scriptures that ancient Indian seekers of the ultimate truth have presented to humanity. Conflicts, strife, wars, battles and violence occur at various intervals, mostly due to ignorance, ego and misinterpretations. The five ideals mentioned earlier that survive eternally: Truth (*Sathya*), *Dharma* (Righteous conduct), Peace (*Shanti*), Love (*Prema*) and Non-violence (*Ahimsa*) are acceptable in every society, faith and religion. These could be expressed in various ways but the essence remains unchanged. Those who internalise these will find equal substance in every religion and faith, an essential requirement for the very survival of the planet earth and the existence of humanity on it. It is a great irony of the present times that religions, which actually should be leading towards social cohesion and religious harmony, are being used to achieve just the opposite. India's age-old wisdom very clearly predicts the way out: "Samavaya eva Sadhuh—Concord alone is correct and proper". This wisdom was not confined only for discourses and discussions amongst the learned scholars but was put to practice as a way of life at each stage.

Once it is accepted that there is a divine spark and limitless potential in every individual irrespective of caste, colour, creed or religion, there shall be no place for aggression, fundamentalism and, hence, violence and terrorism. The human ingenuity would be in a position to devote itself with greater commitment and devotion to further its quest for the search of truth in order to make life better for the fellow human beings. A.P.J. Abdul Kalam (*What can I give You*, 2006) recalls this aspect of the Indian culture in an universally comprehensible manner, recalling the advice of Gandhiji's mother: "Son, in your entire life if you can save or better someone's life, your birth as a human being and your life is a success. You have the blessings of the Almighty." It enlightens the path in search of solutions to the problems of humanity.

From Violence to Peace

It was in 1900 that Gandhiji put down his ideas of the emerging world and what approach would suit India if it were to save itself from the degeneration of human values and norms. These published as '*Hind Swarajya*', created world-wide interest appreciation and even ridicule. Gandhi was only forty years of age at that time. The small compilation, with heavy, pragmatic and prophetic comprehension of the socio-economic and cultural changes and their implications, is being discussed even today. Gandhi himself said that his book: "teaches the gospel of love in place of clamour for hate. It replaces violence with self-sacrifice. It pits soul force again brute force." In 1921 Gandhiji stated that Hind Swaraj sums up his philosophy of life. It is the essence of his life vision, a philosophy for human welfare. It was the philosophy of *Sarvodaya* that encompasses a dream, a blue print and a road map in the march ahead to build a violence-free world. And it was put on paper over hundred years ago. The world faced so much violence even today. Of the 70 million killed during the two world wars, half were women and children. Over 140,000 and 70,000 were massacred when human decisions to drop Atom bombs on Hiroshima and Nagasaki were executed. (Kanti Shah, 2009) What happened in the second half of the 20th century is probably a far darker side of the 'progress and development' that became the key words for the newly independent nations all around the globe. There was no let-off in the violence, exploitation, mutual distrust, bigotry and deceit. Over ten million people lost their lives in Vietnam, Korea, Laos, Cambodia, Afghanistan, Iraq, and Bosnia, India has experienced terrorist attacks in Jammu and Kashmir for several decades by now. Sri Lanka suffered internal strife of the worst nature severely for around two decades.

Every nation and every national in every part of the globe now lives under a sense of persistent insecurity that began with the nuclear arms race and is now a permanent threat to the very survival of humanity on earth. And, secondly, who is not under threat of fundamentalists and terrorists? Obviously, the arms trade is flourishing. The US controls around 50 per cent of Global arms trade. Even the poor and developing nations spend a very substantial part of their GDP on their defence budget. In US, one out of every ten people lives off charity which comes to about 25 million surviving on charity or the state social security. Such provisions are not available in poor and developing countries and millions and millions around the globe sleep hungry every day.

Gandhiji consistently pleaded and practised what he had envisioned in 1909 in the Hind Swaraj referred to above. Can anyone deny the immense need for creating a society 'founded on the philosophy of love and non-violence holding high humane and cultural values?' Such a society would have to adhere to certain eternal values and love for each other and respect for each other and nature shall become internalised in the individual and social psyche. Consumerism leads to violence of varied varieties and has to be abjured. Education can make a visible difference if its content and pedagogy are kept in harmony with the changes in relevant sectors.

Task Ahead

People have high hopes from education which would certainly get universalised in the first quarter of the 21st century, if not earlier. The content of education and its pedagogy have to remain dynamic and flexible. Its suitability shall be determined by the pace of dynamism and capacity to anticipate issues and concerns of the people and society. It would also be adjudged by its capacity to absorb the new and discard obsolesce. The entire content would have to be built around democratic values that must include the essence of democracy: sovereignty, socialism, secularism, justice, liberty, equality, fraternity, individual dignity, national integrity and the like.

The objective of countering violence and to eliminate the very roots of terrorism must be integrated in the process of education in a manner that it works both explicitly and implicitly. The content and process of teacher education and school education must prepare student teachers and students to imbibe democratic values and, more particularly, internalise the concept of secularism as practised in India for over two millennia, as a recorded historical fact. A sense of pride amongst the traditional practices that have encouraged social and religious amity deserves to be generated. Equally important is the need to discard every effort that creates a void amongst different set of communities and people. Programmes for people's awareness could also be organised by schools and colleges in which students take a leading part. Awareness generation materials play a very substantive role on such occasions. Empowerment issues, what good is being done and what could be availed of if the right information is made available to the target group could also help substantially. Issues of exploitation of natural resources by the state is being propagated, and sometimes correctly, by certain terrorist groups in tribal areas to make the life of the community further harsh and hard, resulting in massacres and avoidable bloodshed. Here again, institutions and NGOs could use educated persons from the community and prepare them to let everyone know the real facts. Struggle for rights and against exploitation is a duty but before that, the acquaintance with the issue has to be perfect and based on facts.

Schools and teacher training institutions must have lessons like "Symphony of Human Rights and Duties" or "Eternal Human Values and Human Rights". Activities and materials developed around these ideas would generate an understanding for values and that would include caring for the neighbour in the global village. Activities like annual functions could give a chunk of tie for the presentation of items that convey the essence of the relationship between rights and duties. Both the teachers and teacher educators need some training in understanding how to decipher facts from fiction. Various Human Rights lobbies are doing wonderful work, often educating people in their rights and pointing out the exploitation which they are being subjected to.

The UNESCO Report "Learning: The Treasure Within" explicitly recommends that children must be helped to let "them discover who they are. Only then they would be ready to put themselves in other people's shoes and understand their religion, culture and practices. That would lead to the growth of an emphatic social bonding and would pay rich dividends in future life (Rajput; J.S.; 2006). Education now needs a thorough overhaul that would focus its objectives on cremating a value-based society that honours the human rights of everyone and provides an environment of peace to 'work together for global prosperity'. Wars, it said, are won on the playfields of the educational institutions. Terrorism is the worst of the wars that has been against humanity and the eternal human values that represent the essential unity of the human race. The soldiers against it shall emerge from the classrooms—fully equipped with unbeatable weapons of Truth, Peace, Nonviolence, Righteous Conduct and Love.

References

Gangrade, K.D. 2001, *Religion and Peace: A Gandhian Perspective*, Gandhi Smriti and Darshana Samiti, New Delhi.

Kothari, D.S., 2000, Education and Character Building, Collection of Convocation Addresses (1962-83), National Institute of Science Communication, CSIR, New Delhi.

Shah, Kanti, 2009, *Gandhi's 'Hind Swaraj: A fresh Look'*, Other India Press, Mapusa, Goa.

Akbar, M.J., 2009, COVERT, 15 September–30; September, New Delhi.

Ministry of Education (1966), *Education and National Development; Report* of the Education Commission (Kothari Commission), Government of India, Ministry of Education, New Delhi.

GOI, 1992, National Policy on Education-1986/92, Government of India, Ministry of Human Resources Development, New Delhi.

Dewal, O.S., 2008, *Emerging Issues in School Education*, Sanskaram, New Delhi.

Radhakrishnan, S., 1968, *Religion and Culture*, Orient Paperbacks, New Delhi.

Rajput, J.S. (2008), *Human Values and Education*, Pragun Publication, New Delhi.

Value Education, 86th Report of the Standing Committee of the Members of Parliament for the Ministry of Human Resources Development, Government of India, Rajya Sabha Secretariat, New Delhi, 1999.

NCFSE, 2000 NCERT, (2000), *National Curriculum Framework for School Education*, National Council for Educational Research and Training, New Delhi.

Abdul Kalam, A.P.J., 2006, *What can I give You*, Foundation for Unity of Religions and Enlightened Citizenship, New Delhi.

Rajagoplachari, C., 1978, *Rescue Democracy from Money Power*, Bhartiya Vidya Bhavan, Bombay.

UNESCO, 1996, *Leaning: The Treasure Within*, Report to the UNESCO of the International Commission on Education for the Twenty-first Century, UNESCO Publishing, Paris.

16

Union State Relations in Education

Some Experiential Reflections

The centre-state relations underwent intense deliberations in the constituent Assembly during the formulation of the Constitution of India. The Government of India Act 1935 was the readily available document. Obviously, changes were suggested to shift items and areas from provincial list to central and concurrent lists. It was not an easy task. A strong centre had a very sound rationale in its support. However, none could take the risk of weakening the states. In the Constituent Assembly, H.V. Pataskar emphasised: "the power of the centre must flow from the states, which in the first place, must be strong and powerful. Unless the units are strong, how can you have a federation which is going to be strong?"[1] The general wellbeing of the people had to be the prime responsibility of the state governments and hence basic requirements like health, shelter, food, agriculture, education, roads and the like had to be looked after by the States. These debates had many interesting and thoughtful interventions in favour of a strong centre; but equally significant were the cautions mentioned on this count. Dr Ambedkar expressed his view in these words: "We must resist the tendency to make it (the Centre) stronger. It cannot chew more than it can digest. Its strength must be commensurate with its weight. It would be a folly to make it so strong that it may fall by its own weight."[2] There were strong pleas that in several spheres the nation would require All-India policies and higher education; higher technological institutions would certainly come in this category. In the context of education, it was asserted by Renuka Ray: "where the country has tremendous leeway to make up, particularly in the nation building services, the unifying force must be strong and the Centre should be given some power of a supervisory and coordinating character, in regard to both education and health."[3]

After over six decades, one could argue that education should have been given the priority as was implicit in Article 21-A that the state shall provide free and compulsory education to all children till they attain fourteen years of age. Had India achieved even around 80 per cent of this target in the stipulated ten years, things would have been so different today in terms of the huge measure of India's cognitive capital. It must however be conceded immediately that the conditions prevailing at that juncture were tough and complex. The pains of partition, inadequate resources, food; rehabilitation, security and such other sectors put a heavy demand on the governance in the days the Constitution was under preparation. The situation before the architects of the constitution is very well summarised by Marina Pinto: "Their justification for a degree of centralisation stemmed from their viewpoint that education was an essential instrument in the hands of the centre for national integration and national solidarity. Also, with greater economic resources at its command, it would be possible to prevent duplication and make for better coordination and control.[4] People had different levels of arguments in pleading for centralization, or, also for decentralisation. One of the apprehensions was the possibility of linguistic and cultural barriers becoming impediments in the march towards national integration and social cohesion. The Radhakrishnan Commission on Education (1949) emphasised the place and criticality of ethical and moral values, democratic values and all that was necessary for a cohesive India that reveres its tradition of the acceptance of the diversity. The Constituent Assembly too was deliberating during that period and it retained the following in the List I of the seventh Schedule as entry No. 66: "Coordination and determination of Standards in institutions for higher education or research and scientific and technical institutions." Shortly after the promulgation of the Constitution, the Central Government, in 1951, prepared a bill that proposed the creation of a Central Council of Higher Education to coordinate matters and ensure maintenance of standards. Only it could control the establishment of new universities and lay down norms and standards, etc. It was opposed vehemently by the next Vice Chancellors conference. Those were the days of effective university autonomy. Politicians respected the views of academics. In 1955, another Bill was brought and the University Grants Commission was created in early 1956. It may appear a bit surprising at this juncture but the growth of higher education institutions during 1956 to 1971-02 was considered a mushroom growth. The UGC Act was amended to check it. In 1984, the conference of Vice-Chancellors resolved that there would be no more new colleges and universities. However, neither the 1972 amendment, nor the 1984 resolve could check the growth. The 2010-11 figures are: No. of degree awarding institutions 634; No. of colleges: 33023; student enrolment 16975000; teachers; 816966. Even now our participation rates in higher education are very low and need to be doubled.

In the 1960s, practically all the newly independent nations that had suffered exploitation of resources, illiteracy and poverty for centuries, became aware and convinced of the criticality of universal education in national development, progress and growth. India was no exception. It is reflected in the Kothari Commission Report from its very title "Education for National development". It emphasised: if the pace of national development is to be accelerated, there is a need for a well-defined, bold and imaginative educational policy and for determined and vigorous action to vitalise, improve and expand education. India did extend educational access in a big way, but it is highly debatable whether it could really vitalise and improve its education? If India had unequivocally succeeded on these counts, credit could have been equally shared by the Centre and the States. Now, the need is to find out the fault-lines and attempt improvements in coordination, work culture and in developing a futuristic vision that does not discard the basic premise of nurturing the best 'out of body, mind and spirit'.

It was, and is; impossible to check the growth of educational infrastructure and institutions in India which has more than three times of its population now as compared to the time of independence. India needed to enhance its literacy rates, people were gradually realising the value of and the necessity of acquiring education both for boys and girls. After the initial phase of about three decades, State governments began to withdraw from opening schools and colleges after and, consequently, private initiatives were gradually encouraged. This brought another factor: public schools and private and deemed universities! The source of government support started drying up more and more. Earlier, people did come up with the objective of contributing to education in their area, even communities, were practically assured of government pitching in at some stage and the schools and colleges would become viable and manageable. It was a fine example of public people cooperation which gradually withered away under the increasing influence of and access to commercialisation of education.

Consultation Mechanism

Focusing only on relevant details, one could safely identify the Central Advisory Board of Education (CABE) as the highest Advisory Body in Education both for states and the central government. In 2011-12, the GOI reconstituted the CABE for three years listing the following as its functions:

(a) To review the progress of education from time to time.
(b) To appraise the extent and manner in which the National Policy on Education has been implemented by the Central and State governments, and the concerned agencies and give appropriate advice in the matter.
(c) To advise regarding coordination between Central and State governments/UT Administration, State governments and Non-governmental Agencies for development of education in accordance with the National Policy on Education.
(d) To advise, *suo-moto*, or on a reference made to it by Central Government or any State Government or a Union Territory on any educational question.
(e) To review the National Policy on Education.

It would be interesting to note that CABE is a huge body with a membership exceeding over one hundred and twenty! The Human Resource minister presides over it with two ministers of state in the MHRD as Vice-Chairpersons, there are 12 Central Ministers as ex-officio members from the Central Government, one minister and Lt. Governor from each State and UT, six members of Parliament, another 23 ex-officio members representing ministries, organisations of the central government and other Professional and learned bodies. In addition, there are ten Vice-Chancellors/Heads of Institutions of National importance. There are several categories of nominated members representing different categories. Two media representatives and eleven permanent invitees also adorn the body. The need for coordination function was realised much earlier and it was in 1920 that the CABE was brought into being. Its primary task was delineated as 'keeping in touch with local jurisdictions and assisting the provincial governments with expert advice. However, later development resulted in the dismantling of CABE after the Government of India Act, 1919 financial support from education from centre became practically insignificant. The Coordination function of the Central Government was resumed in 1935 and the CABE was resuscitated. It prepared the "Post-War Educational Development in India" report in 1944. It is also known as Sargent Report. It had proposed a forty year period for universal elementary education. Obviously, in those days of tremendous enthusiasm, it was not liked and a ten year period was stipulated in the Constitution of India! With time the character and functioning of CABE could have become more clear and broad based. But, somehow, its unwieldy composition has often raised question marks on its efficacy.

Over the years it has been noted that the CABE is too unwieldy and there are serious doubts as to whether its composition leaves enough space for its members to express the nations aspirations and desires from education. Is it really representative in character to put before the nation a system of education and an implementation strategy that suits India and has its roots in Indian tradition of knowledge acquisition? Apart from the abundance of Ex-Officio members, all the nominations; except of the six MPs, are made by the minister who invariably is a politician and obviously assembles all those who 'think alike' and are ideologically close to his political line. Past experience has very clearly established such facts. Some serious researches could only confirm the inadequacy of the CABE in getting a truly representative national character and become an effective professional body free from political compulsions. The very size of the CABE has often been the major handicap in making it really effective. In one day meeting, it often becomes a ministry's show, in which a couple of favourite luminaries get the privilege of toeing the ministry's line of thought and action.

Another major consultation mechanism is that of the conference of education ministers of the state. These conference are normally characterised by each minister presenting a printed account of his/her achievements and in the end, making a fervent plea that central assistance must flow to the state concerned as there is 'serious resource crunch'! Over the years, several organizations like the NCERT have been established which provide significant opportunities for Centre-State consultations. All the education ministers of states/UTs are members of the General Body of the Council. It also has experts nominated by its President, the human resources development minister and naturally, the ideological considerations override professional considerations.

General Planning Systems

The most significant consultation mechanisms are the National Development Council and the Planning Commission India. Though the Planning Commission is presided over by its Prime Minister, it is effectively being managed by the Vice-Chairman who invariably is a close confidante of the PM. States have State Planning Boards chaired by the concerned Chief Minister. Even in the early stages, the functioning of the Planning Commission has come under critical scrutiny but the apprehensions have now more or less got routinised without much impact. The Planning Commission is often referred to as a super cabinet and that it has "reduced state autonomy to a shadow in all matters of policy and finance."[5] Generally, the National Development Council (NDC) determines the objectives and considerations that should receive a special focus in the next plan. The Planning Commission sets up detailed technical studies internally. Simultaneously, a number of working groups are set up for different sectors of activity. They study the performance in the concerned sector and taking clues from the same, suggest future strategies and reforms. Experts play a major role in these groups. The Commission also sets up a number of panels and advisory groups. In the entire process inputs are received from specialists and also from those supposed to implement the plans and programmes that may eventually be finalised. This stage ends with the Planning Commission putting up a Draft Memorandum on the Plan to the Union Cabinet. After detailed discussions there, it is again put to NDC in which all states are represented through their chief ministers. It is relevant to mention that while the Draft Plan is under discussion, the Planning Commission also conducts plan discussions with the states. After all this preparatory process, there is a repeat of process of preparing the final memorandum, to be submitted to the Union Cabinet and, then, to NDC. One of the important steps in the process is the preparation of guidelines that are arrived at by the Planning Commission, in consultation with the MHRD. These are meant to help state governments and other institutions and organisations to prepare their plan proposals. Intensive exercises take place in each state. In the education sector, institutions like the IIT's, UGC, AICTE and others prepare their own plan proposals and submit to the MHRD which then goes to the Planning Commission. Inputs from the states and the ministries are examined in the Education Division of the Planning commission. "A final decision regarding the state plan programmes and the outlay in education, as also in other sectors, is taken in a high level meeting between the Deputy Chairman and the state chief minister assisted by appropriate officers on both sides. The state government revises its plan in the light of these decisions."[6]

Essentially, the NDC, conceived as a federal forum has the

responsibility of taking a comprehensive national view of planning in which every state gets its due share. The Administrative Reforms Commission had noted the inadequacy of the NDC on this count and had said: "The degree of consultation has increased with every succeeding plan and so steadily has the influence of the Council. And yet a study of the planning documents and an examination of the planning procedures reveal a paradoxical situation, in which, while consultation with the Council on certain basic matters of policy has been inadequate, the attention bestowed on them by the Council when opportunity has visited it has been even more so."[7]

Invariably, with an experience of over six decades, the process of Educational planning clearly reveals gaps; Take the case of 1968 Policy on education. It laid great emphasis on Vocational education, indicating conversion of around 25 per cent secondary schools into vocational schools. Even today, this percentage is around 5-6 only. We still have schools without buildings, with single teacher only, over six lakh untrained teachers, over ten lakh vacancies of teachers in schools. These do indicate a definite lack of coordination between the centre and states, on one hand and also the scarcity of political will and commitment, on the other, leaving the weaker sections of society in a dilemma after they receive education of inadequate quality.

Current Exemplars: Centre and States

In principle, and also in terms of pragmatic considerations, the Indian education system must respond to following concerns:

1. Providing educational access to elementary education to every child irrespective of any diversity, handicap, location and the like.
2. Ensure adherence to the National Policy on Education; maintain comparability of syllabi and curricula taking due note of the local elements as well.
3. Ensure comparability of learner attainments at the school leaving stage.
4. Ensure modern methods of teaching, evaluation, incorporation of new technologies and pedagogies, nurture creativity, self-learning, ensure pre-service and in-service education of teachers.
5. Nurture talent, ensure international comparability in higher education, develop national and international level institutional networking.

6. Create centres of research and surveys that provide inputs for quality improvement and guide in preparing futuristic plans and programmes.
7. Prepare young persons who understand India, its culture and heritage and are committed to democratic and secular values in addition to universal human values.

The above could always be reworded, but the essence remains the same: to bring out the best from the body mind and spirit of every learner. It would be seen that the study of relationship between the centre and the states must necessarily be made in the light of the goals and objectives of education. And these do not change because of procedural stipulations or rules and regulations. There are umpteen initiatives that could be listed both from the states side and also from the Central Government's side that have been put to implementation. Unfortunately, not many of these could bring out the desired level of results at the implementation stage. One could cite from personal experience the fate of schemes like Operation Blackboard, Non-formal Education and Strengthening of Teacher Education Institutions that were launched after the National Policy on Education, 1986, was accepted for implementation. In 1991, the UP Basic Education Project was launched and World Bank entered the elementary education sector in India for the first time. Other external agencies also pitched in. It was part of a bigger and higher level strategies of the government of India in which there was little say of the consultative mechanism created between states and the centre for educational initiatives. There was a strong lobby that was opposed to foreign collaboration in elementary education in India that was just embarking upon liberalisation and privatisation.

In 1960s and 1970s, there was huge activity in education in every sector; expansion; teacher training, new pedagogy; new institutions and all that. There was a dearth of trained teachers, and deficiency of infrastructural support all around. However, the generation that was managing school education was one that had either witnessed or participated in the freedom struggle. They were so confident of themselves. There were rare instance of any conflict between the centre and the states. Things did change when the consultations mechanisms were not effectively utilised. In the mid-1980s, the Governments of Tamil Nadu and West Bengal refused to go along with the establishment of Navodaya Vidyalayas in the initial stages but eventually these Vidyalayas were accepted and are functioning smoothly in these states. Prior to that there were problems associated with the language formula which too were resolved in due course.

Over the last couple of years, there is general impression of the dilution of consultation mechanisms and hence several problems in implementation and also in legislation. After May 2009, the ministry announced umpteen reform measures which did not emerge out of serious consultations and hence attracted adverse reactions from all over.

The implementation of the RTE, beginning April 1, 2010, should be considered as a very significant event. After two years it was found that practically nothing tangible and visible by way of positive change has really occurred at the grass-roots level. Obviously, this was to be a great joint venture between states and the centre. Most of the funding was to come from the Centre, but the States too had the responsibility of creating a new work culture, motivation and an environment that could invite social participation, considered so essential for the success of every 'movement'. The Centre could not get an active approval of all the states prior to April 1, 2010 for their readiness to plunge in to the implementation in a mission mode. Some of them did not notify the rules and regulations for about two years and kept on complaining that they have no resources. When a programme, that too in a mission mode of such a huge and critical nature is launched, it is both resource intensive and commitment intensive, it is the accepted obligation of the central government to bring all the stake-holders on board.

Major issues are involved in this debate which is the concern of both the centre and the states. With over forty school boards, it is a tough task to achieve comparability of standards in learner attainments. The establishment of the NCERT in 1961 was precisely for this purpose. The NCERT has largely achieved its objectives of bringing out updated curricula and corresponding textbooks. These are made available to the states with clear indications that they must bring in local element of the curricula wherever necessary. Unfortunately in 2010, the MHRD just ignored the presence of the NCERT and declared that COBSE; (Council of Boards of Secondary Education) shall prepare a national curriculum in sciences and mathematics and this would be uniformly applicable. All that COBSE has is an office of one octogenarian person. It has no expertise of its own. Such steps are taken by the centre; either because of the pressure exerted by vested interests, or political or ideological considerations; or sheer ignorance. Sometimes, personal likes and dislikes of the political bosses, or even that of the bureaucrats, make all the difference.

The fact remains that the NCERT has earned credibility nationally and internationally as the most comprehensive research organisation in school education and teacher education. It has trained practically in every State/UT numerous textbook writers, evaluation experts; curriculum developers, experts in Open and Distance Learning, Research methodology trainers and has participated in state level programmes through its experts from Delhi and also from its five regional Institutes functioning from Shillong, Ajmer, Bhopal, Bhubaneswar and Mysore. It prepared national curriculum frameworks in 1975, 1988, 2000, 2005 and these have been accepted by States which have their full authority to develop ones of their own taking local elements into account. An exception must be recalled. The NCERT's National Curriculum Framework for School Education (NCFSE-2000) was opposed by certain elements which carried their objections to the Supreme Court of India. The Court firmly rejected their plea in the judgment delivered on September 12, 2002. However, the Government of the Delhi directed its SCERT to prepare a fresh set of books. Earlier, Delhi schools were just using NCERT books. It was well within their rights and the NCERT did not object.

Centre and Central Institutions

'Talk of decentralization, but ensure centralization at every stage' appears to be the favourite refrain of Central Government functionaries. It has become more visible and evident during the last couple of years. IIMs and IITs are the topmost prestigious institutions which came up after independence and are a unique example of futuristic vision of the leadership of the initial years in free India. In April 2004, all the IIMs decided to reduce their fees. It was said that the HRD minster wanted that to happen. As the governing bodies of all these institutions have representatives from the MHR, the wishes of the government of India were honoured. After the change of government, the new dispensation decided to demolish all that was initiated earlier. Practically the IIMs were chided for reducing the fees. Dutifully and following the procedure, the IIMs decided to raise the fees again! All this happened within two-three months. Obviously, here the issue is that of institutional autonomy and, in a way, it gets linked to centre-state relations also. This approach was also evident when a large number of professional colleges and deemed universities were set up during 2006-09. Approvals and sanctions which were within the purview of national level bodies like AICTE, UGC and the like, were all being directed from the MHRD.

During the first week of 2012, another issue of critical importance emerged in the public domain. This concerns a sudden 'unanimous' decision announced on behalf of the IIT Council by the then Human Resources Development Minister, Kapil Sibal. It meant a common entrance test for all aspirants to IIT's and the NIITs. There would be a general entrance test for all; those who wish to be considered for IIT's would appear, on the same day, in another advanced level test. Further, the School Board results of class XII will get a huge weightage of 50 per cent while the merit list is being prepared. The minister claimed credit for introducing this long-aspired reform and declared that it will come in force right from the year 2013, i.e., within the next couple of months! How the central functionaries bulldozed their own institutions became amply clear with hours of the minister's announcement and the series of protests from the faculty members of the IITs and, also, from the Alumni Associations. Academics and the Alumni of the IITs were upset 'that the government is interfering in academic matters and compromising the autonomy of these institutions'.[8] In fact, about four of the Senates of the IIT's had already rejected this proposal and it is surprising why the same was not projected force fully by their Directors in the Council meeting? If the dissent was put up in the meeting why this significant input was ignored? It has been reported that one of the Directors who 'thinks alike' and is aspirant for another term was sent to another IIT to persuade its faculty to fall inline. He did not succeed in converting them to toe the minister's line. The problem has another angle. All the Directors of these Institutions are appointed only as per the desires of the minister; they have to deal with the ministry practically on a daily basis to get even minor issues resolved. Funds come from the MHRD, which takes full advantage of it in dealing with institutions functioning 'under' it! Having examined the technicalities of the IIT Act, the IITK has found that they are fully authorised to devise their own procedures for the entrance test and they have announced declaration of 'Sibal formula' and conduct their own entrance examinations. Others can join, if they so desire!

Another issue that emerges is: for central institutions, how is the role of the States determined? Should state governments not be consulted in taking major decisions on, say, IIT and NIIT entrance examinations? The process of establishing new central universities has also brought out the issue of Centre-State relations in focus. Normally, the States accept whatever is being proposed by the Centre with its own funds, with the States giving land and related facilities. In Bihar, the State Government had its own considerations and it refused to accept the recommendations of the 'Central Team'. Considerable delay, discussions, controversies and demonstrations followed. The State Government had a point: once they had given a considered opinion, why should not that get weightage. Further, not many would buy the idea that a central university must be located in a convenient place defined as availability of an airport nearby. This is not the India or the government of India of Bapu's dreams! Opinions may differ but a tangible process of consultation must emerge prominently. Proposals like establishment of a National Commission for Higher Education and Research (NCHER), also project a lack of adequate consultation, persuasion and effort to bring everybody on board. The same applies to making the Tenth Board Examination optional and no detention during the first eight years in school education. There are serious reservations, not on their pedagogical soundness, but on the systemic readiness to implement it.[9]

For the Future

There are two major issues that must get top priority, both from Centre and the State: quality deterioration at every stage and gross inadequacy of skill orientation. State governments and also the Central Government schemes and programmes invariably refer to quality aspects, but, in actual practice, these rarely take off. The perpetual question remains unanswered: you need a basic infrastructure and professional support system to build quality on it. Further, one needs constant inputs resulting out of surveys, studies, innovations and researches to infuse dynamism in the system. In-service education, availability of fresh teacher learner materials and particular emphasis on retraining of teachers in the new pedagogy dominated by ICT requires constant additional inputs in the education sector. Needless to say, these would flow in only when both the State and Central Governments realise that it is indeed the most productive investment in human capital for the future. India has a great chance to strengthen its global presence through its young persons well-versed and equipped with market-friendly skills the demand for which is emerging particularly from the ageing societies. With 65 per cent population below 35 years. This is a rare opportunity that must be availed off. Now, it requires very sustained and determined by way of collaboration between the Centre and the States. It is often seen that many of the initiatives get lost because these are termed as either of the State or of the centre. At present, there are several prominent Missions that have been launched by the MHRD. These include: the SSA, Rastriya Madhyamik Shiksha Abhiyan, National Skill development Mission and the Mission on Teacher Education. Such initiatives require intensive coordinated action on the part of the centre and the State concerned. There are avoidable bottlenecks that hinder work in these missions and often the Abhiyan just converts itself into another of the numerous schemes that proceed at a pedestrian pace. The State Councils of Educational Research and Training on one hand and the Higher Education Council for University Education, on the other, are the bodies in States that should be discharging this responsibility with full authority. These would be able to do so, only if the State fully equips them with authority, staff and support systems.

There is not much of research on centre-state relations in education. This must be taken up by independent bodies like ICSSR, NCAER, and a couple of IIM's. This would pave the way for future strengthening of mechanisms linked directly to quality improvement. Essentially, the functionality of central-state relations depends on mutual respect and regard with the common goal of ensuring sound preparation of the future generation. It has to shun politics of all varieties and focus only on human values, morals and ethics.

(June 19, 2012)

Notes

1. Constituent Assembly Debates, Vol. XI, 1949, p. 672.
2. *Ibid.*, Vol. VII, p. 42.
3. *Ibid.*, Vol. VII, p. 358.
4. Marina Pinto, *Federalism and Higher Education: The Indian Perspective*: Orient Longman, Hyderabad, 1984; p. 9.
5. Santhanam, K., *Democratic Planning: Problems and Pitfalls*, 1961, p. 20.
6. Abu Baker, M., *The Union and the States in Education; A study of educational finance and planning*; Shabd Sanchar, Ajmer; 1976, p. 145.
7. The Administrative Reforms Commission, Report of the Study Team on Centre-State Relatioships.
8. Mohan, Dinesh, Time for IITs to discard the JEE; *The Hindu*; Tuesday, June 12, 2012.
9. Rajput, J.S., Does Exam-free Really Mean Stress-free?, *The Sunday Standard*, June 17; 2012; p. 8.

17

Globalisation

The Context of Education

Some fifty years ago, the technocrats of those times organised an exhibition in the World Fair of New York—dedicating it to "Man's achievements on a shrinking globe in an expanding universe". The celebrated science fiction writer, Isaac Asimov, visited this exhibition. Highly excited, he wrote an article about how the world would be 50 years on; in 2014. He wrote, "Communication will become sight-sound and you will see as you will hear the person you telephone. The screen (of the phone) can be used not only to see the people you call but also for studying documents and photographs and reading passages from the books[1]." In the age of smart phones, Skype's, e-books, etc., it all looks so prophetic! He could foresee all of these. Asimov, who passed away in 1992, had several other predictions in most of which he was just on the mark. Change, they say, is the only constant. People observe the change, its impact and also realise how they themselves contribute to the change. Change, its pace, magnitude and enormity as also the consequent challenges, has never before been as daunting as at this stage. Visionaries, like Asimov, guide and motivate others to concretise ideas and even expectations. Today, all of the human beings are 'neighbours'. Huge distances stand reduced to minutes, connectivity within seconds could be universally accessible to anyone. Information, knowledge sources and assistance are just a call away. The glare and glitz of life has been globalised, the fruits of which have upscaled millions and thrown billions backwards. For some, the 'World is Flat'.

For most of the populace, it is hot and crowded world.

There was another visionary who, in his own unique way, visualised the future implications from within the frame of the 'last man in the line'! He wrote[2]: "If I preach against the modern artificial life of sensual enjoyment, and ask men and women to go back to the simple life epitomised in the Charkha, I do so because I know that without an intelligent return to simplicity, there is no escape from our descent to a state lower than brutality." Gandhi was not alone amongst those who were worried the way the world was shaping up after the extended and expanded presence of science, technology and now, the communication technology. It is worthwhile to recall Arnold Toynbee who, after surveying the story of modern materialistic civilization, observed[3]: "It is already becoming clear that a chapter which had a Western beginning will have to have an Indian ending, if it is not to end in the self-destruction of the human race...At this supremely dangerous moment in human history, the only way of salvation for mankind is the Indian way—Emperor Asoka's and Mahatma Gandhi's principle of non-violence and Sri Ramakrishna's testimony to the harmony of religions. Here we have an attitude and spirit that can make it possible for the human race to grow together in to a single family—and, in the Atomic age, this is the only alternative to destroying ourselves." As modernisation and globalisation have engulfed the willing and unwilling alike, the need for a critical review has become urgently relevant and necessary. For the first time, informed human beings are worried even about the very survival of the planet Earth if the present trends leading to the breakdown of the sensitive link of man and nature are persisted further without application of mind and ignoring the basic tenet that natures' resources are to be shared by one and all alike. Further, it is also the responsibility of the generation in control at present to ensure replenishments of these resources wherever possible and necessary. Not only this, globalisation is no longer merely an economic phenomenon, but it impacts every sector of human endeavour and one could prominently mention social, cultural, linguistic concerns, along with the national security, the very concept of patriotism and national identity. The issues of mutual relationships between the nations, the level of mutual trust and faith also come in with equal urgency.

From the Global Discourse

The Positives and Negatives

The turn of the millennium gave rise to a very exhaustive 2K-global debate. International agencies brought the essence of global perceptions on various specialised sectors on whatever was humanly possible to observe and perceive as coming in the near future. In 2005, some of the positives of globalisation were summarized by Cheng:[4]

1. Global sharing of knowledge, skills and intellectual assets that are necessary to multiple developments of individuals, local communities and international communities;
2. Mutual support and benefits to produce energy for various developments of countries, communities, individuals in different parts of the world;
3. Creating values and enhancing efficiency and productivity through the above global sharing and mutual supports to serving local needs and human development;
4. Promoting international understanding, collaboration, harmony and acceptance of cultural diversity across various countries and regions; and
5. Facilitating multi-way communications and multi-cultural appreciations among various groups, countries and regions.

It would be clear from the above and other similar formulations that globalisation would create a new world, in which, theoretically, the key elements of international interactions, national policy formulations and executions would centre on 'sharing experience, knowledge and the know-how'. It would present a very rosy picture of the future particularly for the developing countries which are in need of support that could enhance their knowledge capital and technical proficiency. However, at the grassroots level, everyone knows that self-interest is the first interest of every nation. It would be too naïve to presume that the globalisation would result in altruistic support from developed countries and they would share resources with the developing countries they are eyeing as markets without that fine print of 'terms and conditions apply'! Initially, there were very serious apprehensions about globalisations, particularly in the developing nations, which were already under serious economic stress and growing demand for employment. The most important challenge before them was to ensure human dignity and removal of the blot of being subjects of another power. Even before that, these were required to provide food, health, housing, nutrition, education and equality of opportunity to one and all. Globalisation has created a skewed situation on this front. In several cases, more jobs vanished and only a much lower fraction has emerged as alternative opportunity. The Indian economy faltered during the period 2009-14 considerably and it is reported that only 1.2 million jobs were created! Several negative impacts have indeed been witnessed by the people, particularly in the areas of indigenous skills, crafts, cottage industries and locally produced materials, in which women, who were home-makers, could utilise their free time to add to their earnings. In many cases, national plans are even now being developed without utilising the strong local base of national ingenuity in the sector concerned. A well known example is of the weavers of Varanasi who have suffered all along though everyone would like the traditional purity of their craft maintained as it is a great Indian heritage that has a perpetual place of adoration in India and abroad.

In India, the World Bank assistance in the field of elementary education from 1990-91 onwards, brought with it greater international interaction, foreign visits of Indian bureaucrats and academicians, training programmes, innumerable appraisal missions, and in the overall context, neglect of the local and traditional expertise. Even the content and processes of education were quietly impacted to 'conform to international standards'! The educated class in India, as also in other countries, that extricated themselves from the colonial yoke, has always remained too eager to embrace the Western culture, tradition and the system of governance. With the arrival of the World Bank, such groups were eager and rather happy that they shall have all the international privileges, perks and even gadgets at their beck and call. It may appear a minor consideration for some, but has indeed made a very substantial contribution in accepting the imperatives of globalisation without serious and in-depth analysis of what is locally/regionally available, how the indigenous could be relevant and whether the 'ideology of progress', being borrowed from elsewhere, would really meet the national requirements? It was known to all sensitive citizens everywhere that political colonialisation could now be extended to social, cultural, and economic colonialisation! In several ways, these apprehensions have proved correct. Over a decade ago, the negatives of globalisation, as studied and published from various sources, were visualised[5] as:

1. Increasing the technological gaps and digital divides between advanced countries and less developed countries, that are hindering equal opportunities for global sharing;
2. Creating more apparently legitimate opportunities for a few advanced countries to economically and politically colonise other countries globally;
3. Exploiting local resources and destroying indigenous cultures of the less advanced countries to benefit a few advanced countries;
4. Increasing inequalities and conflicts between areas and cultures; and
5. Promoting the dominant cultures and values of some

advanced areas and accelerating cultural transplantation from advanced areas to less developed areas.

As is now the universal belief, it is education; and the individual prepared through the process of education that must lay fulsome emphasis on the total personality development. Only those prepared, equipped and empowered could actually understand and properly perceive the negatives of the much-hyped global village and only they could prepare appropriate responses to secure national interests. Even this alone may not be sufficient, unless the education systems accept at the policy level that 'education in every country must be rooted to the culture and committed to progress'. It has serious implications that could impact practically every sector of human endeavour and activity. Several newly emerged nations that opted for what looked an easy option, and borrowed systems, plans, programmes, practices and formulations from outside have realised the enormity of the folly committed. No nation could neglect the local knowledge and also the systems of creation, generation, dissemination and utilisation of this knowledge. The significance of the traditional and indigenous knowledge base in now globally recognised and efforts are on to preserve it in its specific locations. Needless to say, not all of it could be relevant in the current context. The essence and utility have to be accepted and the outdated, discarded. Take the example of the systems of indigenous health care like *Ayurveda*, *Unani*, *Siddha* and others that could have easily extended health care facilities up to the last man in the remotest corner of the country. Governments give these a step-motherly treatment as 'other systems of medicines' and the plans to extend the Allopathic systems could not reach the needy! India is still struggling on the health front as are several other nations. India could boast of the best of the modern super-specialty health care centres that match the best anywhere. On paper, these are required to cater to the weaker sections, but, in practice, these have become the exclusive preserves of the resourceful—from India and also from abroad. This gap in health care would widen further as the magnitude of globalisation expands itself. The credibility of the public health care system stands eroded in public estimate. Imagine the plight of a person earning daily wages being forced to visit a private hospital in an emergency! Nearly fifty per cent of the children in India suffer from malnutrition. There is no indication in policies and programmes that it would be corrected in the next five to six years. It has serious implications for education—and also for the growth of the cognitive capital of India.

Globalisation Issues that Confront Education

The first visible signs of globalisation appeared in the 'markets' of the not-yet-developed nations. Immaculate planning and serious research indicated to the colonisers of the past that though they may have lost on retraining the political hegemony, there are alternative strategies to seek social, economic and cultural dominance over the countries struggling to reshape their future after having suffered from alien rule and unbridled exploitation and extortion of their resources for hundreds of years. If handled wisely, these countries could open up enormous centres of economic gains and, more importantly, dominance! The emerging international economic scenario has created new centres of vigorous economic activity that have appeared in several countries like China, India, Japan and others. The disparities are, in fact, growing. In a simpler context, the CEO of a multinational may be earning a couple of crores of rupees per month and the minimum wage of an agriculture labour gets for himself and his family may be just around a couple of a thousand rupees per month, if he is fortunate to get work on all of the days. That around 700 million Indians still need food subsidy clearly indicates the existence of serious flaws inherent in the economic policies, planning and programmes. No one now talks of the wage differential being restricted to 1:10! India now takes pride in its increasing number of billionaires and leaves it to Planning Commission to come forward with apparently ridiculous looking definitions of the poverty line. As globalisation takes firmer roots, crime syndicates also establish international networks. Illegal trade is far less risky or cumbersome. Not only drugs, weapons too are being smuggled to right places, sometimes even the governments are involved in the rackets. There is trafficking in human beings, including children. Theoretically, knowledge sharing is universal and instantaneous, but the real position is that those who can sponsor creation of new knowledge ahead of others do so to exploit it for materialistic gains.

For the young and fortunate in the search of knowledge, it is just a 'click away'! Not many at the policy formulation level care for the digital divide. Whenever such aspects are discussed, the ground level realities are often ignored. Political masters in India still lure educated young persons with freebies like 'free Laptops'. It looks so innovative and acceptable. However, if the young recipient was never given any exposure to the use of computer in their school days, his gains, and even his interest, would just be limited. The advent and wide availability of mobile phones and availability of the television sets are creating new opportunities and challenges in education. Now market is impacting the culture and social tradition to suit its expectations. The dominant cultures are invading every home and hearth. The Malls must sell to survive and hence a no-holds-barred campaign strategy overrides the established social and cultural traditions. Globalisation of food habits, the dress-pattern and use of English, even in personal and family interactions, are clear examples of the market dominating the cultural and social scenario. Any one troubled by these 'trends of modernisation' is immediately declared conservative, rigid, traditionalist and one failing to catch up with times. There is no escape from the media blitz that the market merrily thrusts on one and all. And it is just not simple marketing. It inserts it merchandise cautiously, and sometimes brazenly, in what one must read in the print media and watch on the electronic media. When a sari-clad grandmother selects the shortest of the 'shorts' for the young granddaughter, one is made to believe that India is getting more beautiful and more sexy! Sometimes, it appears India is running a winning race in copying the West!

Diversity

On a serious note, the population of those below 15-16 years has grown up substantially. India, they say, must reap the benefits of the 'golden period of demographic dividend'! India is the nation of the young and ageing societies, particularly in the developed countries, are keen to offer job opportunities to the young, educated and skilled Indians. The only hitch is: are we ready to prepare competent, professionally equipped and mentally alert young manpower? The conditions in our schools and universities are certainly not very encouraging and the downward slide in quality appears unstoppable. India could take advantage of networking with well-reputed international institutions and upgrade its own institutions. It would also require close networking with the industry and corporate houses. The communication systems are now universally available to institutions, if not to individuals in difficult situations. In fact, the culture 'industry' has been monopolised by certain affluent nations and the same is being superimposed on other cultures by those who believe in 'one language, one attire, one menu card, and one culture and uniform social norms and practices'. Some even are busy to ensure one religion for all! The communication and connectivity have even encouraged them rather substantially. It is indeed dreadful to think of a world bereft of the diversities that make this planet a beautiful and colourful place to lead a fullsome life! The fact, and the trend, however, remain that languages are vanishing, scripts are being lost. Across the globe, you could get the food items popularised by the West everywhere, could hear the music and songs of those who, again, could utilise the universal communication systems more effectively than others. The erosion of cultural, linguistic and social distinctiveness that has already taken place is a great loss to humanity, creativity and innovative traits. It deserves to be taken up rather seriously, again by the global community! No one, no nation, would like to suffer the loss of its identity, its cultural heritage and the pride in-built therein! Who would like children not to know the language of their forefathers? But things are happening the other way round. With around thirty per cent of schools now in private hands, the craze for English medium schools is on a sharp rise. Here again, the decline of the credibility of the public school system plays a significant role. When focus shifts merely to earn more in life, such practices gain prominence and also predominance. In India the craze for 'English–Medium' education very clearly exposes the malady that is injurious to the generations ahead. Disconnecting the child from learning through his mother tongue in the initial years is injurious to him and also to the nation and the national identity. One of the essential principles of learning is to ensure a continuity of the home environment to the school environment. This is just not possible when a four year old child is put in a 'play school' and made to learn an alien language from day one in an environment that creates apprehensions—and even fear.

Material progress, skewed as it is, has not effectively contributed towards equity and social justice, since the fruits of progress have not been distributed with transparency and justice. These have been cornered by a few—at the cost of many. Take the case of tribal areas where most of the mineral resources of India are being siphoned off by the corporate and multinationals. Huge scandals are regularly being reported in the media in considerable detail. The squandering of these assets, with the connivance of the government machinery, has all along been in public discourse. Material resources and riches have been harvested indiscriminately by the resourceful and the powerful. The original habitants still squirm in poverty and ill health. To them, all this process of development means dispossession of their meagre holdings if any, attack on their cultural content and humiliation from one and all. On one side, the system of governance deprives them of what has been their due for ages, on the other, the rebellious Maoists and Naxalites force them to take to arms. Only they suffer, none else! All this is well known, the causes are well studied and analysed. The seriousness of the consequences is also adequately known and its implications for external and internal security are equally obvious. Job creation and stopping exploitation of resources is the first step that even a common man would advocate. How long could a nation tolerate the existence of such consequences of incorrect and inhuman policies? The land sharks, exploiters of forest produce and mining mafia have created havoc, which in many cases, is now linked to 'taking advantage of globalisation'!

The Common Cause

It is really strange that with all the acquisition of knowledge and skills and also much higher understanding and control over the forces of nature, mankind continues to suffer increasing violence, bigotry, distrust, fissiparous tendencies and destructive programmes of development that shatter the sensitive link between man and nature. The venom of fundamentalism has led to the rise of terrorism which has sniffed life out of thousands of innocent men, women and children in different parts of the globe. Further, they have converted the entire planet into a place full of fear and insecurity that inflicts great stress and strain on individuals and even governments. Terrorism has created global conditions which make everyone worry what would happen the next day! The challenge before education is to prepare young children on the principles of 'learning to live together'! The logic given is simple: it is a global village in which everyone is the neighbour of everyone else. So, you must learn to respect otherness in all of its shades and colours! How could those unable to live together as a community or as a cohesive society achieve the objective of making their children learn to live together? Education is the only key that could open up alternative solutions.

There is no alternative before the human beings than to sit together and design a common future for all human beings on planet earth, if the human race has to survive. Over the years, it has dawned upon every alert, active and concerned citizen that we are guilty of weakening our own lifeline by the wanton destruction of nature and the resources it provides to one and all. We polluted our rivers, put poisonous gases in the air we breathe, and continue to reduce the forest cover indiscriminately to pander to human greed. The world understood the imperative of the Gandhian warning rather very late: "Nature has sufficient resources to meet the needs of everyone but not the greed of anyone"! The Stockholm Summit was the beginning of the global concern, followed by a couple of others; a lot of positive outcome has been achieved. Much more needs to be accomplished. Apart from immediate steps like cleaning the rivers, arresting deforestation, conserving water resources, it would require a long term strategy to reverse the trend of wanton aggression against each other and against nature by so many. An attitudinal transformation would be required and that can be achieved, only when the nations revert to their schools to find out solutions and seriously strive to equip and prepare the generations ahead with adequate internalisation of values: moral, ethical, democratic and humanistic. Value inculcation, its development and nurturance that leads to internalisation of human values has to be an integral part of every educational activity. The challenge that emerges could also be visualised as the conflict being faced by every individual who witnesses various manifestations of globalisations in his daily life. He is also keen to remain organically linked to his own roots, which instill a sense of identity and belongingness in him and in his heart.

Learning Essentials

The canvas before education opens its various dimensions in response to a simple query: why everyone is keen to get education? The answer is: a new world order is in the process of taking shape. Every individual deserves to be empowered and enabled to develop his talent to the fullest extent. Everyone must be supported to realise his creativity at its best, as that alone could be the backbone of the progress and development which is the essential aim of all the policies, programmes and implementation strategies in every alert and responsive system of governance. The limitations that illiteracy, ignorance and low quality education imposes on the process of growth and progress have been witnessed by practically every country, though to varying extents. When the competition is tough, quality of products and output is the key to remain relevant. The nurturance of the growing up of every future citizen just cannot be taken lightly. It is the quality of education and level of acquisition of skills, which, when upgraded and enhanced through integration of human values, and the emphasis is on character building, would guide the content and process of education in the globalised world. The basic premise of comprehensive education would still be defined by that eternal 3×3 matrix:

Head, Hand and Heart
Self, Society and Nature
Body, Mind and Spirit

Once education systems, right from the planning to the school level implementation stages, take care of these aspects and their interrelationship, education so imparted would truly become an instrument of development. The expected outcomes could be simply put as: "Properly planned educational inputs contribute to the increase in the Gross National Products, cultural richness, build positive attitude towards technology and increase efficiency and effectiveness of the governance. Education opens new horizons for an individual, provides new aspirations and develops new values. It strengthens competencies and develops commitment. Education helps individual develop a critical outlook on social and political realities and sharpens the ability to self-examination, self-monitoring and self-criticism."[6] It appears eternally relevant element in education; only its interpretational dimensions differ and differ heavily in the initial decades of the 21st century. To come up to the expectations of the people and the new emerging global society, the qualitative improvement in education must reflect a change in pedagogical dimensions and lay emphasis on the following[7]:

1. A shift from methods that emphasise passive learning to those that foster the active interest and ability of children to learn on their own;
2. A shift from memorisation to development of the children's capacity for critical thinking;
3. A shift from traditional academic to practically relevant curriculum; and
4. A shift from imparting information to imparting life values such as independent thinking, self-reliance and individual initiative that are essential for success in any field of endeavour.

In the globalised world, the localised initiatives have to be equally strong and prioritised, since the local acquaintance and appreciations developed by local elements of the curriculum would be pre-requisites to become a responsible, capable, active, creative and healthy member of the family and society. Flexibility, dynamism, and readiness to accept innovations have to become hallmarks of the process of curriculum renewal and the assessment of its utility in the labour market.

The Report of the International Commission on Education for the twenty-first century, also known as Delors Report after its Chairperson, identifies four pillars of education: Learning to live together; Learning to know; Learning to do; Learning to be![8] These effectively state all that needs to be said about education and its potential to transform the society and prepare individuals who would usher in the change, take charge of it and make life better in quality and content. The Delors Report further stresses the essential purpose of education and learning: "None of the talents which are hidden like buried treasure in every person must be left untapped." Globalisation promises to present a flat world to one and all. In this fast changing scenario, "the first, and most important, ability you can develop in a flat world is the ability to 'learn how to learn'—to constantly absorb, and teach yourself, new ways of doing old things or new ways of doing new things."[9] Those familiar with the Indian tradition of learning, knowledge creation and its dissemination for the welfare of one and all would immediately recall the presence of the 'idea' all along: *Yavadjivait Adhiyate viprah* (The wise continue their search for knowledge till the very end.). These days, when practically most of the researches are meant for probable commercial gains or towards weaponry, travelling to outer space and the like, it may not be easy to appreciate this Indian tradition. The tragedy is that the Indian education system itself is not realising the universality of the basic premise of the Indian thought: *Vasudhaiv Kutumbakam* (but the world is one family). In case education in India transforms itself on such values, it would pave the path to march on becoming the prime source of spiritual guidance to all those who are suffering due to violence, insecurity, uncertainty, deprivation and even degradation inflicted upon them by their own fellow men! It requires creation of the spirit of belonging to the nation, community and developing a sense of pride in being the inheritors of great tradition that values humanity the most. India, with its great ancient tradition and a highly evolved culture, could just not become another nation that excels in copying the West, without analysing and understanding the intentions and implications that are in the minds, actions and deeds of those promoting materialistic pursuits vigorously, sometimes even unashamedly, instead of global harmony and peace! Those who understand India are aware of the global trends and new techniques and are open to new ideas could sit together and attempt a model of education that could be seen as sprouted from the soil of India, but which aims at the welfare of everyone around the globe. This just cannot be the prerogative of those who are not willing to change with the times and would like to adhere to the tradition, without realising the dynamic nature of the process of education which remains relevant only when it traverses the times like a pious stream that always offers only the fresh and freshness.

It would be worthwhile to recall the following observations of

Thomas Friedman[10] which very succinctly present the 'outcomes' of the existing Indian system, and also indicate very clearly what are we giving to the generation next:

> "Columbus was happy to make the Indians he met his slaves, a pool of free manual labour. I just wanted to understand why the Indians I met were taking our work, why they had become such an important pool for the outsourcing of service and information technology work from America and other industrialized countries. Columbus had more than one hundred men on his three ships; I had a small crew from the Discovery Times channel that fit comfortably into two banged-up vans, with Indian drivers who drove barefoot. When I set sail, so to speak, I too assumed that the world was round, but what I encountered in the real India shook my faith in that nation. Columbus accidently ran into America but thought he had discovered part of India. I actually found India and thought many of the people I met there were Americans. Some had actually taken American names, and others were doing great imitations of American accents at call centers and American business techniques at software labs."

In simple terms, can India devise an education system with potential to restore 'the global faith in the Indian nation'? It is a daunting challenge. The first step is: let the generations ahead learn about India, its treasure of wisdom accumulated over several millennia and its relevance in the emerging global context. Linking the young of India to India has to be the first objective of education, when one speaks of the total quality development of the individual and his personality. History, culture and heritage have to become essential components of educational endeavour right from the beginning stage.

National Identity, Rights, and Responsibilities

Having got rid of such obnoxious practices like slavery, apartheid, caste system, untouchability, colonialism and the like, human rights became, very rightly, the key words in ensuring a 'humane' life to one and all. This 'all' includes those who were discarded, exploited, ignored and made to live a sub-human life. The wars and battles against colonialism were mostly fought on the uniform plank of nationalism and national identity. India presented a unique model to countries under foreign yoke. Indians rose as one nation, forgetting the diversities of caste, creed, religion, language, sect or any other. Against British subjugation, they all became Indians and only Indians! In spite of substantial increase in the migration across the nations and cultures, shift towards languages that offer wider scope and opportunities on a bigger and extended platform, the basic human instinct to remain attached to his roots shall never get diluted. Whatever may be the apprehensions of the transitional times, the spirit of nationalism shall always dominate the urge for internationalism. Linking young persons to their culture, heritage and knowledge pool, as also the distinct ways and means of its creation, strengthens the organic links of the future citizens to their roots and, hence, instills a sense of pride in being citizens of their country. It is worth to recall that the Englishmen understood it and, accordingly, ensured the destruction of the indigenous system of knowledge transfer. They brought in an alien system of education and knowledge. They put to practice their premise that 'to subjugate India, Indians must be delinked from India'!

It would, however, be necessary to take adequate steps in the education system to prepare future citizens of India, who could also make outstanding international contributors in the process of global growth and development. In times of increasing violence, wars, drugs and terrorism, on one hand, and the challenges of poverty, hunger and unemployment are looming large, on the other. Most vulnerable are the young persons. It is clear that things just cannot be allowed to drift 'as usual'! Some alternatives have to be explored to find solutions and find these early. As most of the problems arise because of ignorance, greed, ego manifestations, mistrust, religious differences and the like, the only strategy is to bring the focus back on value-based education as mentioned earlier. Only education has the potential to ensure that, in the name of globalisation, the developed nations are not permitted to exploit the developing nations merely as markets! Further, in a globalised society, the 'man' must become the prime concern and should not be left in lurch! It happens when, say, Indian market is flooded with items from abroad which are normally made in the cottage industry in India. Think of those who prepared various decorations for festivals like Deepavali. When cheaper Chinese materials are poured in the market, as part of a planned strategy, millions could be rendered jobless. Should this be permitted? And as these persons and families belong to the category of common man, not much attention is paid by the government which is ever preoccupied with bigger issues. Here comes the issue of national priorities and also of a sound internalisation of social responsibility by every individual.

Section 51-A was added in the Constitution of India in 1976. It delineated ten fundamental duties (subsequently extended to eleven after the Constitutional amendment of 2002) leading to the Right to Education Act). The first four of these very clearly emphasise the nation and the national identity and projects the future responsibilities on this count. These are worth recalling:

(a) To abide by the Constitution and respect the National Flag and the National Anthem.
(b) To cherish and follow the noble ideals which inspired our national struggle for freedom.
(c) To uphold and protect the sovereignty, unity and integrity of India.
(d) To defend the country and render national service when called upon to do so.

On responsibilities and duties to the nation and, thus, to humanity, the *Mantra* was given by Gandhiji. It is universally true and it alone has the potential to create a world that respects diversity at the individual level and also at the national and global level:[11] "I learnt from my illiterate, but wise, mother that all rights to be deserved and preserved come from duties well done. Thus the very right to live accrues to us, when we do the duty of citizenship of the world. From this one fundamental statement, perhaps it is easy enough to define duties of man and women and correlate every right to some corresponding duty to be first performed..." From this, would emerge a citizenry that would not infringe upon the rights of anyone else, hence, any violation of human rights of anyone anywhere!

Not by ICT Alone

If one confines attention only to the advances in science and technology and more particularly, to ICT impact, it could present a very rosy picture. No doubt, these advances could have been appropriately used to find global solutions to certain basic issues that have confronted human beings for long and are still present in ferocious magnitude before nations and the global community. Billions sleep hungry, deprived of food, shelter and health care. A peaceful world just cannot be created, if social justice, equity, justice, religious co-existence, mutual respect for other cultures and otherness in different aspects, remain mostly only on papers and are not put to practice for "all"! If systems of governance favour some, and ignore or discard others, major chunk of national energy would be spent in resolving internal conflicts. It shall necessarily have international repercussions. International understanding and harmonious dialogue is possible, only when the nation is at peace with itself. Environmental disasters, climate change, food shortages, persistent poverty and the economic crisis being faced by the developing countries reveal the fragility of the 'global village' and universal connectivity. These conditions persist in spite of congenial opportunities for dialogue at every level. Transmigration of young persons to avail of educational opportunities is taking place in increasing numbers. That provides much better opportunities for appreciating otherness. Institutional networking is getting more and more acceptable. Educational opportunities in other countries prepare students develop skills of analytical and critical appreciation which would help them discover alternative solutions in the area of their choice. This comes through in two stages. First, a sound base prepared by good quality school education that imparts initial vocational skills also. The products are then eligible to be prepared for creative and innovative interventions in the process of national development. This may appear just a naive statement, but the position remains that, in actual practice, education remains deficient in quality, content and skill acquisition resulting in lowering the quality at the workplace. Young Indians have done exceptionally well in scientific and technological fields. What India now needs is to extend quality education to all its children in schools. No doubt, that is a tall order, but it is a necessity. Good quality initial education, apart from systemic support, requires good quality teachers. India is seriously deficiently on this front.

All this would take shape only when top priority in the entire process of education at every stage is given to inculcation of values; moral, ethical, humanistic and democratic. The system needs to orient every young person to imbibe the sense of belongingness to the nation, be proud of its culture, traditions and the eternal knowledge-quest. In the process, learners have to be acquainted with the commonality of eternal human values in all religions, cultures and civilizations[12]. Truth, Peace, Non-violence, Righteous Conduct and Love are adored, accepted and recommended by one and all. Every young person has to learn that the world is passing through great advancements, fine, but it is also facing one of its greatest moments of crises in human history. It is far tougher for the educators to impress upon young persons the utility of values, as also their practicability in daily life. The globalised world is full of tensions, machinations, violence, insecurity, fundamentalism, terrorism, distrust and the greed that results in tendencies that make man destroy the sensitive man-nature relationship. Scientists are now calculating how long the planet shall earth last, if the self-destructive tendencies are not checked early! The challenge before societies and, hence, before education is to prepare citizens equipped and willing to accept responsibility to save the planet earth and the bounties that nature has bestowed on mankind.

Only a true national citizen could become an effective international citizen. Only the one who adores his mother could adore all the mothers of the world and hence, every human being.

Action Points

1. India needs manpower at the highest level and at the middle level, apart from serious acquisition of vocational skills at the stage of compulsory education which now must effectively extend up to 16 years of age, if not 18. That requires men and women of character and commitment to handle education policy formulation and implementation. It should not hesitate to develop area-specific and community-relevant models of education, instead of insisting on centralised curricula, as has been the case in the past.
2. Investments in education upscale the nation on all fronts. Delay and inadequacy of resource inputs causes irreparable damage to the quality of education and, consequently, in preparing the right kind of manpower in every sector of human activity. To compete in a global society and to avail of the opportunities that are opening up internationally, India needs to ensure that the dignity of its government school systems is restored on a war-footing. Indian schools need an additional 1.2 million school teachers. There is no visible and serious effort to get these vacant slots getting filled, even in the next couple of years! How could there be effective implementation of curriculum policies? How could teachers in position find time to focus on personality development, value inculcation or making the students understand the national and international contexts?
3. The situation in higher education is indeed alarming. The regulatory mechanisms, developed to ensure dynamism and quality, have failed miserably. If it were not so, how could 80 per cent of professional graduates and 90 per cent of the general graduates are not found fit to take the job? The situation is very complex and the private initiatives have mostly brought in commercialisation inflow. Most of them

are not worried about the quality of output. This is evidenced by the fact that, while India needs to substantially increase participation in higher education, hundreds of its colleges of management and engineering are being closed down; no takers! Professional institutions must be run professionally and the quality of the products needs to be monitored regularly by independent agencies. What an irony that India needs to enhance its participation rates in higher education and hence needs more, the shabby implementation of the policies, burgeoning commercialisation, due to inaction of regulatory bodies and political intrusion, is resulting in the closure of even the existing institutions.

4. Education faces its biggest challenge in the ever-increasing tension between materialistic pursuits and spiritual quest, which, amongst several other tensions, is the cause of real worry for the developing nations. The glamour that mesmerises the minds of sensitive children and young persons 'intrudes' their psyche, rather round the clock. Globalisation has begun the process of creating a 'market society' in full vigour. If materialistic pursuits become uncontrollable, the very survival of the human race would be threatened, People would forget their social responsibilities and what they owe to man and nature relationship. The tendency to acquire materialistic assets could lead to unending desires and may lure one to indulge in unacceptable and unethical means. This has to be prevented by society and through education, that can make young persons take a balanced view of the global dimensions of their role. India must recall and reintroduce the traditional values of non-accumulation, Aparigraha, and let the children understand its significance and import during their impressionable years.
5. The Indian education system must open up to new areas like petroleum, energy, defence equipment, medical equipments, nuclear technologies and others. India requires trained manpower for the outside world, which is keenly observing India's 'golden period of demographic dividend'. That would require a responsive educational initiative that would prepare young persons for jobs in ageing societies, bring in foreign exchange and establish and strengthen socio-cultural ties. Universities and institutions of higher education, earlier perceived purely as intellectual centres, now have the added

responsibility and must keep in mind their role as vehicles of economic development. These have to establish close links with the industry and the corporate world to make requisite changes in their courses and programmes.

6. The content and process of education has to be redefined regularly. Emphasis on the cultural content, heritage, natural resources, and respect for diversity, including religious diversity, must be given adequate priority in schools and institutions. They must understand the role that India could play in the globalised world and what necessary caution and precautions are absolutely essential in dealing with the players of globalisation.

   Globalisation has resulted in several allotropes of exclusion! Multinationals from within, and also from beyond, follow no-holds-barred strategies to influence the decision-makers and indulge in wanton destruction of natural resources invariably at the cost of the local populations. The worst sufferers are the tribals of Jharkhand, Chhattisgarh and Orissa. Bellary mines in Karnataka have created a history of collusion. More than two hundred districts in India suffer from violence and rebellion that are fuelled on the anger and anguish of the uprooted and exploited. This is a worldwide phenomenon that has created islands of affluence, on one side, and that of deprivation and devastation, on the other. Ideology of progress cannot be borrowed from anywhere and it has to be indigenous without, of course, any restrictions on incorporating ideas and experiences from anywhere.

7. On July 13, 2004, the Supreme Court of India delivered a judgement in the MC Mehta vs. Union of India case—making Environmental Education a compulsory subject of school education right from class one to twelve. Before arriving at this decision, the Apex Court had sent the syllabus prepared by the NCERT to all the States/UTs and the Boards of School Education. Each one of these had communicated their consent to accept it. Unfortunately, it was not implemented, because of non-academic considerations. It could be reconsidered as it would prepare more informed and concerned citizens who would understand the import of globalisation in the context of developmental discourse and the need for inclusive growth that remains the major priority in many of the developing countries.

8. Globalisation has enhanced opportunities, and the global movement of students and scholars has increased substantially. Educational expansion has also attracted 'investors' in education who have only the profit motive in view, even at the cost of quality. All this has resulted in certain practices that run contrary to the creation of congenial conditions for equity and social justice. Those who could afford have the option of going to private institutions in India or even abroad. The state funding in higher education has slowed down. Universities, which were traditionally funded by the state, are now being asked to generate their own resources. Universities have increased in numbers, but the level and quality of research is often found to be on the decline. Brilliant young persons are not coming to pure research. As a result, universities and research institutions suffer 40-60 per cent of academic faculty shortage. In a globalised world, every nation has to have its own pool of cognitive capital in every sector of relevance.
9. India needs to prepare special plans to identify talent, nurture it in schools and universities and give them opportunities to carry out the process of knowledge creation, in an environment that gives autonomy, provides opportunity to experiment with ideas and enter into a dialogue and debate with the best minds, with confidence and self-assurance.
10. Public participation in school education, particularly in managing the government schools, remains only on paper. This has to be energised and activated. It should be assisted by the bureaucracy—and not dominated by it—as is the case at present. Schools are the power plants that emanate and disseminate quality within the nation and also outside the nation. The process of transforming India to acquire its respectful place in the comity of the nations must begin in the primary schools of India—and this must begin early.

(May 17, 2014)

Notes

1. *The Week*, May 4, 2004, page 18. Kochi, India.
2. *Young India*, July 21, 1921.
3. Palkhiwala, N.A., *Essential Unity of All Religions*, 2003, Bhartiya Vidya Bhavan, Mumbai.

4. *New Paradigm for Re-engineering Education*; Yin Cheong Cheng; Springer; 2005.
5. *Ibid.*, p. 74.
6. Education: Vision 2020, paper by J.S. Rajput, in the edited volume *India Vision 2020*; Planning Commission, Government of India, New Delhi, 2004.
7. *Ibid.*, p. 83.
8. *Learning: the Treasure Within*, UNESCO, 1996.
9. *The World is Flat*, Thomas L. Friedman, Penguin Books.
10. *Ibid.*
11. Teaching of Fundamental Duties to Citizens, Report of the J.S. Verma Committee, NCERT, 1999.
12. *Human Values and Education*, J.S. Rajput; Pragun Publication, New Delhi, 2006.

18

Academic Excellence and Institutional Leadership

Every discussion on excellence and/or leadership in India invariably deflects to education as the nodal entity. Those imbued with a sense of history and familiar with the glorious tradition of the pursuit of knowledge and wisdom know that it alone led to the global acknowledgement of the primacy of India and Indians in the arena of spirituality. It led to higher philosophical and pragmatic formulations like all human beings are equal, that the world is but one family, that everyone has a right to pursue his religion according to his faith, and that non-violence and non-accumulation must be pursued with unflinching commitment! They had learnt the importance of knowledge and wisdom in making life better and happier on this planet. All this could safely be perceived as an outcome of the pursuit of excellence which would not have been possible in the absence of visionary leadership.

India now has its schools, colleges, universities and a system of transferring knowledge to next generations. Major educational initiatives in the post-independence India centered on the need to universalize access to elementary education. People wanted replacement of the transplanted system of education, a legacy of British rule. Even before independence, significant voices were raised demanding a total transformation of the education system that was created to serve the 'masters'. India deserved a system of education that would assimilate the Indian ethos and shall have its roots deep in the soil of India; its culture, heritage and history: and, simultaneously, ready to accept new ideas, techniques and technologies considered appropriate for moving ahead in national development.

After all, India had developed sound practices of knowledge creation and the legacy of highly regarded institutions of higher learning; Taxila, Nalanda and Vikramshila. Indian contributions to science, mathematics, astronomy, surgery and several other areas had received international appreciation. Taxila continued to flourish in search of excellence from around 700 BC to 6th century AD; after which it was destroyed by the illiterate and uncultured invaders. It remains one of the most outstanding examples of the Indian tradition of knowledge quest and pursuit of excellence. It was an example also of institutional leadership, its products spread not only in India but also in several nations abroad, creating institutions, again, in search of excellence. There was so much of strength and value in the *Gurukula* system that it could be relevant even in modern times.

It was the pragmatic essence of Indian tradition of knowledge quest that is inherent in the conceptualization of *Basic Education*, or *Buniyadi Talim*. Who better than Gandhi understood India, its strengths, weakness, and the contours of diversity? The structure and pedagogy of *Basic Education*, bears the stamp of the strength of Gandhian philosophy of education. Gandhi was convinced that education was the only ray of hope and its foremost objective was to let everyone savor the warmth of this 'ray of enlightenment', without any distinction of any conceivable diversity. *Basic Education* was an all-inclusive conceptualization of what is now internationally known as EFA: 'Education for All'.

Things, however, did not move the way he envisaged for the post-independence period. India decided to continue with the existing system, without explicitly discarding the Gandhian approach and model. Most of the policy makers, both in bureaucracy and political leadership; had their training in decision making and governance that was heavily biased towards the ruling class. Exceptions apart, most of them had inculcated an attitude of acceptance of the 'superiority of all that came from the West'. After all, we had all known for ages that vanquished civilizations do develop a sense of appreciation for the victors; and; consciously and subconsciously; wish to reach their levels. One wonders why it was not realized that a system meant, and structured for a specific objective of educating a few and to keep others out of it, when over stretched to 'all' would just collapse? Forget excellence, even average quality would be a casualty.

Contemporary Concerns

If millions of educated young persons are looking for work and engagements, if around sixty five per cent of schools function in conditions of utter neglect, deprivation and deficiencies, if universities are perpetually short of faculty and funds, would it be too far-fetched to state that the quality of education in the country is on a scary downward slide. Governments regularly present rise in numbers and other statistical details to highlight their achievements and stake claim to progress achieved, but does it carry much weight with those who have seen and studied the system from within? One must hasten to add that there is a bright side in educational achievements which just cannot be ignored. In fact it needs considerable articulation everywhere as that also provides for hope and possibility of putting education system again on the rails so that no generation suffers because of lack of education which alone has the potential to bring out the best in 'body, mind and spirit'! Before one deals with certain contemporary concerns, it must be emphasized that credit must go to the expansion and extension of education that has been achieved during the 68-year period. From a mere 20 per cent literacy rate to move to around 75 per cent is a real commendable achievement, more so as the population during the period has risen from a 330 million to over 1250 million.

Institutions that a nation creates to educate its children and young persons are also required to provide opportunities and environment for creating new knowledge, and in the process, prepare and nurture leaders and visionaries in every sphere of human endeavour and activity. To strengthen the system in totality, it is clearly understood that a sound base of school education is critical to expect high quality innovations and research in higher education. One could recollect several studies that clearly indicate how teacher preparation institutions determine the quality of education in schools that impacts higher education. The quality of school teachers determines the level and magnitude of those who become leaders in their chosen fields.

In the context of school education, one could recall how educationists and scholars vociferously, even now, criticize Thomas Babington Macaulay for his Minutes of 1835. These minutes sowed the seeds of British system of education in India, and simultaneously, also ensured the destruction of the traditional system. Initially, one enthusiastically joined the bandwagon that blamed Macaulay for every ill in Indian Education. Slightly deeper study and analysis has led to a total transformation about the work and ingenuity of Macaulay, one could greatly admire him to give his masters such an effective strategy to 'subjugate India by delinking Indians from India', from its history, heritage, culture, traditions, pursuit of knowledge and the practices of creating, disseminating and utilizing knowledge for the welfare of one and all! In fact, his strategic and futuristic planning is indeed a unique example even for the management Gurus of the 21st century. Colonialism is history, British have left but Independent India has not been able to extricate itself out of the web that Macaulay had woven some 180 years ago. The manner certain Macaulay traits have flourished till today would gladden the hearts of the spirit of the colonial masters of the yore. These are exemplified by our love for English and particularly for English medium schools, and the resultant loss of credibility of government schools.

This must change. As a nation India just cannot ignore that the future belongs to those nations that dexterously enhance their cognitive capital and ensure optimum efficacy in their existing institutions, create new leading institutions, nurture talent and provide avenues for the nurturance of new-age leadership. The existing conditions clearly indicate that India needs a fresh approach in aptitude and attitude towards its education system and institutions. There is ample realization that such a change of enormous magnitude requires a comprehensive analysis of the existing system, a comprehensive understanding of the global scenario, and also of the traditional strengths systems of transfer, creation and generation of knowledge to generation next.

The current professional, public and intellectual discourse on education highlights the need for comprehension of all the relevant parameters that would, and should, impact the formulation of a new education policy. Perceptions on the content and process of education differ rather vastly as different sections visualize the objectives of education with considerable diversity. Pose the query: Education for what? One would find some well known terms emerging out in a gathering of say even twenty individuals, concerned about educational reforms: for life, for living, for value nurturance and development, for character building, to perform its acculturating role, for creating a peaceful global society, for establishing religious harmony, for earning, for skill development, for entrepreneurship training, for providing manpower to ageing societies, the list is endless! Mahatma Gandhi indicated that education is the only ray of hope in the struggle against injustice, tyranny, defective politics and exploitative systems of governance. Swami Vivekananda put it comprehensively, 'man making education'. Yes, education has to transform a lay person in to a personality. Education is a dynamic process and, hence, so long it continues to flow with the times, it remains pollution free. Only a neat, clean, responsive, accommodative, transformative system of education could really become the 'ray of hope' to one and all but particularly to the most deficient, deprived, exploited, socially and culturally traumatized, billions of whom still sleep hungry, suffer ill health, humiliation and indignity round the clock.

When M.K. Gandhi wrote *Hind Swaraj* in 1909, he quoted Professor Huxley's definition of education: "That man I think has had a liberal education who has been so trained in youth that his body is the ready servant of his will and does with ease and pleasure all the work that as a mechanism it is capable of; whose intellect is a clear, cold, logic engine with all its parts of equal strength and in smooth working order...whose mind is stored with a knowledge of the fundamental truths of nature...whose passions are trained to come to heel by a vigorous will, the servant of a tender conscience...who has learnt to hate all vileness and to respect others as himself. Such a one and no other, I conceive, has had a liberal education, for he is in harmony with nature. He will make the best of her and she of him."

The search for such an education continues worldwide and that in itself is a very encouraging sign of civilization growth and evolution. Huxley indicates what could be the output of excellence in education: "The well-developed, well integrated personality is the highest product of evolution, the fullest realization we know of in this world." He goes on further to emphasize; "The exploration of human nature and its possibilities has scarcely begun. A vast new world of unchartered possibilities awaits its Columbus." One could listen to its echo in the words of Bertrand Russell: "Man has no chance of survival if knowledge remains only knowledge but if we could transform knowledge into wisdom, he will not only survive, he will be able to ascend to greater and greater heights of achievements." Dr. Radhakrishnan puts it in total comprehension: "The end-product of education should be a free creative man who can battle against historical circumstances and adversities of nature." Obviously, only those sincerely engaged in knowledge-search can think of unearthing such a potential in individuals, and also within them. Rabindranath Tagore thinks of it in the context of man and nature: "The highest education is that which does not merely give us information but makes our life in harmony with all existence." And who would assist in effort to get such an education? Mahatma Gandhi unfolds the most pragmatic of the answers: "A true teacher regards himself as a student of his students. If you will teach your pupils with this attitude, you will benefit much from it." He, in fact, also clarifies that once the fire to know more, learn more and explore further is ignited, it just cannot be extinguished, the pursuant, the true teacher, shall always live with it. That is the tradition, that is the pedagogy, and that is the pursuit of excellence that survives in living institutions even now, in the days of great turmoil and tension between materialism and spirituality. And to sum up it all, Sri Aurobindo says it in *Life Divine*: "The animal is satisfied with a modicum of necessity; the gods are content with their splendors. But man cannot rest permanently until he reaches some highest good. He is the greatest of living beings because he is the most discontented, because he feels most the pressure of limitations. He alone, perhaps, is capable of being seized by the divine frenzy for remote ideal." Will it not help to link this divine frenzy for a remote ideal to the perpetual quest for excellence in the existing institutional structures on which we fall back upon to prepare our generations ahead? One must acknowledge the seminal contributions in the quest for excellence by stalwarts who created great institutions and, more than that, laid great traditions of self-less devotion and commitment. They, by their own example established how leadership of the scholarly, astute and wise can really pave the path for others to follow. Education must let every learner realize the essence of the pursuit of excellence, no matter what would be the field of his activity in later years.

Excellence needs no formal rigid definition. M.V. Kamath in his excellent essay "The Pursuit of Excellence"; recalls the words of JRD Tata that 'if you aim at perfection, you may achieve excellence'. Kamath emphasizes the use of the word 'may'! I invariably put it as a query to young persons; "You did so well, but why not better than your present best? Strive for the better than the (present) best and shift the goal post further ahead." The pursuit of excellence attracts others on the Path. When Meghnad Saha was elected to the Fellowship of Royal Society in 1924, the event became a source of attraction to young students towards science. Saha was always on the lookout for talent and one of the persons whom he identified was D.S. Kothari whose contributions in physics and education; and also in science and spirituality testify what a great identifier of latent qualities of leadership Saha was! It also indicates the continuity and dynamism of the efforts in pursuance of excellence. There is another instance of the intensity of commitment to be part of effort for excellence. Young Michael Faraday, was fired with a burning desire to get near the great scientist of the times Sir Humphrey Davy. He somehow joined his laboratory as a Janitor, and through sheer dent of his commitment and perseverance, managed to get some scientific experimental work. One day, Sir Davy, before leaving the laboratory to attend a formal dinner, gave him an assignment: he was supposed to record certain changes in an experiment at regular intervals. Davy had assured Faraday that he would come back after the dinner. He forgot, and came back only next morning. Faraday had not left his place and readings were being recorded in full alertness. We all know both of them made seminal contributions to the field of science. But the gem of the sentence came after an award ceremony in honour of Sir Davy, when a query was posed to him; "Sir; which of your discoveries you consider best?" The Answer: "Michael Faraday!" What better example could there be in the context of professional leadership and pursuit of excellence! Let me recount another instance that projects another level of attained excellence indicated by total absorption in its pursuit. Nobel Laureate Neils Bohr was addressing a select gathering of eminent physicists and sitting in the front row, Professor S.N. Bose with eyes closed appeared to be in deep slumber. At one stage, writing his equations on the blackboard, Professor Bohr got stuck at some point, others from the audience offered suggestions but as the next step remained unresolved, gradually total silence engulfed the room. The 'zero decibel' sound level made Prof. Bose open his eyes. Professor! He looked at the blackboard, got up from his seat, wrote the next step and returned back to his seat. And 'slumber'. Everyone was stunned. The speaker proceeded on, as if nothing had really happened! The study of the organic relationship and mutuality amongst Institutional leadership, academic excellence and the growth of leaders could indeed be very exhilarating and rewarding.

Institutional leaders play the most important role in creating, shaping and organizing the future of not only some individuals under their charge, but of the nation. They uplift institutional credibility. They are custodians of the talent, responsible for its nurturance and, are the merchants of hope and faith in future. Human civilizations have flourished on the eternal human quest for a better tomorrow. There are no limits to human ingenuity; inherent desire to explore, excavate, analyze, anticipate, visualize, design and so on. Those who get opportunities of talent nurturance also need encouragement and motivation. They are persons of character and single-minded commitment to succeed. We have great examples of stalwarts like C.V. Raman, Rabindranath Tagore, Prafulla Chandra Ray, Mahatma Gandhi, Sardar Patel, Dr. Rajendra Prasad, Madan Mohan Malviya, Vikram Sarabhai, Homi Bhabha and so many more. Each one of them attributed their rise and achievements to some teacher, mentor or an icon. One may wonder why we do not have the same levels of leadership in different sectors of human endeavour and activity now. John Gardner, in "On Leadership", makes a very interesting calculation in this context, of course, of the USA: "At the time this nation was formed, our population stood at around three million. And we produced out of that three million people perhaps six leaders of world class—Washington, Adams, Jefferson, Franklin, Madison, and Hamilton. Today, our population stands at 245 million, so we might expect at least 80 times as many world-class leaders—480 Jeffersons, Madisons, Adams', Washingtons, Hamiltons, and Franklins. Where are they?"

Will it be out of place to attempt a similar calculation for India? Any study or analysis would certainly reveal the paucity of talent nurturance and development at the initial stages which; unfortunately; is accessible only to a limited number of children and young persons. How did we create the present crisis in education? Our planners and implementers ignored the inherent and in-built dynamism in the Gandhian philosophy; and hence in elementary education, that explicitly emphasized the need to accept ideas from anywhere like fresh breeze, provided these were beneficial to Indian people, and to India. We are yet to build our education system on a sound Indian foundation. This neglect has cost the nation rather heavily.

Those who were in government schools in forties and fifties still remember how the head teachers of these schools played the leadership role. They were indeed role models, agents of social change and were playing the leadership role not only in the school but in the society. These schools had become the places of learning and practising life skills and productive skills as well. The headmasters and teachers could imbibe and develop critical qualities of character, service to the needy and firm conviction in themselves. If we had begun with *Basic Education*, its social, cultural and economic impact would have been immeasurable. Also, at that stage every educated person needed a white-collar job, as that meant prestige, social recognition and financial security. The social structure preferred the literate uneducated over educated illiterates who possessed treasure of talent which, if utilized in schools, could have transformed the entire education system. That was just ignored. The talent that had grown in traditional trades and vocations was gradually lost; expert artisans, artists, creators and innovators were reduced to penury.

Millions of degree holders from universities and even institutions of technical and management education roam for years together to find jobs. It indicates our follies of approach, understanding and visualizing future needs. In the process we also lost the grass-root level leadership which was active and visible in the school head teachers who had access and respectful acceptability amongst one and all. Though the context is different, John Gardner emphasizes this point in his book "Excellence": "We must learn to honour excellence in every socially accepted human activity, however humble the activity, and to scorn shoddiness, however exalted the activity. An excellent plumber is infinitely more admirable than an incompetent philosopher. The society that scorns excellence in plumbing because plumbing is a humble activity and tolerates shoddiness in philosophy because it is an exalted activity will have neither good plumbing nor good philosophy. Neither its pipes nor its theories will hold water." India, to a certain extent has realized its folly and the emphasis on skill development says so very clearly. Only time will tell how effectively that would be implemented.

Faith in oneself is the critical element for the comprehensive transformation of a lay 'person' into a 'personality'. This is the prime job of the education system. An instance is quoted in this regard pertaining to an educational conference in which Martin Luther King Jr. was also in the audience. Someone presented a paper that emphasized: First teach them to read. The majority of the audience, as expected, applauded but King's reaction was different; "first, teach them to believe in themselves!" Once the trait of belief in oneself is acquired, the first seed of leadership is sown. A person with rock-like self-confidence and brimming with self-assurance can take astonishing decisions. When Chauri-Chaura happened, Gandhi Ji suspended the movement. Everyone else had a different opinion, they were shocked. He had complete faith in his principles, and himself. Everybody else fell in line. It is well known that many of his colleagues and even the British government were perplexed when he launched the Dandi-Yatra. And what a miracle it created! It instilled hope amongst all, it firmed the faith of his followers in his vision and pragmatism. He generated hope, the eternal human trait that keeps all of us going even in the worst of circumstance. When Neta Ji Subhash Chandra Bose said, "You give me blood, I shall give you freedom," he was augmenting hope and preparing people to have confidence in him as well as in their own self. Winston Churchill said during World War II that all he had to offer was blood, sweat and tears; and nothing else! He was, in fact strengthening the faith of his people in their own self and igniting the hope that they would eventually succeed. Both of them had sterling qualities of leadership. Winston Churchill won the war, Neta Ji had thoroughly shaken the British Empire and his role in the departure of the British from India is much better understood now than in the initial years.

True leaders, in every sphere, continuously extend and expand their horizons; and that fascinates the young. Great institutions owe their creation and success in playing pioneering leadership role to someone who gets an idea and lives with it, translates it into a reality!

The Stanford University was created by Leland and Jane Stanford in the memory of their son who died of typhoid during a trip to Italy. One sentence that Leland said to his wife indicates how they sublimated their sorrow, expanding their universe to a far bigger horizon; "The children of California shall be our children". Today, Stanford University is the intellectual epicentre of the Silicon Valley. When Mahatma Gandhi was thrown out of the first class compartment at the Pietermaritzburg station in spite of having a valid ticket, he felt insulted and humiliated. He however, had the universality of vision, a total internalization of '*Vasudhaiv Kutumbakam*' and he extended the canvas manifold; individual humiliation was just one more instance of what coloured people were facing everyday; at every step in their life. The traits of leadership within him were further ignited and strengthened. If the world has rejected apartheid totally and completely, the contribution of Pietermaritzburg incident has probably played an outstanding role in it. Gandhi Ji established institutions; beginning with Gujarat Vidyapeeth; Kashi and Nagpur came afterwards. In their heydays, these became centres of character formation and preparing leaders of tomorrow. While Stanford had the resources to acquire 8000 acres of land in the San Francisco peninsula, Madan Mohan Malviya had nil resources. He had the courage of conviction, faith in himself and the people of India and Indian tradition of extending support to the knowledge quest and pursuit of excellence before him. His vision and mission were clear to him and were put forth before the nation with total transparency. Even now, in its hundredth year, every visitor experiences the living presence of Pundit Madan Mohan Malviya on the campus. Banaras Hindu University is a pragmatic manifestation of the premise that education in every country must be 'rooted to culture and committed to progress'. A number of instances can be quoted and cited in which luminaries established institutions for the welfare of the young of India and people of India. Scholars, academics and intellectuals now confront a very different scenario: education is an industry that assures safe and assured dividends!

People have analyzed personality traits of successful persons, the way they persistently and relentlessly went ahead against heavy odds. Some of the qualities that men and women striving to achieve excellence become obvious to everyone as one could say in case of Sachin Tendulkar, George Kurien, M.S. Swaminathan, A.P.J. Abdul Kalam, and the present generation is witness to their contributions and has seen how they have grown up. They were preceded by Jagdish

Chandra Bose, Prafulla Chandra Ray, C.V. Raman, Meghnad Saha, Satyendranath Bose, S.S. Bhatnagar, and other luminaries.

Concerns over Quality

The existing situation on quality; and hence on education; has resulted in widespread concern within the system and also outside it. Somehow, initiatives to put in place remedial measures have not yet made much impact. One often comes across people lamenting that Indian contribution in research output is far below; say, China! Indian universities do not figure in the list of world rankings of universities being brought about by various bodies. Quality decline in education in the days of much-hyped 'golden-period of demographic dividend' is indeed disturbing. Ageing societies are waiting to let young Indians fill in the manpower gaps there but will they agree to compromise on quality? And India is not the only country that has young population aspiring to take advantage of global opportunities. The remedy could come only from sincere, committed and devoted academic leaders. Only a burning lamp can ignite numerous more. Only credible leadership can really prepare leaders at primary schools, and in best of the research and higher education institutions. Think of Gijubhai Vadheka. Recall the impact of the Vice-Chancellors of the level and likes of Dr. Radhakrishnan, Sir Laxmanaswami Mudaliar, Sir Ashutosh Mukherji, Pundit Ganganath Jha and Amaranth Jha on the universities they headed for certain duration! Homi Jahangir Bhabha, Shanti Swarup Bhatnagar, Meghnad Saha, Vikram Sarabhai are amongst outstanding luminaries in the area of scientific and technological advances in India who provided leadership as individuals and also through institutions they created, established or transformed. They envisioned, they implemented, and they achieved and got due recognition. What did not get attention was probably their most outstanding contribution: the institutions they created continue to bear the stamp of their leadership qualities and are providing institutional leadership to many more which came in existence afterwards. These still prepare inspired men and women who lead in their own right. The reputation and recognition Indian talent and leadership qualities have received for its contributions in NASA and Silicon Valley is certainly linked to our leader scientists and Institutions. The level of commitment that scientist receives from his co-workers in a laboratory, or a political crusader gets from his people offers a lot to study how leaders succeed, and who were behind the success but remained in background.

I was always very keen to find out that how the words of the Mahatma could reach every nook and corner of India in the days of negligible literacy, limited media presence? One was equally inquisitive about how people even in remote villages accepted and adopted Khadi, as weapon in the non-violent struggle for freedom from the exploitative and humiliating foreign rule. To understand this puzzle, I called on several prominent freedom fighters. These included, apart from those in political arena, Manubhai Pancholi, Ramlal Bhai Parekh, Kashi Nath Ji Trivedi. It emerged that the grassroots level leadership of the freedom struggle emerged from the schools and training colleges of India that spread the *Vaani* of the Mahatma and his exhortations to use Khadi. Fortunate are those who get an opportunity to interact with such exemplary teachers. I would treasure one of the sentences that reverberated in these interactions: to us teachers, every parent was a leader and every student was a potential leader!

If the institutional leader can rise above the reports of poor work culture; and work-resistant functionaries, and decides to interact with them, repose confidence and assign responsibilities, it brings unexpectedly positive attitudinal change in over three/fourths of the cases. One should be very satisfied with it. No one likes to be controlled, work being thrust on him, directions being imposed and threat of 'action' being repeatedly flashed! As against such an approach, one could have faith that people inherently like work, that work is a source of satisfaction when performed under 'autonomous' circumstances, without undue stress and impositions. Academics are capable of self-direction and self-control. The pursuit of excellence is contagious in institutional climate. This canvas could extend to national scenario as was experienced during freedom struggle. It may be relevant to recall the eternally inspiring poem of Gurudev Rabindranath Tagore:

> Where the mind is without fear and head is held high
> Where knowledge is free
> Where the world has not been broken
> Up into fragments by narrow and domestic walls
> Where words come out from the depth of truth
> Where tireless striving stretches its arms towards perfection
> Where the clear stream of reason has not lost its way into the dreary desert sand of habit
> Where the mind is led forward by Thee into ever widening thought and action
> Into that heaven of freedom, my Father,
> Let my country awake.

When an institution receives accolades, every functionary savours the success and feels rewarded. Institutional attachment of the functionaries plays a great part in the growth of the culture of the pursuit of excellence. Institutional leadership symbolizes equal partnership with every functionary, decentralization, extended involvement and total transparency. For a true leader, institutional leadership is an art, not a craft as is generally perceived in a bureaucratic approach, which usually dominates Indian education systems in many ways, and few of its practices do influence some of the heads of institutions. Academics receive respect, without ever asking for it, or expecting it, it flows to them out of their work and dedication, not because of the hierarchical position they may occupy. They do not 'manage', they think, they envision, they perceive, and they create, innovate and are always ready to move to the next stage. Institutional leaders are persistently under one stress: what shall be the next step in the journey towards excellence. They learn to listen, know the value of empathy, affection, caring and sharing. How do academics and scholars who lead the institutions acquire these attributes? One would like recall the four stages of teaching and learning; and continuing learning; in the Indian tradition (Rama Jois, 1999):

1. Acquire knowledge/education from your parents and teachers.
2. Make your own study, contemplate on what you learnt, and improve your knowledge.
3. Impart value-added knowledge to other individuals that is to your own peers. In your adult life, impart it to your children, other children and to others as teacher or in any other capacity.
4. Use that knowledge for family benefit, as also for the benefit of the society through your profession, avocation or employment, etc.

Evidently, this trusted traditional practice remains relevant even in 21st century. It indicates the presence of trait of 'growing up throughout life in every individual. It is this faith in the potential of every human being that led to the concept of: "*Yavadjieevait Adhiyate Viprah*" (the wise person continues his learning throughout life). It reverberates when one recalls the immortal words of Swami Vivekananda: Every human soul is potentially divine'! The Delores Commission, appointed by the UNESCO to prepare a Report (UNESCO 1996) on the shape of education in the twenty-first century titled it "Learning: The Treasure Within". As such there are no limits to learning, and excelling. Traditionally, Indian premise on excellence has centered on the assertion that human beings can rise to unfathomable levels in worldly knowledge and spirituality; and also in divinity. It has, however, never ignored the mundane side of life, has given due importance and weightage to contemporary advances in science and technology without any hesitation.

And for that one needs institutions. It was the illustrious exponent of spirituality Swami Vivekananda who pleaded with the great visionary and innovator Sir Jamshed Ji Tata to establish an institution that could advance sciences in India. In 1893 they were travelling together in a ship from Yokohama to Vancouver. One was a monk who impressed the West on Indian philosophical and religious traditions as none else has ever done. The other was the father of Indian industry. Both of them were visionaries who were committed to the same cause; betterment and welfare of India and Indians. In that interaction Swami Vivekananda remarked: "How wonderful it would be if we could combine the scientific and technological advances of the West with the asceticism and humanism of India." Jamshed Ji gave deep consideration to the idea and wrote a famous letter to Swami Ji on November23, 1898. The Tata letter contains: "It seems to me that no better use can be made of the ascetic spirit than the establishment of monasteries or residential halls for men dominated by this spirit, where they should live with ordinary decency and devote their lives to the cultivation of sciences—natural and humanistic. I am of the opinion that, if such a crusade in favour of an asceticism of this kind is undertaken by a competent leader, it would greatly help asceticism. Science, and the good name of our common country; and I know not who would make a more fitting general of such a campaign than Vivekananda." Though Swami Ji could not accept the offer due to other preoccupations, he did send Sister Nivedita to meet Jamshed Ji and develop the future plans. Swami Ji passed away in 1902 and Jamshed Ji in 1904; but the seed they had sown sprung to life and the Indian Institute of Sciences, Bangalore was born in 1909. Subsequently, Tata Institute of Social Sciences and the Tata institute of Fundamental Research were established in 1930's and 1940's respectively. The two leaders together paved the path for the creation of leading institutions like BARC and ISRO that have excelled in quality output, preparation of new leaders in their chosen areas and have shown the path to many others. Is it not blissfully relevant premise that an idea given by Swami Vivekananda, and respectfully materialized by Jamshed Ji Tata is the pivot to the success of Indian young persons in NASA and Silicon Valley!

The dimensions of excellence could be manifold. People do perceive it in their own way, though some elements would, obviously be common. Emphasis could vary in the context of the area of pursuit. M.V. Kamath (2003) has discussed in great details what factors make a difference in the path of pursuit of excellence. He includes amongst these: success, toil, the discovery of talent, the quest for individuality, the nature of path, hope, charity, self, knowledge, courage, persistence, competition, commitment, the need for standards, the spirit of sacrifice, responsibility, and space within heart. He uses another term also amongst these, *Dasoha*, which he finds is a 'study in excellence'. "The term implies humility, service, understanding, compassion, respect for one's fellow citizens, self-abnegation, in fact, a whole range of virtues with which we are familiar." Gandhi wanted that all that you wish to do first think of the last man in the line and how your proposition would upgrade his life! One clearly sees the urge for inclusion of the elements of excellence on the canvas of human existence on the planet earth. Success, they say, comes to those who dare, defy and devote! Socrates pursued excellence. He was forced to commit suicide but remained steadfast to his pursuit. Galileo suffered a similar fate. Their excellence is remembered and recalled with universal reverence, no one knows, or wishes to know about their detractors. Right from Jesus Christ to Gandhi, Martin Luther King Jr. and several others paid the highest price for their steadfast march to achieve their goals. They changed the course of history and gave human dignity to billions, and transformed the minds of human beings. Nelson Mandela endured the worst of the conditions for around three decades but never gave up hope. All of them were just pursuing the path towards human excellence: a world where every human being shall get his liberty, dignity, honour and justice. We all have that dream—move towards a just world, free from violence, wars, fanatical killings of innocents, hatred, bigotry, insecurity. The path is shown in educational institutions by the academic leaders who realize how necessary it is to accelerate the march towards a better world.

The Indian system of the pursuit of excellence is known for its longevity, and also for its survival instinct in difficult conditions. Its objectives were always humane and humanistic. No doubt, it is also a pursuit of bliss; and the manner this bliss is perceived in *Hitopadesh* would remain eternally relevant:

> *Vidya dadati Vinayam, Vinyad yaati Patratam*
> *Patratwad dhanam aapnoti, Dhanad dharmam tatah sukham*
> (Education imparts intellectual culture;
> Intellectual culture secures capacity and stability.

Capacity and stability enables to secure wealth;
Wealth so secured enables to conform to Dhrama;
Which in turns secures happiness.)

In the globalized world, materialistic pursuits have relegated spiritual quest to background, it is however realized by concerned individuals that affluence, acquisition and accumulation are no harbingers of real happiness and bliss. There is an intervening stage; *Dharma*, the righteous conduct! This is the strength of India, and the Indian tradition. The transition towards a better, substantive and creative life shall take shape in schools, colleges and universities and other institutions of higher learning. Only those who understand India, its culture and traditions shall lead the quest for better and blissful life for one and all.

The *Guru* leads from humanity to divinity. Good teachers, and good pupils shall create a far better world, a humane world, a caring and sharing world. That is the expectation, that there is the hope, and that shall sustain the eternal human quest for excellence.

(September 18, 2015)

Notes and References

The author has extensively drawn from available literature and from his personal experiences and interactions with young persons and the learned. No claim to originality is being made in this presentation. The following sources deserve special mention.

1. Kamath, M. V., *The pursuit of Excellence*, 2003, Rupa and Company, New Delhi.
2. *Learning the Treasure Within*, UNESCO Report, 1996, UNESCO Publications, Geneva.
3. *Excellence*, John W. Gardner; 1984, W.W. Norton and Company, New York.
4. *On Becoming a Leader*, Warren Bennis, 2003, Magna Publishing Company Ltd., Mumbai.
5. *Optimizing Institutional Functioning*, J.S. Rajput in Experiences in School Education, 2001, NCERT, New Delhi.
6. *Ethics for Governance*, B.P. Mathur, 2014; Routledge; New Delhi.
7. "Leaders of Institutions can Boost Learner Attainments," J.S. Rajput, *The New Indian Express*, August 23, 2015, Chennai.
8. *An Inverted Life, Reflections on Leadership and Change*, Warren Bennis, 2003, Magna Publishing Company Ltd., Mumbai.
9. Rama Jois, Human Rights and Indian Values, 1999, NCTE, New Delhi.
10. *The Essence of Leadership; Explorations from Literature*; S. Manikutty and Sampat P. Singh, 2015; Bloomsbury Publishing India Ltd, New Delhi.

Index